Television in Black-and-White America

CULTURE AMERICA

Karal Ann Marling & Erika Doss, Series Editors

Television in Black-and-White America

Race and

National Identity

Alan Nadel

University Press of Kansas

Published by the

University Press of Kansas

(Lawrence, Kansas 66045),

which was organized by the

Kansas Board of Regents

and is operated and funded

by Emporia State University,

Fort Hays State University,

Kansas State University,

Pittsburg State University,

the University of Kansas, and

Wichita State University

Library of Congress Cataloging-in-Publication Data

Nadel, Alan, 1947–
  Television in black-and-white America: race and national
  identity / Alan Nadel
  p. cm.—(Culture America)
Includes bibliographical references and index.
ISBN 0-7006-1398-6 (cloth : alk. paper)
  1. Blacks on television—United States. 2. Whites on
  television—United States. 3. Television broadcasting—
  Social aspects—United States. 4. National characteristics,
  American. 5. United States—Race relations—History—
  20th century. I. Title. II. Series.
PN1992.8.A34N33 2005
  791.45'6552—dc22   2005012610

British Library Cataloguing in Publication Data is available.

10 9 8 7 6 5 4 3 2 1

The paper used in this publication meets the minimum
requirements of the American National Standard for
Permanence of Paper for Printed Library Materials
Z39.48-1984.

This book is dedicated

to the memory of my wife,

Amy Perkins, 1952–2003.

CONTENTS

Acknowledgments ix

1. Black Bodies, White Space, and a Televisual Nation 1

2. Television, Reality, and Cold War Citizenship 15

3. Disneyland, the Interstate, and National Space 43

4. The Adult Western and the Western Bloc 86

5. Rebel Integrity, Southern Injustice, and Civil Rights 112

6. The New Frontier 157

Conclusion 182

Notes 187

Bibliography 201

Index 211

ACKNOWLEDGMENTS

This manuscript benefited greatly from the superb editorial work of Nancy Scott Jackson and research assistance from Hilary Lowe, both at the University Press of Kansas, and from the excellent copyediting of Connie Oehring. Maureen Duffy helped with some research as well as a number of computer glitches. I am also very grateful to Donald Pease, Ellen Schrecker, and Eric Smoodin for valuable comments and suggestions. I studied hundreds of television episodes (from which much quoted material comes) at the Museum of Television and Radio in New York City and at the UCLA archives. The staffs at both places were excellent, and James Friedman, at the UCLA archives, was extremely helpful.

Television in Black-and-White America

1 Black Bodies, White Space, and a Televisual Nation

The distinguished scholar Cornel West, while driving from New York to teach at Williams College, was stopped by police, who suspected him of trafficking in cocaine. When he said that he was a professor of religion, the police officer replied, "Yeah, and I'm the Flying Nun. Let's go, nigger!"[1]

In 1931 nine black youths riding the rails through Alabama were arrested and accused of raping two white women whom they had never even seen. In less than three weeks, each was tried and convicted; all were sentenced to death. Although—after two U.S. Supreme Court rulings in their favor and four retrials—the sentences were never carried out, each of the Scottsboro boys, as they were known, spent between six and nineteen years in jail.[2]

The Hyde Park, Chicago, *Property Owner's Journal* of 1919 and 1920 stated unequivocally: "Every colored man who moves into Hyde Park knows that he is damaging his white neighbor's property. Therefore, he is making war on the white man."[3]

The State of Oregon's 1859 constitution prohibited blacks from immigrating to that state, and the last vestiges of the constitution's prohibitive clause were not repealed until 1971.[4]

According to the 1852 *Code of Alabama*, Article II, no. 1033: "Every free colored person who has come to this state since the first day of February [1832], has been admonished . . . that he cannot, by law, remain in this state; and does not, within thirty days, depart there from, must, on conviction, be punished by imprisonment in the penitentiary for two years."[5]

Over the full half century between 1884 and 1937, a black person in the United States of America was lynched, on average, once every five to six days. In the worst single year, 1892, a black person was lynched every 2.2 days.[6]

These are not anomalous details of American history. Examples of this sort, prolific and continuous, constitute a chronicle of discrimination and persecution nearly four hundred years long and three thousand miles wide, rooted at first benignly, then with growing ferocity, and finally through a complex system of denial in the tacit assumption of Anglo-Saxon privilege.

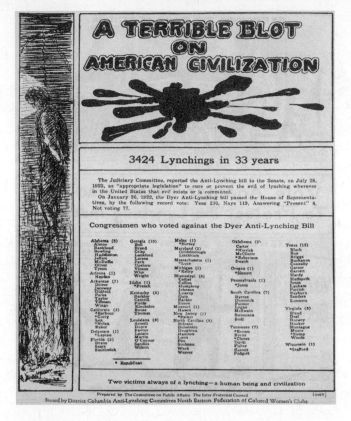

One of many unsuccessful attempts to get the U.S. Senate to pass an antilynching law. *Library of Congress, Rare Book and Special Collections Division.*

As Toni Morrison reminds us, "Africanism is the vehicle by which the American self knows itself as not enslaved, but free; not repulsive, but desirable; not helpless, but licensed and powerful; not history-less, but historical; not damned, but innocent; not a blind accident of evolution, but a progressive fulfillment of destiny."[7]

Although the black profile, since the early colonization of North America, has been construed as a stain on white civilization, this view of black and white was neither inherent in Western discourse nor uniform throughout the "New World." Rather it was an elaborate construction, local and unique. Racial categories are exceptionally unstable and very historically specific. And even within racial discourse, "white" is a particularly imprecise designation. "White people," as Richard Dyer notes, "are neither literally nor symbolically white."[8] Yet the myth of whiteness has retained such unspoken power as to structure profoundly several centuries of Western thought and underpin in numerous discrete incarnations the social dynamics of American life and law. As Cheryl Harris has demonstrated, "whiteness" is not a physical property so much as a legal right, in that it has functioned as a category, not a physical or biological property, based on historical conditions under which it "was solely through being white that property could be acquired and secured under law. Only whites possessed whiteness, a highly valued and exclusive form of property."[9]

That property is as elusive as it is exclusive, tied not to pigmentation but to something else, of which pigmentation is a sign, although a very unreliable one. Thus, we have many historical incidents of "light-skinned" blacks passing for white. Their mere ability to "pass" demonstrates, of course, that they are white, to the extent that whiteness is a visible trait, just as "dark-skinned" whites are often not perceived as white by the same visible measure. "White as a skin colour is just as unstable, unbounded a category as white as a hue, and therein lies its strength. It enables whiteness to be presented as an apparently attainable, flexible, varied category, while setting up an always moveable criterion of inclusion, the ascribed whiteness of your skin."[10] Thus, Jewish and Irish people, to name two of many groups, have at times been regarded as nonwhite. Such a distinction would be meaningless were it without consequence. But as the Holocaust or the slave trade or the history of Native Americans (or, arguably, Hiroshima) has shown, the consequences of being considered nonwhite can be horrific, even if whiteness itself is impossible to define or measure. It is what Roland Barthes would call a myth, that is, an instance of Nature being confused with History.[11] That persistent set of confusions not only enables people to pass for white but, much more importantly, it enables whiteness to pass as the norm. "White" names a category defined not by visible traits and certainly not by DNA but by an invisible essence connected to an equally invisible privilege and power.

Part of that power—the part I am concerned with in this book—emanates from television during the Cold War era. Certainly television did not invent the "whiteness" of America as a set of white colonies, as a white postrevolutionary nation, as a white post–Civil War nation, or as a white post–World War I nation. What it did do was impressively help codify and deploy whiteness as the norm for the United States in the nuclear age. Technology in combination with mythology, as we shall see, made television an instrument of Cold War consensus that offered compelling instructions in normal American life. One of its most consistent instructions was that normal Americans normally lived in white communities. Television was instrumental in constructing those communities and in affirming them.

It is virtually a cliché among students of Western culture that domestic space has been treated as feminine and public space as masculine. Less highlighted and more tacitly accepted is the fact that these spaces have acquired not only gender but also racial distinctions. Put simply, from the symbolic image of the *White* House to the literal conditions of the streets of Howard Beach, New York, much of public policy, legal sanction, and popular discourse relies on the unspoken assumption that the public space is white. This assumption underpins, for example, "the Age of Exploration" as much as it does the privileged gaze focused on "native" populations by *National Geographic* photographers.[12] It fatally infects the implementation of treaties with Native American peoples, and it has been a profound determinant in public and private housing policies, which have ramifications throughout the full range of life-quality factors such as schooling, real estate values, street safety, health resources, police protection, and access to jobs or entrepreneurial opportunity.

However compelling seems our nation's historical attachment to the idea of race and, particularly, to black/white distinctions, such an attachment was no more inevitable than it is irrevocable. At numerous points of crisis or decision, the black-and-white character of racial classifications—their perception and their implications—might have been drastically reconfigured. Our understanding of racial difference in the United States might have been reimagined, even if such a reconfiguration may seem almost unimaginable from the perspective of 350 years of racialized history, especially in light of the tenacious way that racial notions infect virtually every aspect of contemporary American life.

And that in part is my point: Maintaining America's black-and-white profile was neither inevitable nor accidental; this dichotomy represents the triumph of numerous direct and indirect strategies, and of the groups who benefited from them. Retrospectively, we can recount numerous moments when things *might* have been otherwise. The formation of colonial law was one such moment, the framing of the Constitution another, as were the early decades of the new nation, Reconstruction, or the beginning of the twentieth century. That the opportunities were multiple should come as no surprise, given America's penchant for reinventing itself.

America is what Ralph Ellison has called a "conscious nation," by which he means that it derives its authority not from tradition or bloodline but from a conscious, intellectual decision. The founders of the United States declared their independence. They identified inalienable rights. They framed their constitution so as to invent a specific form of government, one that resembled a well-made eighteenth-century contraption, segmented, balanced, checked, and counterbalanced, equipped with functional attachments, suitable for repair and periodic upgrading.

For good reason, invention, pragmatism, and self-reliance have long been associated with the American character. American history dating back to the earliest colonial settlements comprises a virtual catalogue of social, technological, and political invention. And reinvention. Americans, even before they came to think of themselves as Americans, thought of themselves as conquering a new environment or taming a new frontier, constructing a new social order or forging a new world. In many ways the Declaration of Independence announced not so much the beginning of political independence as the culmination of more than a century of independent thought and act.

Perhaps this practice in adaptation helped the crafters of the American nation construct a governing document that has become renowned for its flexibility. That document, in any case, contributed greatly to this tradition of reinvention, a tradition that some have referred to as the "American Experiment." President Abraham Lincoln alluded to that experiment when he said at Gettysburg that the Civil War was "testing" whether a nation "conceived in liberty and dedicated to the proposition that all men were created equal" could endure. Indeed, the Civil War was a crucial moment of "reinvention," that is, a moment when the governing framework had to accommodate new social, political, and economic priorities and assumptions. While the accommodations following that armed conflict characterized America's most dramatic reinvention, other than the Revolutionary War itself, numerous shifts—for example, from an agrarian to an industrial economy, a colonial to an imperial nation, a hemispheric to a global power, a rural to an urban to a suburban populace, to name a very few—have had profound impacts on the sense of American identity that contribute to any notion of national character or national space.

This book is about one moment of reinvention that has had a huge and not fully acknowledged impact on the racial profile of late-twentieth-century

America: the post–World War II era. In particular, this book is about the role of black-and-white television during that period. If television was a remarkable technology, it was an even more remarkable social phenomenon, for it provided in midcentury a shared set of experiences and narratives consolidated visually within a homogeneous space. It produced and distributed the common nation that radio portended and to which the stories of the America of the day alluded. In many ways, television appeared to make visually concrete the necessarily imaginary space of the United States.

I am not suggesting that the United States did not exist before its citizens watched television. The United States, of course, had a real government and specific geographical boundaries; it had law, enforcement, and a legal identity that was recognized internally and internationally. I am suggesting only that because the composite of a nation's institutions and its acreage cannot be comprehended as a visual totality, construing any nation, and particularly one as vast and diversified as the United States, requires an act of imagination, just as inventing it did. Television thus contributed profoundly to solidifying what we could call a "national imaginary," that is, a set of common images and narratives that people shared when they thought of America as a nation and of themselves as its citizens.

This televisual imaginary was forged, moreover, at a time when great importance was placed on national homogeneity. The Cold War mandated widespread conformity and concomitant suspicion of "nonconformists." This call for conformity affected the full spectrum of American life, encompassing dating rituals and dress codes, political affiliations, and gender roles. The imaginary America that television represented, in other words, was one particularly distrustful of diversity. The popular image of the "melting pot" suggested as much: America was a place where immigrants exchanged their heterogeneous backgrounds for the opportunity to be part of a homogeneous nation.

For several reasons, which I will be discussing in Chapter 2, television constructed, even within Cold War parameters, a particularly narrow and conservative vision of America. That vision was channeled in black-and-white first through two and then, by the mid-1950s, three monopolistic national networks to a captive audience composed of baby boomers and their home-bound parents. Although the audience was black and white (and Asian, Hispanic, and Native American), the images were overwhelmingly white. Speaking of 1950s television, Henry Louis Gates says in his memoir that he "first got to know white people as 'people' through their flickering images on television shows."[13] "Lord knows," he explained, "we weren't going to learn about being colored by watching television. Seeing somebody colored on TV was an event."[14]

"Colored people," in fact, were not completely absent from black-and-white television. Especially before 1952—when the end of the Federal Communications Commission (FCC) license freeze allowed television broadcasting to proliferate in the South—black faces were seen on television with more frequency than in other areas of mass media, including film. Throughout the late 1940s and 1950s, Ed Sullivan's very successful variety show regularly featured black performers. And in the early period, the all-black comedy *Amos 'n' Andy* was a big hit. The show was, however, an extreme anomaly, one that despite high ratings could not last on network television, incurring as it did assaults both from civil rights groups that found it derogatory and from white racists who objected to the prominence and autonomy it gave to black characters. In an adaptation of the John O'Hara novel *Appointment in Samarra*, a black actor played the role of a waiter who stopped the principal character from fighting with another man. "No one would think twice about the role—it's so slight," television historian Donald Bogle points out, "were it not for the fact that it was one of the few that featured a serious Black actor during the era; and the drama itself was one of the few to incorporate the Negro in some manner into American life."[15] Sponsors were just as fearful as networks about alienating the South. In regard to race, "dramatic footage of the actual strife gets people riled up," *Variety* reported in 1962, "and such an experience might alienate customers and outlets of national advertisers, especially in the South."[16]

Because black faces on television entertainment shows overwhelmingly belonged to athletes, musical entertainers, and actors playing menial roles, Gates is correct that somebody colored on TV was an event. Some things were even more rare. Completely excluded from Cold War television were double beds, which married people usually slept in, or the word "pregnant," which married women sometimes got, although not nearly so frequently when they avoided double beds. Also missing, for the most part, were people with political opinions, critiques of the social order, or nonheterosexual desires, to name some obvious categories. That television omitted, ignored, or distorted just about everything in American life is less surprising than that it did so at the same time it touted itself as the definitive source of "reality." Even before 2 percent of American households had television sets, the nation was primed to regard television as the apparatus of truth, sine qua non.

As such, with growing intensity throughout the 1950s, it provided definitive representations of America and of the West, grounded in countless assumptions of normative whiteness. Prior to the American Revolution, a powerfully simple notion of racial difference—of superiority and inferiority—had already emerged, tied to a vague concept of "whiteness." It proliferated in North America with tenacious cogency. Certainly that cogency reflected the ever-increasing interests vested in the idea of racial supremacy. Throughout American history, this idea's form is protean, but its theme is etched in the proverbial stone: the United States of America—like its original colonizers—is white, and the black man or woman is always the dangerous outsider. White Americans, both North and South, pro- and antislavery shared a common fear that a black population jeopardized the liberties to which the founding fathers pledged their lives, fortunes, and sacred honor.

These fears arose out of a sense, dating to the seventeenth century, that for the white colonial American, as Winthrop Jordan succinctly puts it, "virtually every quality in the Negro invited pejorative feelings."[17] The colonists' fears were grounded in, as Jordan aptly states, "a revealing assumption: that free Negroes were essentially more Negro than free."[18] Being "more Negro" meant not only being more loyal to race than to citizenship but also being driven more by natural tendencies than by social sanctions or legal restrictions. The fear of the free black, in other words, was the fear of a less-than-human nature, an aggressive instinct not subject to the control of legal or moral principles. This fear of the black's imagined affiliation to a natural rather than a social order consolidated the racial themes of the seventeenth and eighteenth centuries: that the black is heathen, apelike, bestial. Since in the colonial period bestiality had strong sexual connotations, from very early in the settlement of America the black's unsuitability for freedom was connected to the way that black freedom threatened white women.

The free black thus posed numerous problems for white America, especially after the American Revolution. Since by the late 1700s racial distinction was fundamental to the institution of slavery, the free black was in a position to demonstrate that the constructed opposition between blackness and freedom was completely bogus. At the same time, free blacks could provide living affirmation of the egalitarian principles upon which the American Revolution was based. So strong was the national commitment to these principles in the fervid decades immediately after the Revolution that at that moment the United States might well have reinvented itself as a slave-free nation.

Unfortunately, the abolitionist strains were consolidated around putting an end to the slave trade, a feat that was accomplished in 1808, rather than to slavery itself. Many people believed that the latter would inevitably follow from the former, and others saw the step as a particularly efficacious compromise between slave and free states because it avoided dealing with the "problem" of a massive increase in the free black population. Instead, throughout the first half of the nineteenth century, the restrictions on free blacks increased until, by the 1850s, many Southern states had even passed or were attempting to pass laws allowing—in one case requiring—free blacks to return to slavery.[19]

Another attempt to save the United States from the perceived danger of an unrestrained black population was the colonization movement, which sought to ship blacks back to Africa. Although it had many abolitionist supporters, the colonization movement was deeply conservative in that it saw the growing black population as inherently threatening to public welfare. The colonization movement failed because it was as economically impractical as it was inchoate, but it remains vividly symptomatic of the apprehension attached to the idea of a free black population, an apprehension that was to grow as the century progressed. Throughout the South, by the mid-nineteenth century, the slave codes were extensive and extremely repressive.

By the time of the Civil War, the narrative of the black man set loose on white America had plagued race policy in the country for over 150 years. Within both the abolitionist and the proslavery camps, debate raged over the containment and disposition of manumitted blacks. Where should they go? At stake was freedom of movement—how ought black figures to be allowed to move about in white space? This conflation of the racial and the spatial informed the Fugitive Slave Laws, in that those laws negated legal sanction for the idea that a geographical site could exist in which the human rights of blacks took precedence over the property rights of whites.

Since the Civil War resolved the issue of the (black) human being as property, the war might have reinvented the United States as a racially integrated nation. Certainly the Thirteenth, Fourteenth, and Fifteenth Amendments to the U.S. Constitution assert the foundations for legal integration. As early as 1865, however, states started passing laws establishing racial discrimination. Black Codes were passed in most Southern states, extending some basic rights to blacks (e.g., marriage, right to ownership, right to enter into contracts, etc.) while in numerous ways restricting and subordinating them, often in ways that limited the right to sell their labor to the point that the effect sometimes came close to replicating slavery. This was both the cause of and the response to the advent of black mobility in the South.[20] With the collapse of Reconstruction, a widespread system of segregation was soon in place, supplemented by extralegal violence. Within a few decades after the Civil War, it was clear that the war had done little to abolish a racial caste system in the South. But it had, as I argued in my first book, *Invisible Criticism*, importantly shifted surveillance and discipline from the personal master to the impersonal state.[21] One consequence of the universalization of discipline was capricious enforcement, which in turn made invisibility advantageous for the black community. Thus, the postbellum organization of power encouraged a symbiotic relationship between black invisibility and transparent whiteness, even in Southern states where more than one-quarter of the population was black and where any random snapshot of life (except in officially segregated activities) would evidence a heterogeneous culture.

If the twentieth century did anything, it made these conditions less specific to the South. Between 1913 and 1916, boll-weevil epidemics and a series of severe floods led to a serious collapse in Southern agriculture. This hardship had the greatest impact on the poorer black laborers, fostering what has been termed the "Great Migration" of black populations to Northern urban centers. Between 1916 and 1918, more than one million blacks left the South, that is, more than 15 percent of all the blacks in those states. This large influx of blacks was not, in general, well received by Northern whites, especially because between 1890 and 1930 Northern industrialists used blacks as strike-breakers, a role that might not have been unexpected, given that many unions at that time practiced racial discrimination. In the North, in other words, the black's physical menace was coupled with economic menace. Since the Great Migration was heavily motivated by economics, the freely moving black body now signified a double threat.

Violence was used in the North not only to act out aggression against the imagined threat that the black posed but also to spatialize racial divisions. "Residential segregation," as Douglas Massey and Nancy Denton succinctly state, "is the principal organizational feature of American society that is responsible for the creation of the urban underclass."[22] "The emergence of the black ghetto," they further pointed out, "did not happen as a chance by-product of other socioeconomic processes. Rather, white

Americans made a series of deliberate decisions to deny blacks access to urban housing markets and to reinforce their spatial segregation."23 In their implementation in the North and the South, these decisions almost indistinguishably blended together public policy, private-sector efforts, legal sanction, law enforcement, and extralegal actions. At the beginning of the twentieth century, when black populations were growing in Northern cities, for example, fifty-eight black homes were bombed in Chicago alone between 1917 and 1921—an average of one every twenty days.24

By the mid-1920s, however, economic coercion had in large part replaced direct assault and intimidation. During the Depression, the federal government introduced mortgage assistance programs. The policies of these programs, unfortunately, tended to echo the goals of neighborhood associations. The federal Home Owner's Loan Corporation (HOLC) was established in 1933 to help people buy homes, or save their homes from foreclosure. To allocate its funds, HOLC ranked neighborhoods in one of four categories, financing relatively few homes in the third category and virtually none in the fourth. This policy "systematically undervalued older central city neighborhoods that were racially or ethnically mixed" by putting them in the third category, and "black areas were invariably rated as fourth grade."25 The HOLC policies, which did not invent but rather bureaucratized and nationalized extant ad hoc practice, diverted funds away from neighborhoods that might become black as well as those that already were. Their standard, moreover, was emulated by private lending agencies.

The Levittown developments, for example, that initiated and facilitated the middle-class emigration to the suburbs after World War II, officially prohibited black ownership, as did numerous other neighborhoods unofficially. "Curiously, the Federal Housing Administration appeared to condone Levitt's race discrimination. It chose to ignore a 1948 Supreme Court ruling that outlawed such covenants as Levittown included in its deeds. The FHA concerned itself only with the plans, materials, and financial backing of houses, said the agency's [New York] state director. It could not intrude in the area of 'social values.'"26

The beginning of the war in Europe and the subsequent U.S. entrance into the war had effected some changes in race relations while also underscoring in many ways the de facto national policy of insulating blacks from the general public. Although the Selective Service Act of 1940 brought many blacks into the armed forces, blacks were rejected at a rate twice as high as whites. Throughout the war, all military units were racially segregated so that the defense of the nation could appear to be a white-on-white activity. "Experience on the home front," moreover, "drove the morale of African-Americans to a new low."[27] Race riots broke out in many cities. The worst started in Detroit with a fistfight that snowballed into a brawl involving several hundred people, then escalated to the point where whites were roaming the streets, beating black people and burning their cars.

Given this context and the history of enforced racial divisions that have haunted the nation, the black "ghetto" denotes a space delimited by violence, within the confines of a "neutral" white space. During television's black-and-white era, particularly, that white space comprising the public domain became increasingly a televisual space. If we consider the virtual impossibility that any event will acquire "historical" status if it escapes the scrutiny of television; if we consider, furthermore, that no other medium of communication in the second half of the twentieth century conferred the same legitimacy and that television's power to legitimize has been matched only by its speed and ubiquity, we can see the great degree to which television does not report news of the public sphere but rather comprises the most significant domain that allows the possibility of news and of history. By many criteria, for the baby boom generation, television has been the fundamental public space and, therefore, is a necessary condition of historical possibility.

By looking at the arrival of television, its initial axioms, and its early programs, I hope to provide some understanding of how it established its authority and how it then adapted its conventions when it converted from a primarily live to a primarily filmed medium. Crucial in that conversion was Disney, the first film studio to produce regular shows for network television. Because of television, Disney Productions, a marginal studio that had verged on bankruptcy, came into its own. Television put Walt Disney in direct, eye-to-eye contact with the audience he was born to mold, the baby boomer who would set trends, values, and priorities throughout the second half of the century.

The Disneyland theme park, central to Disney's vision and its heft, both extended and validated the televisual reality that it promoted. It also marked the intersection of television with another growing network of homogeneous space, the national highway system. The superhighways and newly available airwaves wove Disneyland, the park, and *Disneyland*, the show, into one resilient cord tying suburban America to the frontier and, through that frontier, to the values of the American West and the Cold War West.

By the end of the 1950s, much of prime-time television had become a virtual frontierland, with "adult Westerns" comprising as much as 80 percent of the top ten shows and over 50 percent of the top twenty. Abounding with Cold War messages and themes, these Westerns seemed to speak simultaneously the nation's history, destiny, and mythology, defining the American West (erroneously) and, by extension, the Cold War West as a definitively white space. At the same time, the consequences of the civil rights movement and the Supreme Court school-desegregation decision gave visibility to the racism and brutality of some American practices, making them hard for the national public to overlook.

This book will attempt to show some of the ways that late-1950s and early-1960s prime-time television attempted to reread the news coverage and, in several subtle ways, reassert the ethics of conflating the racial and the spatial. This tendency can also be found in a number of extremely significant Kennedy-era shows, from *Bonanza*-like "property" Westerns to "New Frontier" Western updates such as *Route 66* and *The Fugitive*.

Finally, as well as initially, this book was motivated by an attempt to understand the Rodney King incident, that is, the beating of King by Los Angeles police officers after a car chase; the capturing of that beating on video; and the reactions—social, legal, and extralegal—to the video. If one reads *Presumed Guilty*, officer Stacy Koon's defense of his involvement in the beating of Rodney King, it is easy to see that he and King have completely different narratives not just of the events of May 3, 1991, but of the nation in which they both live. Less in Koon's description of the specific event than in his discussion of his job experiences in general, one can see that he thinks he is protecting public space, doing a necessary, vital, and indeed very dangerous job. The event of the beating, in fact, could be fairly described as a collision of King's fears with Koon's fears.

Although the moment of that collision of fears and of the norms that they represented occurred decades after the hegemonic era of black-and-white television, the King video still marks the legacy of the version of community projected as the real America by Cold War television. It also stands in sharp contrast to that moment by demonstrating how the authority of video recording had usurped that of television as the premier representative of reality. Television's authority had been on the wane for decades, just as the hazards of "driving while black" had been around for decades. The Rodney King video, therefore, is just a vivid bookmark indicating that we are solidly in a new chapter in the relationship between technology and the perception of reality. In light of that bookmark, it may be a little easier for us to recall a preceding chapter, when television monopolized the nation's vision in such a way as to create, for the only time in American history, a common visual space.

2 Television, Reality, and Cold War Citizenship

On February 26, 1939, twelve years after Philo Farnsworth's first demonstration of a television transmission, broadcast television had its official debut via an experimental pickup from the unfinished fairgrounds of the 1939 World's Fair. The National Broadcasting Company (NBC) telecast its popular radio comedy *Amos 'n' Andy*. The unique telecast of this situation comedy (sitcom) about urban African Americans featured an all-white cast wearing blackface makeup.[1] Layered with irony, television's black-and-white era thus began with a juxtaposition of black imagery and white reality so that the black face was simply an illusion, a semiopaque overlay on *real* white men, an optical convenience intended to supplement verbal humor with the suggestion of visual reality.

More than a suggestion, it was indeed a moment of stunning truth, in that the debut of what would be the definitive instrument of American veracity for the next half century was marked by pervasive contrivance. First of all, the presentation was not actually a broadcast but rather an experimental pickup, one *broadcasting* to an audience so *narrow* as to be nearly nonexistent. This episode of *Amos 'n' Andy*, moreover, was the first program of a medium that had no programming schedule, performed at a World's Fair site that as yet had no world's fair. Broadcasting's first television audience saw on that incomplete site, "for real," its favorite black characters, who were not really black people and who lived in an imaginary place very different from the one chosen for the broadcast. Circumscribed by artifice, this first moment of broadcast television seemed unintentionally to assert a fundamental premise: that blackness was a figment of white imagination.[2]

No medium could have been better suited for conveying such a message, as television from the outset was a technology positioned to define Western reality. It would convey in a manner simultaneously unique and traditional a notion of the American *e pluribus unum* that would represent democratic ideals as a seamless blending of the historical past, the quotidian present, and the mythic future. Television offered a relentless set of lessons in nationalism,

In blackface, the white radio creators and performers of the "black" comedy show *Amos 'n' Andy*. *Library of Congress, Prints and Photographs Division* [LC-USZ62-95690].

"living room lectures," as Nina Leibman calls them.[3] "In the span of roughly four years," Lynn Spigel explains, "television *itself* became *the* central image of the American home; it became the cultural symbol par excellence of family life."[4]

But in the Cold War, family life itself was a symbol in a global competition. If Spigel is correct that the term "togetherness" was coined in 1954 by *McCall's* magazine,[5] that moment represented not the initiation but the culmination of nearly a decade of Cold War containment strategies that identified the god-fearing nuclear family as a fundamental response to communism. "Togetherness," in such a context, connoted the merger of national solidarity with individual resolve, of domestic security with the cult of domesticity. The importance of togetherness as a national value evoked the idea that America's future depended upon an infinite number of tight units that were, implicitly, mirror opposites of communist cells. Whereas the cells were bound by communal rather than familial ties and met in secret, the true American family visibly displayed its togetherness. Whereas the cell members were atheists, "the family that prays together," as TV public service announcements of the period repeatedly pointed out, "stays together."

Religion, in this sense, was so much a part of a national agenda that it virtually acquired a secular status. "Our Government makes no sense unless it is founded in deeply felt religious faith," President Dwight Eisenhower proclaimed, "and I don't care what it is."[6] Eisenhower's secretary of state, John Foster Dulles, stated, "There is no way to solve the great perplexing international problems except by bringing to bear on them the force of Christianity."[7] From 1952 to 1957, Catholic bishop Fulton J. Sheen was the star of *Life Is Worth Living*, a successful television show (until it was pitted against Groucho Marx's *You Bet Your Life*) in which Sheen, with the aid of a blackboard, instructed the audience in values and global politics from a Catholic (or more generally Judeo-Christian) perspective. "Sheen came forth as an authentic Christian optimist," media historian Thomas Doherty explains, "preaching a message of joyful deliverance. He represented a kind of normative anticommunism."[8]

His medium explicitly televisual, his zeal particularly focused on anticommunism, his conviction unquestionable, his message a sacred version of Cold War togetherness, Sheen in many ways accentuated the qualities that typified Cold War television as the source of social norms, the live connection with unmediated truth, and the repository of Western values. Appearing live in the living rooms of average Americans, delivering a spiritual message for a commercial sponsor, providing sacred rationales for a political agenda, *Life Is Worth Living* consolidated many of the traits that characterized television in its first decade of national broadcasting and in the years leading up to that decade.

For technological, economic, social, and political reasons, television during the black-and-white era projected a version of America with extreme authority. During the Cold War, the television industry developed specific strategies to facilitate a relentlessly consumer society that was inextricably connected to establishing television in the public imagination as the authoritative source of reality. That authority impacted profoundly the post–World War II character of American race relations. To understand that impact, we first need to look at the emergence of American television.

The Television Monopoly

In the earliest years of regular programming (1948–1951), by far the top show—the best of the best—was *Texaco Star Theater*, which starred Milton

Berle. So great was Berle's popularity that in 1951, after three seasons as television's top performer, he was given a thirty-year contract by NBC, guaranteeing him $200,000 a year whether he worked or not. In five years, however, his Tuesday-night show was off the air; in less than a decade he was reduced to hosting (the unsuccessful) *Jackpot Bowling*. Much accounts for the rapid demise of Berle's celebrity. His humor appealed to the heavily Northeastern, ethnic Jewish viewers who composed a disproportionate percentage of television's early audience. Until the early 1950s, there also wasn't much competition in terms of program variety or alternate channels; many markets that received television broadcasts were limited to one, two, or three signals. Since television touted itself as the source of endless variety, any show was likely, in light of the potential that TV alleged, to grow stale in a relatively short period of time.

Even though Berle's contract was an anomaly and something of a publicity gimmick, the folly of the thirty-year contract reflects, I think, more than inadequate marketing data or limited understanding of the medium's inherent volatility. The Berle fiasco may also reflect the naïveté of a specific historical moment that maintained, despite the immense changes occurring over the preceding twenty-five years, inordinate faith in stability. It was as if the boom of the 1920s, Prohibition, the stock market crash, the Great Depression, and World War II were all part of a nightmare from which the nation had awoken, ready to resume normal, everyday life.

Yet another implication of the Berle contract was the way it exemplified an aspect of American television central to its character: Television from its inception was heavily monopolistic. Monopolized patents and monopolized airwaves combined to create a viewing experience that monopolized domestic space, national attention, and credulity. Just as one network monopolized Berle's talents, the industry would attempt to monopolize the control of technology, the production of signals, and the attention of viewers.

During the 1930s, the most powerful influence on the development of television technology and the laws governing its implementation was the Radio Corporation of America (RCA). With RCA as the chief patent holder and the most influential lobbyist, and with the strongest competition coming from another major radio network, the Columbia Broadcasting System (CBS), before the first television set was commercially marketed, it was almost certain that the new industry would be modeled on radio broadcasting as it existed in the 1930s. By that point, radio, which had started as a bottom-up medium, was dominated not by an array of independent stations or by a plethora of amateur broadcasters, like those that had sprung up in its early days, but by powerful national corporations. During the 1920s and early 1930s, in the process of consolidating the production of transmitters, receivers, and programs, RCA had honed the art of broadcasting. Using litigation and cooperative agreements with other corporations, RCA was able to squeeze out the small stations and over six hundred amateur transmitters that had sprung up in the 1920s.

In the same manner that it had monopolized much of the radio industry, RCA was positioning itself throughout the 1930s to control the production of television transmitters and receivers as well as to dominate the production and distribution of telecasts. RCA needed government cooperation. In 1928, when it applied to the Federal Radio Commission for a television license, RCA stated that "only an experienced and responsible organization, such as the Radio Corporation of America, can be depended upon to uphold high standards of service."9 While RCA continued to buy up patents, it also pressed relentlessly for government rulings that would favor the technological systems it had monopolized.

Regulation of the airwaves, that is, of the frequencies at which a transmitter would be allowed to send out its signal, was vital. Obviously, if anyone were to send signals from anywhere, using any means available, no signal would be decipherable. AM radio signals would trip over FM radio signals; high-definition and low-definition signals would trip over one another as well as over radio signals; even neighboring competitors with the same kind of signal—AM, FM, TV, etc.—would relentlessly jam one another.

Any form of airwave communication required rules with national standards and federal enforcement capabilities, in the same way that airplane routes had to be controlled and regulated. Airwaves, like plane routes, were not "public," therefore, in the way that public streets were. Airwaves were not open to public use but instead regulated in public interest. Without a system of federal regulation—a limited-access interstate skyway system of sorts—signals of the same type in close proximity would overlap, and signals of sundry types in collision would turn every message into audiovisual nonsense.

The government had to decide where along the spectrum of possible frequencies to assign television signals. RCA wanted the lower end, VHF spectrum (channels 1–13) because its patents were not fully operative at the higher UHF frequencies. When RCA succeeded in convincing the FCC that assigning television to the VHF spectrum was in the public interest, the consequences were profound. Assigning television to the VHF spectrum committed television to lower quality standards because higher-definition pictures and the technology at the time for transmission of color images both required larger-frequency bandwidths than those available in the VHF range. It also meant blocking the allocation of VHF frequencies to the newly developed FM radio technology, a decision that would forestall the broad use of FM radio for several decades, despite its clear superiority to AM transmission. The VHF spectrum also favored private over public television, as most of the germane patents held by the government operated in the UHF range. Most important, however, was the fact that the VHF range created an artificial scarcity of licenses that would have a profound effect on the phenomenon of broadcast television. As a trio of media economists noted in 1974, "The artificial scarcity of VHF licenses has [created] a system of powerful vested interests which continue to stand in the path of reform and change—particularly change involving increased competition and viewer choice."[10]

The outcome of nearly two decades of deliberations and rulings by government agencies determined that Americans would experience television as a black-and-white image of relatively poor resolution, with a small number of large corporations controlling the technology and monopolizing most of the content. The revenue for this venture would accrue to a small number of manufacturers of transmitters and receivers, most of whom would also produce programming that they would try to network, in the same way that radio programming had been networked but, owing to the restricted number of available stations, with much less competition.

The means for profiting from the programming was much more complex than the means for profiting from equipment sales. Since the airwaves belonged to the public, the television industry could not *sell* airtime. Rather, it used programs to attract viewers and then sold the viewers to sponsors. To sponsor a television show was to pay for giving the show away, with the signal cast as broadly as possible. (The concept of "broadcasting," a term first used metaphorically to describe the rise of the radio medium, came from a farming term that denoted spreading seed widely rather than planting one hole at a time.[11]) In return for this form of sponsorship, the sponsor was allowed to address the people who had been attracted to the freely distributed show. For this right, the sponsor paid the producer and the distributor of the show. So potentially lucrative was this arrangement that as early as 1949 a talent agent at the William Morris Agency noted, "Television has the impact of an atomic bomb. It is increasing the people's intellect in proportion to a bomb's destructive power for blowing them to pieces. And it's a foregone conclusion that national advertisers will go into TV or go out of business."[12]

None of this, of course, would have been possible without government regulation of the airwaves, which remained public property. The use of public property, like any other distinctions between public and private, was unavoidably implicated in Cold War ideology. According to American Cold War rhetoric, private control fostered competition, free enterprise, and personal liberty, whereas government control fostered rigidity, lack of enterprise, and the suppression of individual expression. According to American dogma, free enterprise preserved freedom, whereas state control threatened it. In short, private ownership was capitalist and public ownership communist. Television therefore occupied a peculiar position in that its free enterprise required government-supervised disposition of airwaves, making the government the agency by which public property was used to sell public attention to private corporations for corporate profit.

The Public Interest

Since the mandate for this relationship entailed demonstrating that licensing airwaves was in the public interest, the immense profits that the television industry has accrued over half a century have always been, at least rhetorically, connected to a definition of "public interests." However much it has been fluid, debated, and debatable, the public interest has remained an important element in all arguments for private control of the airwaves. Public interest, in this context, has been substituted for public ownership, a practice that was not deemed to be in the public interest in the Cold War West.

When it came to television, therefore, the public interest was served in ways that would not impinge on the monopolistic aspects of commercial television. One way that the public was served was through a series of public service announcements, and another was through religious programming. The FCC also reserved frequencies for educational television, primarily in the UHF bandwidth, where they would not impinge on the scarce availability of channels in the VHF range. News programming also played an important role in demonstrating television's ostensible commitment to public interests, Nancy Bernhard has shown, while broadcasters mediated between self-regulation and censorship, public service and entertainment, sponsor-supported and government-subsidized production.

In the immediate post–World War II period, the television industry was being conceived within the context of a national imperative for government to "control information campaigns that would vanquish world communism."13 Between 1948 and 1953, therefore, television news created an aura of objectivity by "reporting closely and without comment on the activities of high-ranking officials, the very practice federal information officers most wanted"14 because it allowed the government to control the interpretation of the news without interfering with the free-market system of American broadcast television. In this way, while actually being a funnel for government propaganda, television asserted independence and objectivity. That independence and objectivity, in turn, legitimized government press releases by representing the content as "news." As a result, television news became a government asset, and access to public officials therefore became routine. The interdependence between broadcasters and officials blurred the issue of control and "left television's news collaborations with the national security state unseen in American culture."15

The Truman administration became particularly interested in, if not always successful at, exploiting government's symbiotic relationship with television news to promote its foreign policy. During the Korean War, a voluntary Broadcasters Advisory Council, consulting with cabinet officials, established the efficacy of a self-censorship that not only forestalled government intervention but also secured government assistance in developing programs that supported the war effort. On NBC, the weekly show *Battle Report—Washington* provided reports on the war's progress, as did the DuMont series *Pentagon* and the CBS show *The Facts We Face.*

Both *The Facts We Face* and *Battle Report—Washington* gradually expanded their scope to cover a full spectrum of Cold War activities. *Battle Report—Washington* was actually produced in a White House office and hosted by President Truman's assistant, Dr. John Steelman. It mixed stock government documentaries with news footage shot for the show and federal officials addressing the audience with scripts written by government information officers.

When it came to war coverage, such assistance was invaluable to both the government, because it could exercise extensive control over content, and the broadcasters, because they could use government assistance to cut production costs. The Department of Defense (DOD) was particularly effective in helping the networks develop increasingly popular forms of news entertainment that, by the end of the 1950s, obscured the DOD's cooperation with private broadcasters. "In return for the substantial air time donated by the networks, [the DOD radio-TV branch] provided . . . free programming . . . public affairs announcements, personnel to appear on discussion programs, archival footage. They even arranged for naval maneuvers to be performed for network cameras."[16] If network television relied on the government for program information, the government and especially the military collaborated in the production of mass entertainment for clearly political reasons, even going to the point of staging events if appropriate archival footage was unavailable.[17]

As part of the Korean War effort, the now defunct DuMont network ran *Our Secret Weapon—The Truth*, a counterpropaganda show. CBS fueled nuclear frenzy with "What to Do During a Nuclear Attack," a documentary hosted by Walter Cronkite.[18] Like the widely shown 1950s public service short, "Duck and Cover," "What to Do During a Nuclear Attack" conveyed a dual message—that nuclear assault could occur at any moment, and that with the right preparation Americans could avoid serious personal harm. This odd mixture of universal paranoia and mundane pragmatism, simultaneously apocalyptic and optimistic, affirmed television's role as avatar of the American surveillance state, a cultural model that invested surveillance with an aura of civic pride rather than a fear of secret police. In the cultural lexicon, the Federal Bureau of Investigation (FBI) protected rather than threatened personal liberty; it uprooted communists and their sympathizers. Hypervigilance thus combined duty and pleasure, for in assisting the surveillance state, the private citizen was preserving his or her own freedom. This mind-set required, of course, delimiting freedom within very narrow parameters, ignoring what could have been seen as an inherent conflict between surveillance and freedom.

Just as "What to Do During a Nuclear Attack" (other than oxidize) in effect eliminated the controversial poles of the issue—either the hopelessness of surviving a nuclear war or the extreme improbability of its occurring—so television news narrowed the spectrum of political debate. Network news shows such as *Meet the Press* (first televised in 1947) played a vigorous role in the anticommunist campaign, operating to define an "objective" distrust of a (perceived) communist position.

The Instrument of Truth

Television fostered its reputation for objectivity from its status as a technological phenomenon even more than from its programming. Part of television's power, in this regard, was owed to a faith in visual representation that has dominated Western thought since the Renaissance. "Seeing is be-lieving," we have come to believe. "Pictures never lie." "Ocular proof," Othello demanded of Iago before he would accept assertions of Desdemona's infidelity. Modern science depends on the empirical method. The solution to every mystery, Sherlock Holmes demonstrated, begins with observation. Noting the commercial value of television, a 1946 article about the use of the close-up, by H. G. Christensen, in the fledgling trade journal *Television* explains "another important thing: By *visual* demonstration *actual proof* can be submitted of many things that now must be accepted on mere statement."[19]

Christensen was not referring to news, science, nature, or education but to a sponsor's claim about the storage capacity of a refrigerator. As another example, Christensen describes a show that demonstrated that Chef Boy-ardee spaghetti could be prepared in twelve minutes: "During the entire broadcast, with all the changes of camera angles, the pot on the stove *was always* in the scene." The climax of the show was that the meal was served to the audience members. "There was an integrated commercial that not only didn't interfere with the rest of the show but certainly did a better sell-ing job than ever could be done by oratorical radio."[20] The quality of the food was validated by the sight of the audience eating it.

For some people, television even represented an extension of the natural order. "A man will come home at night," stated a 1949 book, "and open the magic window of television, which will bring him information and enter-tainment from all over the world. . . . He will have lost the habit of using his ears for what they were never meant to do, and sight will have been restored to its natural place in his life."[21] Television was predicted to be so powerful a medium as to activate more than the natural senses of sight and sound. "So magic is the performance of the electron tube," wrote one commenta-tor in 1942, "and so diversified is the service it already performs, that an en-gineer in describing its versatility reports that it can hear, see, taste, feel, smell, remember, calculate, count, measure and talk."[22]

Television's stunning visual power was enhanced by its potential for im-mediacy. Television gave Americans access to a new level of truth not only because it let people see things but allegedly let them see things *immediately*, before reality could undergo alteration. Rather than perform actions, televi-sion ostensibly allowed events to be performed.

"The public," James Caddigan wrote in *Television*, "is being given the promise now of 'seeing things as they happen.' It is their most enthusiastic expectation of the immediacy of television that will present a challenge to every station to present the 'scoop' news in as speedy and complete manner as possible." Unlike print media, which have to wait for the story to unfold, then write it up, print it, and distribute it, television would, in effect, eliminate the middlemen. The television public, Caddigan believed, would expect to witness news rather than read about it.

Clearly the public that Caddigan had in mind in 1947, when he wrote this dictum, was the general American populace, not the tiny minority that actually owned television sets. Caddigan's huge imaginary audience, moreover, would have access to a competing array of news broadcasts integrated into a constant flow of programming, for "the immediacy of television" was as much temporal as physical. Gilbert Seldes, an early pioneer in television programming and one of the medium's most articulate critics, wrote, "The fact that television can transmit actuality is of prime psychological importance. It invites us to 'the conception of things as they are'; it sets us on the way to maturity. . . . The essential thing is to determine that television will satisfy the deep human desire to look, at times, on the face of reality."[23]

A significant pillar of the argument rested on underscoring "spontaneity." As Orin Dunlap pointed out in 1942, "Telecasting of spot news is mostly a matter of luck. The biggest thrills in newscasting are likely to be surprises." And, as early as 1948, *Time* was lauding television's power of the spontaneous: "The unexpected makes some of television's brightest moments: a rainstorm breaks, and the camera shows ground keepers covering the pitcher's box with canvas, then sweeps across the bleachers, singling out soaked fans huddling under newspapers. The key man is the camera director, who must watch on small screens the action of three or four cameras, to decide which image to send over the air at any moment."[24]

The newscasts, the same article noted, were generally disappointing, with the exception of "such foreseeable events as political rallies where the cameras, being set in place, catch unscheduled incidents."[25] In this interesting mix of the "foreseeable" and the "unexpected," wherein surprise depends on prediction, we can see in the moments of television's initial mass reception that the television viewer was in effect seen as a paragon of the surveillance state. The viewer tuned in to one event, but because that event was live, the viewer might unexpectedly find a second event hidden within the first. The brightest moments were those in which orchestrated order was disrupted, and the anonymous spectator glimpsed moments of something "unexpected." Even though the event—a ball game, a speech, a performance—came with the immediacy of a live broadcast, it was validated by the unexpected, as if its claim to be real required the proof of a second level of reality. In order to appreciate the full richness of television's potential, therefore, the viewer had to be on the alert.

That glowing reality—"some of television's *brightest* moments"—relied crucially on the camera, which must already be in place so as to "catch unscheduled events," and the camera director, who must "decide which image to send at any moment." The unexpected constituted both the bane of television programming and its validation. It gave people an extra reason to watch the limited and fuzzy perspective that it afforded; it invested the ordinary with extraordinary value and untapped potential. Caddigan noted,

> Many of the so-called special events productions give little warning of their coming, and should a television production staff wait until an incident or a story is looming over the production horizon, before moving toward preparation, the story will either be poorly produced or lost entirely. Preparation for the unexpected seems like a larger order to fill, yet, that is exactly the job that must be handled if the special event or news incident is to be produced with the "immediacy" that television promises. The television audience of the future is being educated at the present time to expect sight of an incident "as it happens."[26]

Although television heavily encouraged that expectation, in 1952 less than half of all households had television sets, and because of an FCC licensing freeze between 1948 and 1952, broadcasting was concentrated regionally. As a whole, therefore, the nation was incapable of seeing things as they happened. Beyond that, the technology of broadcasting—the size and cost of the cameras, the expense and difficulty of remote hookups, the limited picture quality—rendered "spontaneity" a relatively rare commodity. Far more regularly, television offered a mix of staged, rehearsed performances, broadcast live, and action or adventure shows on film, augmented by old movies, often cut into bits. Aside from sports, few events were presented as they happened, and the total amount of sportscasting, especially on network television, was very low.

While the capacity for the whole nation to see something "as it happened" was facilitated by the completion in 1953 of the transcontinental coaxial cable, connecting television signals from coast to coast, such moments were still infrequent. The cable facilitated viewing such national events as, for example, President Eisenhower's inauguration, but it contributed relatively little, in the regular flow of programming, to support television's promise to put all Americans in touch with everything at exactly the moment that everything happened. It is vital to keep in mind, nevertheless, how pervasively the television industry in its formative years asserted that it was providing a conduit to reality, and consequently how many of its programming strategies contributed to bolstering that assertion.

Television projected a sense of intimacy, surrounded by an aura of verisimilitude, as if to augment its less-than-fulfilled promise of immediacy. To that end, even talk shows such as *Today* manifested "togetherness" by bringing the world to the viewer, filtered through an ersatz family of hosts and assistants. One early *Today* host, Ernie Kovacs, used his wife, Edie Adams, as part of the cast; another host, Dave Garroway, included in his morning family J. Fred Muggs, a chimp who vividly merged the traits of the viewers' diapered baby boomer infants and their adored house pets.

Perhaps the most interesting ways in which television programming asserted the medium's veracity clustered around those portions of the schedule lacking the prima facie assumption of "truth" that accrued, for example, to a live sporting event. Arthur Godfrey, who in the early 1950s had three separate, highly successful television shows running simultaneously, owed much of his success to his ability to capitalize on television's investment in intimacy and reality. Although no one argued that he was an exceptionally talented performer, Godfrey was popular both with daytime and prime-time audiences because his ad libs and informal conversational style conveyed the sense that he was expressing his true personality, that he was genuine. As one pair of television historians succinctly noted, "people did not tire of him because he was an interesting person to listen to. He was himself."[27]

Godfrey epitomized an attitude toward television as the magic place where things were themselves. Most early sitcoms were live, and when they were not, they used obligatory laugh tracks to suggest spontaneity. Many of those shows employed what has been called an "I-me-mine" formula in which a celebrity played him- or herself or appeared as a fictional character who had much in common with the real-life performer. The "real" personality of the performer thus created a sense of intimacy that diminished the show's fictional aspects and created a comfort zone: The viewers were taking the performers into their living rooms, and the performers seemed to be reciprocating.

One particularly successful early sitcom of this sort, *The Adventures of Ozzie and Harriet* (1952–1966), focused on the domestic setting of the real band leader Ozzie Nelson, his real wife and former lead singer, Harriet, and their two sons, all of whom played themselves. The *Burns and Allen Show* similarly had George Burns and Gracie Allen playing themselves, enacting episodes chiefly from their domestic rather than professional lives. *Make Room for Daddy*, starring Danny Thomas as himself, followed a similar formula, as did a number of less successful shows such as *Mary Kay and Johnny* (1948), a sitcom about the trials and tribulations of a real married couple of entertainers.[28]

At a very slight remove from these shows were those in which celebrity performers played characters with fictional names and, sometimes, fictional occupations, who nevertheless very closely resembled the celebrities who played them. These included *Where's Raymond*, starring Ray Bolger; *Bonino*, starring Ezio Pinza; and perhaps the most famous sitcom of all time, *I Love Lucy*. In that series the character Lucy, played by Lucille Ball, was married to Ricky Ricardo, a Cuban band leader, played by Desi Arnaz, the Cuban band leader to whom Ball was actually married. The show, which premiered in 1950, quickly became the most popular sitcom in the country, and Lucille Ball's pregnancy, mirrored on the show by Lucy's pregnancy, became the focus of the 1952–1953 season. In the midst of the postwar baby boom, pregnancy no doubt was one of the greatest common denominators shared by the television audience, so the pregnant Lucille Ball mirrored not only her character but also her viewers. In Lucy's pregnancy, television was providing the newest member of the family at the same time that the television set was becoming the newest addition. Millions of homebound new mothers welcomed television into their growing family with the same alacrity with which they awaited Lucy's delivery.

Indeed, this visual instrument not only functioned as a member of the household and a figure of authority; it also self-consciously positioned itself as the representative of religious and domestic norms. To that end, for example, a rabbi, a priest, and a minister were present on the set for the filming of all the Lucy episodes dealing with the pregnancy. Throughout those episodes, the word "pregnant" was never used, nor, throughout the entire run of the series, were Lucy and Ricky ever portrayed as sleeping in the same bed.

The Surveillance State

The members of the clergy observing the filming of the pregnant-Lucy episodes, while guaranteeing that the episodes were in good taste, could

The pregnant Lucille Ball mirrored not only her character but also her viewers. *Photofest.*

also guard against some indecency that went undetected by the actors, writers, producers, directors, that is, by the normal mechanisms of television production. These religious leaders served as the invited agents of the ultimate surveillance state; under their watchful eyes, it would be impossible, even inadvertently, to subvert American mores, to deviate from the approved domestic norms. This need for elaborately self-conscious layers of censorship in the form of self-observation, like the odd symbiotic relationship between the planned and the unpredictable so valued by early television critics, implicitly identified television with the surveillance-state mentality that informed American life at the moment of the medium's proliferation.

As has been extensively noted, the manifestations of Cold War containment extended to all aspects of American life.[29] Loyalty oaths proliferated. College faculties were being purged.[30] The U.S. Senate and House of Representatives were conducting continuous investigations to safeguard the nation from subversion. The FBI, the Central Intelligence Agency (CIA), and sundry private organizations were gathering files on people whose actions might reveal disloyalty. Television, as the technology that allowed one to see everything, fitted well into the cultural logic of Cold War observation and intelligence gathering.

"Television's surveillance potential," Jeanne Allen points out, "was quickly associated with aircraft intelligence gathering."[31] Army intelligence, in fact, was the model Caddigan recommended for television newsgathering. News divisions, he believed, should set up for each area a "television intelligence file" that would include notification contacts, topographic data, weather reports, and correct credentials because, "at the time of an incident, intelligence from the field will be most important to the production staff working on the script at the station."[32] This form of military-style intelligence gathering was "a never ending job as each new production will provide added information that can be used to advantage on some future show."[33]

A world under surveillance made sense to post–World War II Americans locked in the throes of the Cold War frenzy. At exactly the moment that the television curtain rose, the iron curtain was descending not only on Eastern Europe but also on world consciousness. Fears of the spread of communism outside American borders and the subversion of American ideals from within inundated the nation with an aura of suspicion. Thus, at every turn television differentiated American acts and values from un-American activities and objectives. People who did not consider religious broadcasts a form of public service, people who had not allowed their families to pray or stay together, people who embraced controversial positions or associated with those who did (or were even accused of associating with them)—these people were suspect.

The search for subversion, for deviance, after all, requires a set of norms against which to measure deviation, and nothing would supply the norms more prolifically and more rigidly than television. Enabling Americans to distinguish the true American from the imposter was therefore a task fundamentally consistent with the idea of television. As we have seen, television promoted itself as the medium of truth, not artifice. This describes to an equal degree the industry's self-image and the public image it promoted. With extreme versatility, television devoted its strong authority to the cause of the Cold War. The anticommunist message, as J. Fred MacDonald has extensively documented, took numerous forms.[34] Bishop Fulton J. Sheen may have been the most successful and the most explicitly anticommunist of the religious broadcasters, but he was far from the only one performing the public service of helping the nation align itself on the side of God in confirmed opposition to the godless communists. "The fundamental depravity explaining all Red actions was alleged to be the atheism basic to Communism."[35]

The broadcast schedule, through the mid-1950s, was replete with spy series, action-adventure series, and military and space adventure shows that shared a set of common Cold War motifs. Each episode of *Superman* reminded us that he was the superhuman, interplanetary agent of "truth, justice, and the American way." *Captain Video*'s Video Rangers swore "to support forever the cause of Freedom, Truth, and Justice throughout the universe," and children watching *Rod Brown of the Rocket Rangers* in order to join the Junior Rocket Rangers had to pledge to "always chart my course according to the Constitution of the United States of America."[36] *Captain Midnight*, a jet pilot and the commander of a secret squadron based in a secret mountaintop location, so regularly dealt with issues of national defense and problems caused by enemy agents that J. Fred MacDonald calls it "thoroughly Cold War in its orientation."[37]

Television documentaries on the U.S. military also dotted the programming landscape. One of the most successful, *The Big Picture*, filmed by the U.S. Army Signal Corps, produced 828 episodes between 1951 and 1971,[38] each beginning with the announcement: "From Korea to Germany, from Alaska to Puerto Rico, all over the world the United States Army is on the alert to defend our country—you, the American people—against aggression."[39] This connection between foreign policy and "you, the American people" at home watching television is very revealing. Television was indeed the instrument that connected the everyday life, the leisure activity of the American people, to their national agenda: "Our country" meant "you the television viewer."

If watching television made one the definitive citizen, we need to consider how that practice defined citizenship. Certainly the connections to the monopolistic aspects of television broadcasting are implicit. If watching television were a multifarious, diversified, and fragmentary experience, each person's participation would be somewhat unique. Assorted Americans would receive sundry messages and be exposed to wide-ranging values and opinions. (Consider for example the fact that although most of the European countries in the Western bloc—the North Atlantic Treaty Organization [NATO] nations—had active, often successful socialist parties, a socialist's acquiring any serious television exposure in America would be impossible even today, much less during the black-and-white era.) Under a more diversified broadcast system, citizenship might have been defined by the right to watch and respond to an array of viewpoints and values, not by the message one received. Exactly the opposite was true under the heavily monopolized system of American Cold War television, in which a small number of stations conformed to very similar norms. "The aim of television," as David Marc so aptly puts it, "is to be normal. The industry is obsessed with the problem of norms."[40]

The (white) nuclear family watching *The Big Picture* was the normative unit of domestic security in the nuclear age. As such, it received relentless instructions on how to be normal at the same time that it was the measure of television's normal range of expression. From its inception, radio sought to reach the broadest audience by presenting that which was most common. Television not only inherited the informing principle of broadcasting but also turned that principle into a national ideal.

Its monopolistic structure allowed television programming to be dominated by two networks, each competing for a simple majority of viewers. Each week in the months of January and February 1957, for example, the CBS half-hour adventure show *Robin Hood* was watched on between 48 percent and 51 percent of the sets in use, composing just under one-third of the total potential television audience. In none of those weeks, however, did *Robin Hood*'s ratings put it among the top twenty shows.[41] Under such circumstances, alienating even a relatively small segment of the audience could put a broadcaster or network at a great disadvantage. If the FCC had not created an artificial scarcity of stations, then worsened the scarcity by freezing the issuing of licenses for three years; if it had not aligned itself so strongly with patents and technology controlled by one company and ignored the need for public television, one could, in theory, imagine circumstances in the early 1950s that would have allowed most populated areas to have over a dozen stations, and for the thousands of stations throughout the country to be affiliated with one or more of a few dozen networks, producing shows that spanned a broad range of opinions, ideas, and interests. One could imagine, for example, stations and networks organized around the interests of targeted minorities, or political values, or regional and local concerns. The narrower the broadcast frequency spectrum, the lower the frequency of dissent and the smaller the spectrum of opinion. Under the commercial, legal, and technological structure of television in its formative years, the safe, the clichéd, and the uncontroversial had an enormous advantage over the experimental, the original, and the challenging.

The economic pressure to maximize the number of viewers when applied to the concept of citizenship thus encouraged a very conservative citizen, so that television could be the site of debate in the public forum only so long as the parameters of the debate did not exceed the most common of accepted notions. At the height of the Cold War in America, any position fell outside the normal spectrum if it could be associated, for example, with socialism. Although national health care was becoming the norm in post–World War II Europe and the bulk of the industrialized world, because it was branded "creeping socialism" or "socialized medicine" it could not be treated seriously in U.S. news coverage, public affairs broadcasting, or television dramas. Homosexuality, premarital sex, and atheism were as unacceptable as plunging necklines or, for the most part, men with facial hair. An unqualified endorsement of capitalism and Judeo-Christian religious belief provided a tacit foundation for all of the positions expressed in virtually all programming.

This set of conditions mandated many programming decisions. Because delivering consumers to sponsors seemed, at least ostensibly, connected to head counting, the network or program that could deliver the largest audience was the most valuable. Unlike industries that rely chiefly on niche audiences, television, especially in the first decades, sought a degree of universality. The consequent pressure to maintain huge audiences demanded inoffensive programming.

In order to assure that programming was inoffensive, the National Association of Radio and Television Broadcasters in 1956 codified its norms with a television code. The preamble, stressing the fact that television was a common national activity, began with its informing principle: "Television is seen and heard in every type of American home."[42] Therefore, "it is the responsibility of television to bear constantly in mind that the audience is primarily a home audience, and consequently that television's relationship to the viewers is that between guest and host."[43] This metaphor treated the viewer and the show as equal in kind. The television show was not some object to be accepted, rejected, evaluated, or consumed; it was a guest, someone like the viewer, to be invited in and attended to.

At the same time that the broadcasters were guests who must display good manners, they also had to provide the viewer with the best: "American businesses . . . are reminded that their responsibilities are not limited to the sales of goods and the creation of a favorable attitude toward the sponsor. . . . They include, as well, responsibility for utilizing television to bring the best programs . . . into the American home."[44]

The notion that television had the capacity to deliver the best was a long-accepted axiom of the medium. During World War II, television was used in New York City to train air-raid wardens, who received their lessons from sets installed at local police stations. This program of instruction was based on the idea that "there is always a best lecturer for any subject and through television he can actually instruct all the parties instantly and uniformly. Standardization of training is thus introduced into the defense plans."[45]

The technology of television, as its use in police stations in the interest of national defense illustrated, allowed Americans to receive the best as a universal standard. "In this war program," Dunlap explains, "light has been shed on the ability of television to put into practical use the unlimited possibilities envisaged for it after the war."[46] After the war, through television, the best would become the standard; the standard would become uniform and available for universal access. The broadcasters' code merely codified that prediction by elaborately detailing the characteristics of the best programming. It included using television as a "means of augmenting the educational and cultural influences of schools, institutions of learning, the home, the church, museums," with the understanding that education "via television may be taken as to mean that process by which the individual is brought toward informed adjustment to his society."[47]

Televisual education, in other words, is a form of regulation that validates social norms and brings the individual in line with them.

Here are some examples of appropriate adjustments found in the code's twenty-nine-item list of acceptable program material: "Reverence is to mark any mention of the name of God, His attributes and powers"; "illicit sex relations are not to be treated as commendable"; "law enforcement shall be upheld, and the officers of the law are to be portrayed with respect and dignity"; "camera angles shall avoid such views of performers as to emphasize anatomical details indecently."[48] As part of television's obligation to provide the best programming, the code unequivocally stated, "It is the responsibility of a television broadcaster to make available to the community as part of a well-balanced program schedule adequate opportunity for religious presentations."[49]

This code clearly delimited television's options within a rigid Cold War agenda that supplemented the medium's role as a virtual arm of government propaganda. The power of propaganda, of course, is directly correlated with its invisibility, that is, its ability to disappear beneath the veil of "truth." During the height of the Cold War, American "truth" comprised a narrowly construed and pervasively deployed consensus. The strategy of "containment," as originally articulated by George Kennan, charged all American citizens with the task of checking the spread of communism through a combination of vigilance and self-scrutiny that would produce a uniformly attractive image of American life.[50] Because the Cold War was being fought for hearts and minds, on a chiefly symbolic battleground, the ability to deliver and solidify images proved as effective in some ways as any form of hardware, just as the principle of "deterrence" depended on the symbolic rather than the material value of planes, missiles, and nuclear warheads.

Since containment rendered the American family a form of symbolic capital, the best programming taught Americans how, implicitly in the national interest, to be normal. If television was a guest, it was a very knowledgeable and instructive guest visiting a compliant and amenable host, one who was receptive to a national agenda and in touch with national norms and mores. Dedicated to normalizing and affirming the values and lifestyles of its audience, the television broadcasting system aimed, one could argue, at becoming a seamless extension of the television set, the piece of living room furniture that made those projections part of the flow of everyday life. "Television," *House Beautiful* announced in 1951, "has become a member of the family."[51] As such, of course, it could not be controversial, for the home, after all, was the repository of postwar values, and the nuclear family, by consolidating the values for which the Cold War was being fought, implicitly validated the nuclear arms race.

A stunning example of television's avoidance of controversy could be seen in the treatment of the actress Jeanne Muir, a regular in the early hit sitcom The Aldrich Family. Muir was charged with participation in left-wing activities. Although she denied the charges, General Foods, the show's sponsor, indicated that it made no difference whether or not she were guilty; the mere fact that she had been accused could hurt sales. "This reasoning became a model for other blacklisting cases. . . . The very fact that someone had been charged made them guilty of being too controversial."52 In the obsessively normal world of black-and-white television, a person innocent of any substantive charge could nevertheless be guilty of being controversial. This latter category—being controversial—which comprised the blacklist's largest group by far was, as Thomas Doherty points out, "infinitely elastic in application and maddeningly circular in reasoning."53 If television was the site of exemplary citizenship—the apotheosis of democracy—it was a new kind of democracy, one forging consensus by precluding controversy. And since television was the American activity, anything not suitable for broadcast, by implication, was un-American.

With the outbreak of the Korean War, suspicion became an even more overt obligation. "At home the question of Communist influence in America was no longer restricted to the theoretical level—the nation was at war. With American boys being felled by Red bullets, no sponsor wanted to be charged with satisfying the Communists by putting one of their fellow-travelers on national television. Publications such as Red Channels became the unofficial Madison Avenue bibles on performers with alleged Communist connections."54 Red Channels, published in June 1950, was devoted to identifying "subversives." The American Communist Party newspaper, The Daily Worker, "as vetted by Red Channels was not the only source of names," Doherty explained. "Page after page of lists and publications, notations culled from rumor, supplemented by innuendo, and littered with transcription errors, might also render a personality controversial."55

Despite the need to rely on dubious information, networks and ad agencies vetted prospective hires in all aspects of production. A company executive in charge of personnel security reviewed the names with "consultants" working for organizations such as AWARE, Incorporated, an anticommunist arm of the broadcast industry founded by Vincent Hartnett, the chief author of *Red Channels*. Producer David Susskind testified to having submitted for approval about *five thousand* names.[56] People who were not approved were virtually unemployable unless they were cleared by AWARE. For such clearance, Hartnett received substantial fees and/or exacted favors as proof of loyalty. Since producers were instructed never to reveal the reason they had failed to hire someone, it often took people time to discover that they were being blacklisted—and, unless they overtly succumbed to a financial or ethical shakedown, even longer to find out they had been removed from the list.

Such was the case of Philip Loeb, the costar of *The Goldbergs*, a hit comedy in the late 1940s. In 1950 he was named by *Red Channels* because of his progressive political activities in the 1930s and the show's sponsor attempted to buy out his contract. He refused and continued to appear on the show until the end of the season, when CBS canceled it despite its high ratings. When NBC picked it up, the new network required, despite the protestations of the show's producer and star, Gertrude Berg, that Loeb be replaced. From 1952 on, the FBI kept Loeb under surveillance while he struggled to find sparse work. In August 1955, the bureau decided that Loeb should be removed from its list of suspects. One month later, with no knowledge of his cleared status, Loeb committed suicide.

One sign of a possible subversive was an interest in civil rights. Security investigators often regarded a black employee's participation in civil rights activities as incriminating evidence.[57] Hazel Scott, a black singer and performer, in 1950 briefly had a program on the DuMont network until she was listed by *Red Channels*. Although she testified before the House Un-American Activities Committee (HUAC) at her own request, categorically denying any interest in the Communist Party, she was unable to save her show. Even if Scott had, for some unlikely reason, triumphed over the blacklist, there's a strong chance she would not have survived the end of the FCC license freeze in 1952, for that moment marked the point at which television would enter the South on a large scale. Once the South made up a significant portion of the market, any network found that alienating viewers in that region was a risk it could not take. It was fear of Southern backlash, not the complaints of the National Association for the Advancement of Colored People (NAACP), that led to *Amos 'n' Andy's* cancellation. The South simply was not ready to accept a black television show. That attitude made black shows controversial, and controversy was anathema to television. In 1954, for example, a woman in CBS's personnel department asserted that the network did not practice discrimination in hiring but that in certain positions, such as receptionist or "script girls who sit in on shows with the client," it "might not be advisable to use Negroes."[58] Blacks were clearly too controversial for visible roles. Even more shocking evidence came from NBC's failed attempt at *The Nat King Cole Show* in 1956. The content of the show was not controversial, nor was the star. It was basic high-quality music entertainment, which started out as a fifteen-minute show and was later expanded to half an hour. It was tried out in a number of time slots. Because it was clear that the show's success would be a breakthrough for blacks in television, it got a great deal of support from major stars—black and white—who offered to appear on the show for scale (a few hundred dollars) instead of the five-figure salaries that they normally received for television appearances. Thus, Cole's guests included Sammy Davis, Jr., Mel Torme, Ella Fitzgerald, and Peggy Lee. Nevertheless, no matter how NBC packaged the deal, the show was unable to attract a major sponsor. With its ratings slowing, even a plan allowing local affiliates to elect the show and sell the time locally met with inadequate success. "The collapse of the *Nat King Cole Show* served only to reaffirm what many felt to be true: television was no place for Afro-American talents to seek success."[59]

Series featuring blacks or even individual dramas about blacks were too controversial for television. In an exemplary case, Rod Serling's attempt to dramatize the story of Emmett Till (a Northern black teenager brutally killed for looking at a white woman while visiting family in the South) underwent so many changes that in the final version the victim was no longer black and the locale was not Southern.[60] According to a 1957 *Television Age* article, "in the matter of segregation, it would be difficult to present a dramatization dealing with some aspects of this problem on a sponsored program, particularly at a time when the subject is considered highly inflammatory. . . . It would be impossible to maintain any balance of dramatization highlighting one side of such a currently explosive issue as segregation in a sponsored *entertainment* program."[61]

The network was thus applying the same principle to the episode's content that it applied to hiring: It didn't want to be controversial. This principle not only drove black faces from the air but also curbed the anthology shows of the sort that Serling worked for in that period, such as *Playhouse 90* or *Kraft Theater*, which provided weekly hour-long or ninety-minute dramas. Although these shows might engage slightly more controversial themes, they too became normalized by the realities of commercial television, which saw the triumph of the Hollywood-influenced, West Coast sensibility over the Broadway-influenced East Coast approach. The Hollywood sensibility valued entertainment above serious engagement with social or moral issues, a system that resulted in even less divergence from the already narrow, normative Cold War agenda. The motivation was as much commercial as political. Fred Wizbar, director of the Hollywood-based filmed drama series *Fireside Theater*, explained, "We sell little pieces of soap, so our approach must be the broadest possible . . . we never take a depressing story."[62]

Public Space, National Identity, White Consumer

If television was constructing an ideal citizen, that citizen not only believed in truth, justice, and the American way but also understood that his or her defining role was as a consumer. Henry Clay Gipson made the same assumption about television as an educational tool:

As the world grows older, people are bound to have more leisure. These people must find something to do with their non-reproductive time. . . . Almost everyone will have a hobby and want to learn something. Through television we can give people the proper knowhow. We can acquaint them with the skill required to use many varied products. *And what could be finer advertising than to actually show the use of a product?* (italics in the original).[63]

In some ways, television's role in the production of consumers was an implicit possibility from the outset: In his 1927 exhibition in a department store, Philo Farnsworth gave the first public demonstration of television by transmitting to a small screen for sixty seconds the image of a dollar sign.[64] In a manner of speaking, we could say that television began with a commercial and the shows were filled in later. Much evidence would support this premise, but "television," as James Monaco pointed out, "did not cause consumer capitalism, it just made it easier to construct a society built on waste and economic exploitation."[65]

If the televisual citizen was the consumer, then everything he or she saw was the object of consumption. Like Farnsworth's first televised dollar sign, the message, the commercial, and the implicit meaning coalesced under a single visual image so that every television show constituted a form of product placement, a point not lost, for example, on Mary Gannon, commenting on a 1945 television show presented by *Mademoiselle* magazine: "Beyond the opening and closing announcement which said simply CBS presents this program as a public service prepared in collaboration with the staff of *Mademoiselle*, no further mention was made that the merchandize came from the pages of the magazine—it was just inferred." The sequences were used as "natural incidents in a closely related theme."[66]

Since people were more likely to consume when they were happy, television favored happy endings. Viewers also had to consume the appropriate products. Nina Leibman cites, for example, this 1959 memo from the J Walter Thompson advertising agency to the Screen Gems advertising liaison, regarding an episode of *Father Knows Best* sponsored by the agency's client Scott Paper:

> Unfortunately, I notice there is a very grievous error on Page 2, namely the business where Margaret wipes the paint off the refrigerator. The author has boldly written, "She gets a *cloth* and wipes off the paint." Were Mr. Elliotte a new and untried author I would not have been so shocked. Surely this young man has been most derelict in failing to watch the Scott commercials. Else, he would not possibly have failed to realize that no material performs the disagreeable task of absorbing paint so well as a Scott Paper Towel.
>
> From past experience I am sure that when this scene is shot Margaret will instinctively use a Scott Paper Towel. Correct? If so, you may consider this letter to constitute client approval.[67]

Notably, this memo situated the sponsor as the protector of reality rather than the promoter of contrivance, indicating that the writer was being unrealistic. In reality "no material performs the disagreeable task of absorbing paint so well as a Scott Paper Towel," a fact established by Scott commercials. Ignoring the commercials, the writer was not being true to life, thus differentiating himself from the character, Margaret, who in reality would never succumb to the writer's unnatural instructions. Margaret, the ad man was sure, remaining true to her instinct, would use a Scott Paper towel. The script from this viewpoint did not provide an artificial display for consumer products but rather reflected accurately the truth contained in the Scott commercials.

Television, as this memo illustrated, uniquely merged the economic realities of its production with the reality it professed to deliver, establishing itself in the postwar American scene as a two-way circuit. It professed to bring the real world to the viewers and to bring the viewers to the reality of consumerism. Scott Paper, like almost all Cold War television sponsors, was doing more than commodifying reality; it was keeping that reality shiny white by adhering to the principle articulated by network executives to writer-producer Robert Alan Arthur when he tried to limit the number of commercials: "The Crest story is really very important. The strange thing about television is that the Crest story is really more important, and the drama is something that goes between the commercials and will be sacrificed at any given time for that purpose."[68] Crest toothpaste and Scott Paper towels were doing more than selling white teeth and refrigerators with shiny white surfaces. They were promoting the notion of a stable, transparently normal nation, unambiguous and without controversy or dissent. Lacking partisan emotions, political positions, or minority opinions, much less minority complexions, the Americans featured by television mirrored the products they were supposed to consume: white bread, vanilla. In this sense, whiteness means the absence of emotional, political, or philosophical pigmentation. Cold War television—in regard to anything but communism—was white in the sense that white is the most neutral of colors, deployed by a medium that had honed the craft of equating neutrality with normality.

American Destiny

By the mid-1950s, television was fulfilling its destiny as the apparatus that would allow Americans to fulfill theirs. In 1942, when less than one in a thousand Americans had ever seen a television program, one author predicted that "television is destined to bring into the home total means for participation in the sights and sounds of the entire world. When it projects the instantaneous present rather than the past it will be more realistic than the motion picture. The sense of being present as a living witness of distant events as they transpire is one utterly unique."[69]

The emphasis on "participation" rather than simply on seeing is very significant. Television not only delivered the messages of reality but also brought those messages home in such a way as to make the viewer a participant. To put it another way, watching television became a form of participation—but participation in *what?* The simple answer was "everything." Television would allow the viewer to participate in the nation and the world.

Perhaps the most powerful expression of this perception came in 1952 from Pat Weaver, at the time a vice president at the Young and Rubicam advertising agency, who would shortly become the head of NBC programming:

Having the all-family, all-home circulation through a planned radio-television schedule, we can create a new stature in our citizens. The miracles of attending every event of importance, meeting every personality of importance in your world, getting to observe members of every group, racial, national, sectional, cultural, religious; recognizing every city, every country, every river and mountain on sight; having full contact with the explanations of every mystery of physics, mechanics and the sciences; sitting at the feet of the most brilliant teachers, and being exposed to the whole range of diversity of mankind's past, present, and the aspirations for mankind's future—these and many other miracles are not assessed yet. But I believe that we vastly underestimate what will happen.[70]

Like others a decade earlier, Weaver connected the immediacy of television with a notion of citizenship. Televisual citizenship, technically superior to more ignorant, more pedestrian, more limited, and secondhand citizenship, represented the ideal to which each American could aspire.

This ideal of course narrowed the range of debate over political or social issues, whether that debate took the form of news or drama. Television could function, therefore, as the site of "democracy" to the extent that "democracy"—representing what the most people had in common—was defined in opposition to "idiosyncrasy." Broadcasting nationalized the common person in every way that his or her values were common rather than unique, clichéd rather than original, status quo rather than progressive. Necessarily entrenched in the past not the future, broadcasting proliferated narratives of a conservative utopia, sine qua non: what "ought to have been"—America in the past-perfect conditional tense—as the model for "what ought to be." Instead of delivering entertainment to audiences, it constructed "reality" as a form of entertainment, allowed free consumption of that entertainment, and then delivered the consumers to the organizations that sponsored the delivery. When Lucille Ball and Lucy Ricardo gave birth within twenty-four hours of one another, on the eve of Dwight Eisenhower's nationally broadcast presidential inauguration, the show in fact delivered "Little Ricky" to America at the same moment that it delivered America to televisual reality, an odd hyper-reality that substituted immediacy for veracity, normality for individuality, idolatry for religion.

3   Disneyland, the Interstate, and National Space

In the history of Cold War television, 1954 was a watershed year, one that marked the beginning of the end of the preference for live television and the start of a powerful relationship between film studios and the television industry. It was the last year of operation for the heavily undercapitalized DuMont television network, and it saw the emergence of the American Broadcasting Company (ABC) as a third national network in a three-way sharing of airwaves and audience that would define national television programming for the next quarter century.[1]

At the beginning of that season, the transcontinental coaxial cable had been in place for less than two years. As a consequence of the FCC's lifting, in 1952, a three-year freeze on new television stations, numerous new stations were coming on line, most notably in the South. With television sales booming, by the end of the 1954–1955 season over half of American households would own sets. That season, in other words, marked the moment when, in several ways, television began to fulfill its potential to create a coherent national space, one unified visually, temporally, and iconographically.

For several reasons, television and film were promoted through the early 1950s as alternative rather than complementary media, with television providing "live" entertainment in small parcels for families with a presumed low attention span and movies providing large-scale, elaborate productions that demanded and earned full attention. Television foregrounded its immediacy—consider such titles as *See It Now, You Are There, Face the Nation, Today,* or *Tonight*—while film often emphasized the length of production time ("two years in the making"); television worked to improve its delivery mechanisms while film stressed the way in which it contrived to enhance its projected image. Thus, in the early 1950s, while the film industry introduced its new wide-screen format, CinemaScope, the television industry completed the construction of the transcontinental coaxial cable that allowed simultaneous broadcast of live shows throughout the nation.

If rapprochement between the two entertainment industries was inevitable, it is still important to understand that one of the obstacles to that merger was the perception of difference in the public imagination produced by the early rivalry. So strong was television's myth of immediacy that well into the late 1950s, long after the bulk of prime time was broadcast in telefilm format, *TV Guide* still notified viewers that a show was not live with the parenthetical word "film," thus indicating that the show would not contain the "sense of immediacy" that viewers had come to expect.

Although the time was right and commercial interests were pressing for a broad shift to telefilm, Disney's role (in conjunction with ABC) in the shift was highly significant. ABC in the early 1950s had a lot of capital and relatively little competitive programming, a situation it sought to alter by forging connections with motion-picture studios. Its bait was its ability to help bankroll a studio's television projects. In a 1953 deal with Hal Roach, Jr., for example, ABC helped fund production in exchange for "syndication rights and a profit share in the series."[2]

The arrangement for Disney's weekly show, *Disneyland*—ABC's first bona fide hit—was somewhat different. Over the preceding years, Disney Studios had produced two exceptionally successful Christmas specials for NBC and had held negotiations with all three networks regarding a weekly television show. Only ABC, however, agreed to help finance the huge amusement park, Disneyland, for the construction of which Disney had acquired 160 acres in Anaheim, California. An hour-long weekly film series entailed, by television standards, very high production costs. The typical television series in 1954 was composed of thirty-six to thirty-nine original episodes. Even though Disney planned to use material from his other projects so that only 60 percent of the television production would be new, and devote half the episodes to reruns, he still did not expect to turn a profit on the actual show.[3] Rather, Disney expected the value of the show to come from ancillary benefits. As *TV Guide* explained:

> By an odd coincidence, both the amusement park and the TV show will be called "Disneyland." By another coincidence, both the amusement park and the TV show will be divided into four parts: Fantasy Land, Adventure Land, Frontier Land, and the World of Tomorrow. The amusement park will be opened to the public July 1955, just nine months after the television show goes on the air.

"By that time," a Disney aide muses, "there will be hardly a living soul in the United States who won't have heard about the Disneyland amusement park and who won't be dying to come to see it. Yessir, television is a wonderful thing."4

The wonderful thing about television, in other words, was its ability to turn a dream into a reality, and thus at every turn television and Disneyland were interconnected. ABC's financial backing enabled the construction of the amusement park that provided the basis for the ABC television show, and the show served as an elaborate commercial for the amusement park, from which ABC received profits from food concessions. The popularity of the show, moreover, established the network that had backed it, making that network a platform for promoting the products of Disney Studios. The success of that symbiotic relationship also initiated the rush of movie studios into telefilm production that, in about half a decade, would reformulate television programming. As TV Guide reported in 1955: "It all started, of course, with Walt Disney, whose incredible success with Disneyland forced the hand of the other studios. All by itself, Disneyland made a senior partner out of what had been a junior TV network, provided an unparalleled publicity platform for the Disney theatrical pictures [and] won two Emmy awards."5

One of those Emmys was for the episode that showcased the Disneyland park, providing a detailed chronicle of its construction. A park named Disneyland was the subject of the television show Disneyland and was also the star of the show, which modeled its format—four separate thematic kingdoms—on that of the park. The park was the geographic, architectural, and thematic reference point for the television show at the same time that it was the commercial product sold by the television show. Because the economic structure of television does not involve selling products to audiences but audiences to sponsors, Disney was able to demonstrate the medium's capacity to create a seamless commercial loop. At the same time that the show advertised the park, it delivered viewers to sponsors whose products, tied in with Disney imagery, were also commercials for the park. In the aisles of American supermarkets, the labels on Peter Pan peanut butter alluded to Disneyland and Disneyland, just as Disneyland brought audiences to the Peter Pan in the amusement park and to the one in the supermarket aisle.

Both the show and the park were also sponsors of an ideal America, one that in the 1950s prolifically announced itself as both normal and normative. In the name or the guise of reality, Disney presented the ideal America to the population that would, ideally, consume the products made by Disney or his sponsors. One of those products, of course, was an automobile, which would take that population along the ideal roadways—interstates 90 percent federally financed—to the happiest place on earth, that is, the place where their own national narratives would, as if in a dream, come startlingly true.

Reality and Telefilm

It might seem ironic that Disney, the film studio most heavily invested in the overt production of fantasy, would be the studio most initially crucial in the history of television, a medium initially invested in communicating "reality." Disney, however, could also be viewed as being uniquely in synch with television's understanding of reality, that is, with the understanding of reality expressed in the memo regarding Scott Paper Towels discussed in Chapter Two. The reality of palpable commercial products entering into a flow of economic exchange through the immediacy of television arose only secondarily out of the medium's "live" broadcasts and primarily out of its insertion into the life of consumers. By 1956, it was clear that television actually had induced families to stay home more often.[6] The television set was a multifaceted member of the family. As the television broadcasters' code pointed out, it was a guest—or a horde of different guests—as well as the appliance that transported the guests. It was also a piece of furniture, an everyday possession situated among other possessions, such that the television set constantly reminded the viewers of the material world to which the broadcasts—whether "live" or film, fiction or nonfiction—connected them.

Disneyland became the medium for insinuating its imagery into the world of its sponsors' daily exchanges. The television show's corporate sponsors—American Motors, Derby Foods, the American Dairy Association—used prominent ad agencies to market their products, and the campaigns all had strong Disney tie-ins. Peter Pan peanut butter, for example, was hawked with the assistance of the figures from Disney's 1953 animated feature *Peter Pan*.[7] The ads, the products, the figures in the movie theater and on the television screen became a seamless reality, a real food, a real brand, with real endorsements from real animated characters, made all the more real by virtue of their connection with television. By 1954 television had become less the test of reality than its measure. "Realism," Karal Ann Marling writes, "whether of the calendar, the Grandma Moses, or the paint-by-the-numbers variety—representational art that is—drew strength from television, from the sudden intrusion into 1950s living rooms of framed, moving pictures that reduced the objets d'art hanging over the sectional to the status of wallpaper. Like a calendar, television presented images . . . of real things, in astonishing variety. Like Grandma Moses, it conjured up collective memories of bygone times when, for example, Davy Crockett died at the Alamo (on ABC's Wednesday-night *Disneyland* program during the 1954–55 season)."[8]

Even before his foray into television, Walt Disney had established his studio as the source of truth. Winning eight Oscars in the postwar period for nature documentaries, Disney had an unassailable reputation as the nation's foremost cinematic scribe of the natural world. The nature films, combining grandeur and intimacy, seemed to allow almost voyeuristic insight into both the natural order and the myriad details of nature on which that order was based. With confidence and authority, Disney seemed not only to observe nature but also to speak on its behalf.

Although these nature documentaries may seem antithetical to the animated features and shorts that gave Disney Studios its unique identity, the studio earned remarkable authority in both genres by employing the same techniques. Technological supremacy, obsessive attention to detail, and an unshakable belief in the human quality of all living things gave credibility equally to characters in animated films such as *Bambi*, *Bear Country*, and *Lady and the Tramp* and to documentaries such as *The Vanishing Prairie*.

In *Snow White*, Disney said, "we had cute little animals, more on the fantasy side. In *Bambi* we had to get closer to nature. So we had to train our artists in animal locomotion and anatomy."[9] At the same time, Disney's "True-Life Adventure pictures used techniques learned in cartoons," Robert De Roos explains, quoting one of Disney's writers: "Any time we saw an animal doing something with style or personality—say a bear scratching its back—we were quick to capitalize on it. . . . This anthropomorphism is resented by some people—they say we are putting people into animal suits. But we've always tried to stay within the framework of the real scene."[10]

Cinderella, dressing and naming her mice in the opening scene of the 1959 animated film, in other words, was a surrogate for Walt Disney himself. In his meticulous transformation of a mouse into a person, Disney, like Cinderella, was able to serve as both the protector of and spokesperson for the animal kingdom. Employing a multiplane camera (developed for *Snow White*) that gave the "astonishing effect of depth and motion,"[11] using changing perspectives and contact shadows, Disney produced animated films developed from narratives employing cinematic storyboards and edited in the classical Hollywood style. Three-dimensional nature looked real in Disney's documentaries, in other words, because he had already mastered the more difficult task of fashioning credible reality in two dimensions. Disney treated his animated nature as though it were real, and his audiences did the same: They believed Disney's photographed animals in part because they accurately emulated his animated creatures.

Even with this experience in nature documentaries and the credentials they provided, presenting a filmed television show in prime time still entailed the potential pitfall, conventional wisdom held, that using film—a form not thought to be well suited for a small screen—would play to television's weakness at the expense of its chief asset: reality. *Disneyland* therefore used several strategies to link itself to "reality." Most important was its connection to Disneyland, a real place with a geographical design and mapped coordinates, even though when *Disneyland* first aired Disneyland was only an image, designated by that design and those coordinates. The image, however, was the real dream of a real man, Walt Disney, who was the live host (recorded on film) of *Disneyland* and the real mind behind the show's (and the planned park's) animated characters. That real man had the same name as the trademark that connected those characters to the material uses of their images. Looking directly at the camera, the real Walt Disney spoke to the real boys and girls of America (and many of their parents) about his real plans to build a fantasy land (as well as an adventure land, a frontier land, and a world of tomorrow). These imaginary lands, the show constantly reminded its audience, provided the segments of the television show they were really watching.

That show, moreover, strategically blurred the boundaries of the real. Under the trademark "Walt Disney," the man of the same name was constructing a real park that did not exist but was represented by a television show of the same name that did. The show did not have the actual rides and restaurants that its namesake would have, but in their stead it had the real narratives upon which those amusements would be based, narratives about fantasies, adventures, dreams for the future, or legends from the past. Those narratives were brought to life through the reality of film production and brought home through the reality of television technology.

In several significant ways, the park (Disneyland) may have been as pivotal as the TV show (*Disneyland*) in converting television to a film medium. It is not just that, as one journalist wrote, "the sudden removal of Hollywood's mental block on TV can be traced almost directly to the success of Walt Disney's 'Disneyland' show."[12] Certainly, Disney demonstrated that television's popularity did not depend on its being broadcast live. More important, however, he did so by appealing to a higher sense of reality, the national fantasy of seeing Cold War America as the culmination of a utopian destiny. In direct distinction to communist utopianism, which anticipated a withering away of the state and all the institutions—banks, stock markets, churches—that supported class oppression, America's Cold War alternative combined theological mandate and social Darwinism to promote the blossoming of institutions that distributed capital to the worthy. The marketplace in this model was the route to perfection, be it economic, spiritual, civil, or technological, so that history, freedom, and prosperity all came together in the same matrix of commercial realities. Disney's genius was to weave the three hallmarks of midcentury American middle-classdom—the car, the home, and the television—into a seamless commercial loop. At the center of that loop resided Disneyland, the place where America's future and past, its natural world and fantasy life came together in order to create, as the plaque on its Main Street proclaimed, "the happiest place on earth."

Disneyland, the first "theme" park of its magnitude, is crucial to this examination of Cold War television because television provided the parameters of the happiness Disneyland manifested, the means for accessing that magic kingdom, and the template for comprehending it. Disneyland provided visible "proof" that safe, homogeneous, family-oriented immediacy was indeed the reality television had promised it would be. The park, in other words, exemplified televisual reality, and through television Americans were citizens of Disneyland. It was the urban plan, the technology of everyday life, that proved the American Dream was real and hence, implicitly, that communism was false. In this way, Disneyland represented the West, as that term referred to the as yet unsettled global dispute between Cold War blocs, while also echoing the settlement of the American West.

The historical significance of the famous moment when Soviet Premier Khrushchev was forbidden to visit Disneyland lay in its symbolic capital. No doubt the site, as Khrushchev was told, posed insurmountable security problems, but his inability to pass through the portal of this magic kingdom also signified the presumption that no communist would ever see paradise, even though its gates were open to any average middle-class American family. The most powerful communist in the world would neither see nor sully this capitalist heaven.

The Road to Somewhere

To help understand how Disneyland came to play its role in the Cold War reinvention of America, we can start with the park's most important precursor, the 1939 World's Fair. "It all began with the 1939 World's Fair," Marling writes in her history of the Disney theme parks. "Like other fairs, this was an instant city, a city (or cities) in miniature, thrown up overnight to celebrate progress and forward thinking. The fair was American urbanism as it ought to be."[13] The 1939 World's Fair, in other words, marked a profound turning point for urban planning. Representing the culmination of a centuries-long industrial revolution and appearing to transform tangibly—almost miraculously—technology's promise into commercial realities, the fair portrayed America as a place of "miraculous reality," an oxymoronic phrase that, as we have seen, also all too aptly described television.

Equally well, it applied to a new American landscape that would share cogent qualities with the television medium destined to turn that landscape into a national community. Like television, the landscape would privilege its homogeneity, its commercial accessibility, and its conformity to cinematic reality. Everywhere at the 1939 World's Fair, reality functioned under a utopian mandate. What reason for a fair, after all, if not to represent the best that the present and the future have to offer? Thus, the fair's implicit and explicit messages were virtually indistinguishable from one another. The goal of promoting automobile travel, for example, was synonymous with showing how such travel improved American life. General Motors' "Futurama" exhibit, the fair's most popular attraction,[14] provided visitors with an idealized version of auto travel, promising fourteen-lane express roads by 1960 that would allow traffic to move at 50, 75, and 100 miles per hour. The exhibit redefined urban space as much as it did the role the car would play in it, and the fair made the city of tomorrow seem all but inevitable: "It was a tangible fact, this Democracity, this Futurama, as real as the clever dioramas in which autos of the future winked past shrunken skyscrapers on tiny freeways, bound for suburbs laid out in tidy, geometric patterns."[15]

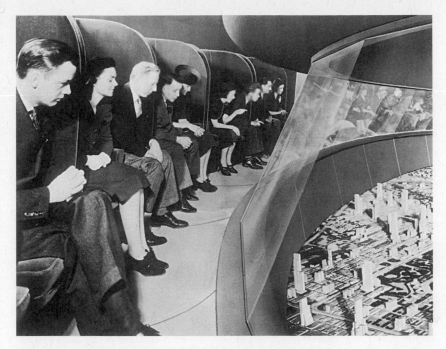

GM's "Futurama," the most popular exhibit at the 1939 World's Fair.

The sense of mobility that Futurama asserted was not antithetical to stability but rather endemic to it. America, after all, was a place of infinite mobility, facilitated not only by its open spaces but also by the narratives that propelled people into them. Dependent as much on geographical as on social progress, America's narrative of upward mobility had long been connected to the possibility of moving from log cabin to White House, of pulling oneself up by the bootstraps, of finding a place in the sun, or crossing some great divide.

Whatever the destination, fulfillment entailed the capacity to get there on one's own. The city of the future was thus envisioned as one with limitless access and egress: the freedom to come and go as one pleased. The same held true of the ideal domestic setting, at once insulated from and intimately tied to the urban hub, so that while at home the citizen could sense his or her household as the center of the universe. The citizen-viewer was both a satellite to and a hub of industry, culture, and adventure. Thus, the motion of these respective hubs provided the gravitational counterpoise that stabilized them, created knowable public and private spaces, and facilitated commerce between them.

In the history of European exploration and development of North America for the last five centuries, one could argue, the continent has been constructed as a road to somewhere: the route to India, the northwest passage, the Oregon Trail, the underground railroad, the transcontinental railroad, the interstate highway system. The nation provided the road to happiness as well as the end of that road, where the past could be discarded and simultaneously reconstituted as the ideal version of itself. Disneyland effected this reconstitution by encapsulating a technologically honed idealization of the past. The Main Street that brings people into the "happiest place on earth" reconstitutes the turn-of-the-century small town as an ideal site of American life. Situated at the western edge of the nation, Disneyland sits at the end of the line, in the place where the highway can go no farther and the frontier must deliver the reinvention that constituted the implicit promise of the West. In this sense and in many others, Disneyland and the interstate highway system come out of the same vision of the frontier nation.

In providing the reward at the end of the trail, Disneyland was in fact replicating a relationship that dated back to the invention of amusement parks at the turn of the twentieth century. Because electric companies charged trolleys a flat rate, Judith Adams explains, the trolley companies "sought to increase rides during slow weekends and evenings. The ingenious solution was to create a lure at the end of the line, a pleasure park for leisure and enjoyment. Beginning as shady picnic groves often located near a body of water, the parks rapidly expanded with the addition of regular entertainments, mechanical amusements, dance halls, sports fields, boat rides, restaurants, and other resort facilities."[16] These parks, like Disneyland after them, were seen between 1900 and 1920 as realizing the American Dream: quintessential democracy configured as the New Eden, combining safety and thrills.[17]

Adams's description of the amusement park provides a virtual summary of Disneyland offerings. Disney, in other words, had captured in his 160-acre American Dream (two-thirds of the acreage devoted to parking) not only the moment but also the ethos of the first amusement parks. At the same time, he performed a deft inversion so that instead of taking the trolley to the park, people took the interstate to the trolley. The mode of *geographical* transportation to the early American parks was thus converted into the park's mode of *temporal* transportation back to an earlier (yet cleaner and more appealing) America.

To this updating of the amusement park Disney added the visionary qualities of the millennial exhibition. The expositions, as Neil Harris correctly points out, helped to "establish the most fundamental feature of all, and one that Disney eagerly built upon: a periodically recurring rhythm of mass movement, a faith in destination as social restorative, a system of travel designed to reaffirm belief—in the future, in the past, or, especially for twentieth-century Americans, in one another. . . . The transforming dream, so long nurtured by the expositions, that search for social happiness, remained in place."[18]

The 1939 World's Fair was important in this regard because in promoting the particular utopian vision to which it was committed, it would foreground and accurately predict the significance of two technologies crucial to the success of Disneyland—television and auto transportation. The American Dream is not a split-level house, A. Q. Mowbray reminds us, but "to drive coast to coast without encountering a traffic light."[19] The interstate highway system, television, and Disneyland—all creatures of the 1950s—shared the decade's obsession with conformity. The same principles of standardization that made possible the auto assembly line in the first half of the century ultimately shaped the postwar roads those massproduced cars traversed, the motels at which their drivers stopped, the food those drivers ate, and the signals they received on the TV antennae protruding from the suburban tract houses where the autos rested between journeys. Every detail in this social topography proclaimed its regularity. In its relentless consistency, the postwar America of highways and TVs demonstrated unequivocally that, as the newly amended Pledge of Allegiance proclaimed, this really was *one nation under God*.

The interstate and the television—perhaps two of the most powerful unifying technologies in the history of civilization—intersected at Disneyland. Crucial to the selection of the Anaheim site was the newly constructed Santa Ana freeway. A 1952 study conducted for Disney by the Stanford Research Institute recommended Anaheim because the "projected Santa Ana Freeway would make it less than an hour's drive from Los Angeles."[20] The park and the freeway combined, in fact, to make Anaheim the fastestgrowing city in the fastest-growing county in the nation over the period of the 1950s. "From its very inception, the Anaheim playground took shape as a vacation mecca for America on wheels, promoting the gospel of leisure. *Disneyland Holiday*, a special company publication for tourists, captured this impulse, describing the facility as 'America's favorite vacationland'

and offering information on the park's many attractions, the unique appeal of southern California, travel games and puzzles for children, and maps of the Los Angeles freeway system."[21]

Another way to think about the Disney phenomenon is to understand that Disney mastered the art of combining the figurative and the literal. He understood that the freeway was merely an extension of America's westward movement, the search for an ideal place to be free, the paved path to a cliché banquet. In this sense, his park would literalize escapism. "If Disneyland was a place of escape and amusement, it was also, in its own way . . . a better, cleaner, more pleasant and resonant American place than 1955 afforded the average urbanite who drove to Anaheim on the interstate and the Santa Ana Freeway."[22]

Similarly, its vision of the future would assert facticity, no matter how faulty the presumed clairvoyance of Tomorrowland turned out to be. "Of all the zones inside the park," John Findlay pointed out, "Tomorrowland gave management the most problems, because it constantly grew obsolete." Understandably, the only aspect of Tomorrowland that remained continuous was Autotopia—"the freeway of the future"—which provided children with "a dose of the automotive world that seemed so pervasive outside the gates of Disneyland."[23] Like the General Motors Futurama, Autotopia infused the fantastic with credibility. While it indulged the child's fantasy to drive a car, to have access to the American road to adventure, it also rendered that road perfect: perfectly safe, comfortable, and uncongested. In Disneyland, parent and child alike discovered the real freeway: free of accidents, transient populations, migrants and immigrants, old cars and the people who could barely afford to maintain them. Although one might wait on line to ride the Autotopia, once the ride started it functioned perfectly, the way roads were *really* designed to operate.

Autotopia thus acted as the complement to Main Street's trolley and the freeway that brought people to the place where they could board it. A magical navigation allowed the trolley to return people to the freeway—the road that had gotten them to Disneyland—redesigned into a perfected version of itself. In the process, the journey from tract home to interstate to freeway to parking lot to Main Street to Tomorrowland to Autotopia became a pilgrim's progress, a return to origins as a world both visionary and uncannily quotidian, such that imitating the experience of driving to work could become entertaining by virtue of its absolute predictability, normality, standardization, control.

Autotopia, in other words, replicated the experience of turning on a television set. Whatever the imperfections that filled postwar life en route from workplace to home, they all disappeared when television put Americans in touch with life as it was really supposed to be, life sans the annoying discrepancies that topical abnormalities may produce.

The Place of Televisual Reality

In this regard, Disney was merely saying about television what television, as we have seen, was saying about itself. It is very important to remember how extensively, throughout the 1940s and early 1950s, television's promoters touted it as the technology of the real. It was the instrument that would connect every household with real life in real time. When television employed drama, it would be "real" drama, in the sense that it would be witnessed in the way that drama was really witnessed, that is, as it occurred. Film, to the extent that it was used, would also be integrated into a flow of experience that was real, surrounded at the broadcast end by live announcers, live shows, live news and sports and at the reception end by live people going about their real home life.

It would unfold, furthermore, with infinite stability, the end of an episode resembling not the end of a story or the end of a life but the end of a daily routine; as they did in real life, things would recur on a daily and weekly schedule, incorporating into the pattern predictable variations on a theme. If, as the cliché goes, all tragedies end with a death and all comedies with a marriage, all TV episodes end with a commercial, that is, a reincorporation of the topical narrative into the reality of quotidian postwar consumerism. Disneyland, as George Lipsitz astutely explains, served a similar end. It "provided an alternative to the heterogeneous public spaces of the city, and it powerfully projected its image of the middle-class suburban consumer culture as a norm to which other groups should aspire."[24]

Clearly, myriad aspects of early television were completely consistent with the Disney ethos, a fact of which he was acutely aware. "As early as 1938, the official handbook of the studio had observed that television 'although in its infancy, opens up a vast field of entertainment', and in 1944 the studio had briefly undertaken an educational project about this medium called 'The World in Your Living Room.'"[25] Even in the 1940s, Disney, virtually alone among studio heads, understood that television need not be a threat to film. One reason for Disney's attitude was that he took the same approach to film that television took to almost all its productions: He explicitly believed in the motion picture's obligation to family entertainment.[26] Beyond the perfect suitability of his films to television, Disney also saw the huge sales potential of the new medium. He strongly believed that television could be very effective in selling motion pictures and in 1951 called television the "greatest sales medium of the age."[27]

The planning of Disneyland thus drew heavily on the principles of television production, not only because the park needed to be completely consistent with the television show that was spending a year promoting it but also because television was fundamentally consistent with Disney's informing philosophy. Thus, at every turn the influence of television on the park's design was apparent. First, Disneyland uniquely employed, as did television, the techniques of stagecraft developed by set designers and adapted by filmmakers to create a controlled illusion. The design scheme known as the "Disney effect" derived not from the studio's films or the television show but from the planning of Disneyland. It referred to "the subtly integrated variations of color carried from one building to the next, in effect creating a deliberately color-coordinated landscape, a chromoscape made possible by Disney's total environmental control."[28] From the start, the Disney organization saw designing the park as a task for moviemakers, not city planners or amusement park designers.[29] The designers used the film design technique of "forced perspective" that "tricked the eye into seeing structures as taller than they were" by making the first story 90 percent scale and the higher stories each at an increasingly diminished scale.[30] They also understood that at a time when at least four out of every five Americans had grown up with motion pictures, the perfected, harmonious design of the movies superseded personal experience as the chief source of collective memory. "The sensation of Disneyland's Main Street," therefore, as Findlay noted, "is that one is experiencing a very familiar milieu—something akin to a memory yet hauntingly like a movie or film set."[31] The memories rang true because we had seen them at the movies. The same was true of the jungle cruise, which Marling described as

> a visceral, sensual experience, like stepping, somehow, into the Technicolor confines of *The African Queen* and becoming a member of the cast, bound for some exotic coast in the company of Bogart and Hepburn.
> In fact, the ride had been loosely based on the adventure described in that popular film and on its picturesque river craft. . . . What Disney's

so-called Imagineers added to the film by transferring it in three dimensions to Anaheim was a missing quotient of "reality."[32]

Despite its reliance on film techniques and, more important, the history of America's seduction by those techniques, Disneyland successfully transcended the limitations that Disney, who often indicated during the 1950s that he was becoming bored with movies, saw in the film medium. Films, he felt, were cut short by external reality: "When they were done, they were done."[33] "Because it was *real*, Disneyland could never be completed. . . . The tension between perfection and reality, between the real and the more or less real, was the primary source of the visitor's delight."[34] Disneyland, in other words, transcended the limitations of film by becoming more like television.

Disney "thought of the park in transitory terms," George Lipsitz reminds us, "like a television series that could undergo revisions over time."[35] Resembling the interstate and the rapidly spreading television networks, Disneyland was an ongoing construction project, one that applied narratives to space as a way of creating public identity and delimiting the public domain. Those narratives were planned to stress transition from scene to scene and a story line that would yield an "undilutedly rosy view of the world; contradiction or confusion were qualities the planners of Disneyland associated with the defective, poorly planned, conventional amusement park."[36]

Disney's challenge, therefore, was constructing a narrative space that was thematically consistent, lacking contradiction, and as multifarious as an amusement park (with a main street and four discrete lands). Television once again provided the model for his solution. Characterized by discontinuous narrative, the park was, as Marling notes, "like the weekly TV show called *Disneyland*. Narrative was what separated Disneyland from all those other places. So each part of Disneyland became its own narrative . . . like a lineup of half-hour shows on any given Wednesday evening in Televisionland."[37] But Disneyland was programmed not for just a segment of prime time: "It meant to attract customers for an entire day of amusement, during which they would never become distracted or lost or bored."[38]

The park was designed, in other words, to be received in the same way as television, that is, as a constant flow of discrete experiences manageably integrated into the daily life of the guests. Emulating a quintessential trait of television, Disneyland, *Look* magazine pointed out, exhibited the "relentless urge to reduce reality, somehow, to smaller, more graspable terms."[39]

Disney stressed, moreover, that Disneyland would "be a place for California to be at home, to bring its guests, to demonstrate its faith in the future."[40] The park would replicate, in other words, the early–1950s experience of inviting guests into one's living room to watch television. In consequence, the park would have the effect—which I noted in the preceding chapter was predicted by early television commentary and promoted by its programmers—of elevating the ordinary citizen. The designer John Hench, a close Disney associate, said that "in touring lands devoted to fantasy, adventure, and the future, visitors could escape their unnatural present day cares, 'drop their defenses,' and 'be more like *themselves.*'"[41]

Citizenry, Disney Nation, and the Cold War

Because Americans were *really* themselves when insulated by Disney narratives, Disneyland was a logical extension of television, effecting the social mutations that television promised by surrounding people with the realities that television could only lay before their eyes. Adams points out, "One of the park's primary attractions is that it allows visitors to walk right into and experience the historical environments and fantasy worlds they passively watch on the television screens in the living rooms. They can immerse themselves and participate in the worlds that tantalize them nightly but from which the television screen separates and limits them to the status of observers."[42] But that experience, like watching television, was supposed to be more than vicarious; it was supposed to become integral to the visitors' real lives. Like television comedy, variety, drama, and advertising, Disneyland was supposed to improve their "stature," as Pat Weaver had said of the prospective television audience. The park's emphasis in engineering visitors' responses was on making them feel better about themselves. [43] Disneyland's "smooth blend of sentimental modernism, sentimental populism, nostalgia, consumerism, family virtue, and corporate abundance [proved intoxicating] for millions of Americans who passed through its gates," Steven Watts writes. "It allowed visitors to revel in the fantasy life of their culture during the halcyon days of the American century and ritually reaffirm an idealistic view of themselves."[44]

"Actually, what we're selling throughout the Park is reassurance," Hench explained, reflecting on his fifty-year career with Disney. "We offer adventures in which you survive a kind of personal challenge. . . . We let your survival instinct triumph over adversity. A trip to Disneyland is an exercise in reassurance about oneself and one's ability to maybe even handle the real challenges of life."45

Like television, Disneyland employed elaborate artifice to maintain its claim on reality. By surrounding the park with a berm, or earthen wall, twenty-five feet high and by running all the electrical lines underground— at great expense to Disney—the designers prevented views of the "outside" world from destroying their illusions.46 The design techniques, in other words, not only turned the Anaheim site into a television or movie set but Orange County into the studio lot that contained the set. America itself was the studio that literally housed and figuratively produced Disneyland, connected by the interstate and the coaxial cable to the rest of the nation.

Marling is perfectly correct, therefore, in viewing Disneyland as "the first made-for-TV place, in which the fictive content of the programming dictated the honest-to-gosh activity of Americans in physical space."47 Just as *Disneyland* was proving that film could be adapted for television, Disneyland was demonstrating that television could provide a model for public space. Disneyland, the historian William Irwin Thompson writes in a description that stunningly conflates televisual and automotive travel, "is a kind of TV set for one flips from mediaeval castles to submarines and rockets as easily as one can move, in . . . Los Angeles, from the plaza on the Mexican Olvera Street . . . to the modern Civic Center."48

Repeatedly, Disney associated reality with purification. He distinguished his middle-class and family-oriented park from the lower-class "carny" atmosphere of traditional amusement parks, which he called "dirty, phony places, run by tough-looking people."49 Disneyland's Main Street is thus "a kind of universally-true Main Street—it's better than the real Main Street of the turn of the century ever could be."50

"Reality" in Disney's lexicon meant things as they ought to be. According to Hench, "To achieve 'Disney Realism' . . . we program out all negative, unwanted elements and program in positive elements." This resulted, the designers felt, in a recaptured rather than a distorted reality. "We've taken and purified the statement," Hench explained, "so it says what it was intended to."51 Disney in fact was relentless in his commitment to his definition of reality. When the evangelist Billy Graham, after visiting the park, said that he had had a nice fantasy at Disneyland, Walt Disney replied, "You know the fantasy isn't here. This is very real. . . . The park is reality. The people are natural here; they're having a good time; they're communicating. This is what people really are. The fantasy is—out there, outside the gates of Disneyland, where people have hatreds and people have prejudices. It's not really real!"[52]

Given Disney's monomaniacal insistence, it becomes hard not to see the emphasis on purification, the obsession with what *ought* to be, as less idealistic than proscriptive. Disney, testifying in 1947 as a "friendly" HUAC witness,[53] suggested this belief in purity and fear of contamination when he described communism as "an un-American thing" because communists infiltrated and subverted well-meaning groups of "100 per cent Americans."[54] The repurification, the return of Americans to what they really were thus functioned for Disney as a national mandate embracing everything from entertainment to legislation, discrete group activities to mass media.

In proliferating normativity, in other words, Disneyland joined television in its concerted Cold War agenda. Hence, the control of the park aimed not only at engineering Disneyland activities but also, through them, reengineering the American spirit (or, dare we say, "soul"). The Disney staff, Richard Schickel explains, entered a whole new field of "public engineering," drawing on social psychology, urban technology, and the new study of proxemics.[55] In addition, making clear that the world as it ought be was a place where even spontaneity must be planned, an executive order instructed Disneyland employees that "any ad libs must be approved before use."[56] At stake in this order, of course, was not just a fear of the unruly but also a commitment to standards. The park's regimentation guaranteed a uniform product: No visitor on any ride would see or hear anything that another visitor did not. This was part of the process of reassuring the visitors, part of the renewed faith that a pilgrimage to Disneyland was supposed to produce.

My point is that Disney's understanding of things as they ought be drew more profoundly on the ideals of consumerism than on family values. The park presumed that Americans ought to want out of life what they wanted out of mass-produced appliances: uniform consistency. Main Street was pleasing, Findlay made clear, not only because it emulated visual aspects of a small town but also because "its scale and proportions make for nearly perfect visual/architectural homogeneity."[57] The product uniformity that characterized Disney's standard for reality (which the park encapsulated) exemplified Disney's obsession with control. Judith Adams sums up this aspect of the park's dynamics: "Total control of space, movement, and mood create a succession of visual stereotypes so profound in effect that they quickly achieve the status of national popular images. Everything about the park, including the behavior of the 'guests,' is engineered to promote a spirit of optimism, a belief in progressive improvement toward perfection. Elements within the park achieve mythic, religious significance as treasured icons protecting us against infusion or assault by evil in any form, including our own faults."[58]

Because the control of the park extended in this way very naturally to control of the employees, whose lives were extensions of their association with Disneyland, the employee manuals, not surprisingly, instructed the employees to uphold company standards even when away from the park.[59] In the Disneyland model, in other words, control of public space is not simply a proscription for amusement parks; it represents the ideals of "real" America.

Disney's mediations, Watts reminded us, helped Americans acquire a perspective on their role as midcentury historical figures: "Disney operated not only as an entertainer but as a historical mediator. His creations helped Americans come to terms with the unsettling transformations of the twentieth century."[60] Watts did not point out, however, that the terms to which Disney helped us come were profoundly televisual. Disney, *Disneyland*, and Disneyland all helped (white middle-class) Americans to discover imaginative perspectives that reconciled them to the oddity of seeing reality—the thing that was supposed to circumscribe and consume them—contained by a piece of living room furniture, surrounded by slipcovers and bric-a-brac, by the plethora of real life's most tangible, ephemeral, and ultimately dispensable items. Disney helped them come to terms, in other words, with the most startling transformation of all: that reality existed elsewhere, that without television they lived incomplete, aberrant, slightly un*real* lives.

He did this by attaching reality to a set of consumable narratives that made reality, by virtue of its homogeneity, its normativity, its commodification, seem potentially accessible to all. He validated the acquisitive ethos of postwar America by representing that ethos as the means to complete historical reality, to meet the appointment with destiny that took place less on December 7, 1941, or even August 6, 1945, than on the day on which the coaxial cable created a coherent, uniform, simultaneous America of which Disneyland was to be the most tangible proof.

But, as many have noted, Disneyland provided the model not only for Cold War entertainment but also for much postwar urban living. Identifying Disneyland, the Stanford Industrial Park, the Seattle World's Fair, and Sun City, Arizona, as "Magic Kingdoms" (after their Disney prototype), Findlay convincingly argues that "magic kingdoms of the urban West helped to define a new standard for what was normal on the American cityscape, and their proliferation sustained at least some of the thinking that had helped to create them during the postwar years."[61] Of these places, Disneyland was unique in that it not only combined the goals of all the others but also articulated the thematic connection between those sites and American history, purpose, and destiny. To put it another way, Disneyland demonstrated the inextricable connection between idealized living and televisual reality. A full—and fulfilling—life needed to be as safe and as predictable as television; if television was the apparatus of unmediated reality, if it defined postwar citizenship, then a world that fell short of television's standards was a prima facie failure:

> Through the medium of *Disneyland*, the American family became part of the process of building the park and acquired an emotional stake in its success. It was Walt's own Williamsburg, his American Versailles, but it was part of the Wednesday-night home lives of countless viewers, too. And by rehearsing the proposed features of the park, the TV show eliminated all grounds for apprehension: Disneyland—the theme park— was just as safe, wholesome, and predictable as the living room setting in which the family gathered every week to watch Walt talk about it. Add a little sunshine and a few hot dogs and going to Disneyland would be just like watching that other *Disneyland* on TV.[62]

To see Disneyland, as Paul Goldberger did, as a "testing grounds for urban technology" as well as a testimony to "Disney's faith in the ultimate rightness of technological progress"[63] is simply to recognize the postwar lifestyle as a logical extension of everything Disney represented. He was indeed reinventing American community after the model impelled by television and facilitated by the interstate. In so doing, he was prophetically endowing a new understanding of public space with potent credibility. "Architect Charles Moore attributed Disneyland's success to its ability to provide Californians with a 'public environment' in the midst of a region dominated by the private spaces of suburban subdivisions and automobile interiors. Just as Main Street functioned as the town square of Disneyland, Moore described Disneyland itself as the 'town square of Los Angeles.'"[64]

Part of Disney's power was his mastery over time combined with an almost Einsteinian appreciation of the relative relationship between time and space. At the most mundane level, of course, that relationship informed the governing principle of the freeway; distance was not a function of how far one lived from a given place but of how long it took to get there. By cutting the driving time, the Santa Ana freeway brought the park close enough to downtown Los Angeles. Beyond that, the park blended seamlessly discrete temporal trajectories—prediction, memory, fantasy, adventure, and historical chronology—by spatializing them. Disney understood that there is no difference between what we remember having fantasized and what we fantasize that we remember. Fantasy and history alike reside with relative privilege within each person's memory bank, reached with equal ease, bracketed with equal convenience. If we remember the time we did something, we are also remembering a place, and by giving every time its own place Disneyland not only charted the mind's topography but, more importantly, gave that topography a permanent, public home.

This home, furthermore, had its own television time in a historical period when life was becoming more and more oriented around network time slots and the national community created by them. From coast to coast, America in prime time regularly looked at a small selection of shared images so that in the same way that Disneyland provided Los Angeles with its town square, *Disneyland* and television in general provided America with its town hall. In this way, Disneyland/*Disneyland* conflated the ubiquitous and the eternal. It gave a real locale to what David Marc termed the "eternal present" of television. At the same time, it imbued that locale with television's timelessness. "'In Disneyland,' publicists explained, 'clocks and watches will lose all meaning, for there is no present. There are only yesterday, tomorrow, and the timeless land of fantasy.'"[65]

This control of time had, as George Lipsitz explains, important social implications: "Disneyland also spoke to the break with the past that formed an important part of the lives of Los Angeles residents. In a city made up of migrants from all over the country, no common heritage served to underpin individual or collective identity. But by presenting images of familiar figures from television and motion pictures, Disneyland spoke to the commonality of experience made possible by popular culture. People came to Disneyland with a variety of experiences and beliefs, but the reach and scope of electronic mass media guaranteed that they all shared familiarity and knowledge about Disney stories and products."[66]

The West

Disney was bringing the spirit of westward expansion into the age of television, for the West had always been a temporal rather than a geographical place, the place—be it New York's Mohawk Valley, Indiana's plains,

Iowa's prairie, Arizona's canyons, or Oregon's coast—with which time had not yet caught up. The West was that place with the time for one more reinvention. "In California and throughout the West," Findlay noted, "rapid growth had tended to obliterate continuity between past, present, and future. . . . The local past vanished under the onslaught of population after 1940, which effectively remade the cities again and again."[67]

The settlement of the West—the imposing of order on unruly space and history on timelessness—was a task for which Disney had exceptional skill if not the perfect historical opportunity. Deployed through the astounding apparatus of television, this disparity between Disney's vision and his historical circumstance created the excess that so profoundly affected postwar American culture. "Few could deny," Findlay assures us, "that Disneyland's ability to create order out of chaos affected the urban patterns outside its walls."[68] But the Disney urban model for Westernizing America came attached to a body of Cold War narratives that helped combine the historical and geographical West with the Western bloc, of which America was the self-proclaimed leader. "One of Disney's great achievements" Watts explains, "was to gather [the strands of Cold War Liberalism—corporate liberalism, corporate capitalism, provincial conservatism, and urban technocracy], relax the tensions among them, and braid them together emotionally into a resilient political culture of Americanism."[69] However, as William Graebner reminds us, "it is well to consider that Disneyland was the success it was because the founder's fantasy so closely resembled the shared desires of millions of Americans. To what extent then," Graebner asks, "does the Disneyland experience merely reflect American values? Were the white, middle-class Americans who patronized Disneyland in search of uniformity, homogeneity, and passivity?"[70]

Another way to phrase Graebner's question is: To what extent is Disneyland merely a symptom of a Cold War television culture? In many ways Disney's success was a quintessential symptom of his times in the same way that Hitler's message was far more likely to succeed in 1930s Germany than, for instance, in 1950s Israel. Disney's reception was no doubt a product of the times, but the times were unquestionably shaped by the legacy of his astonishing achievement. Disney was the perfect Cold Warrior because he could fight the Cold War, and enable ordinary citizens to do the same, in nonpolitical terms. From its inception, this was an articulated strategy of "containment," as laid out by George Kennan in his famous 1948 "X" document that named and focused a quarter of a century, at least, of American

foreign policy.71 According to Kennan, a crucial role in containing and ultimately defeating communism fell to average American citizens, who
through their way of life would demonstrate to the world the superiority of
capitalism and democracy, thereby making the United States a more attractive partner for other nations and depriving the Soviet Union of allies until
it collapsed of internal frustration.

The strategies of containment, as I have demonstrated at length elsewhere, infused a broad spectrum of American activities, productions, and
behaviors.72 The important point is that the Cold War stood for more than
a competition with another world power: It represented a narrowly defined
and broadly endorsed way of life that affected most mainstream tastes and
trends of the 1950s. When Findlay states that Disneyland "capitalized on
postwar tastes and trends. It enshrined the Cold War and all the things for
which it stood—competition with the Soviets in productivity, in space, in
ways of life," 73 he is explaining how Disneyland represented the West.

That mode of representation drew on Disney's inclinations, as clearly
demonstrated by the nature films that garnered him so much acclaim just
before his development of Disneyland. "Nature did not really appear here
on its own terms," Watts explains. "It was a kind of cultural canvas upon
which Disney and the audience painted an array of Cold War concerns and
values."74 Like the park, the documentaries imposed narratives on the
landscape that revealed the appearance of order amid the chaos of nature,
and like the Disney animated films, they did so by anthropomorphizing the
animal world. In this nature, made to look more real by virtue of its ostensible compatibility with human narratives, the struggle for survival seems
to advocate free competition while the landscape seems to embrace family
values and the evolution of the frontier. That evolving landscape, moreover,
evoked a symbolic reverence for Americana (in much the way as did John
Ford's use of Monument Valley). At the same time, and in much the same
way that Disneyland would, these documentaries, through their remarkable
technical accomplishments, affirmed American technological expertise,
without which supremacy over the Soviets, of course, would have been impossible. As Watts aptly states, "Disney's technological wizardry brought re-
assurances that American ingenuity would prevail in an uncertain modern
world."75 Finally, the miraculous penetration of nature enabled by astonishing technology and demonstrated by the equally astonishing pictures appeared to articulate a divine scheme; they seemed, as one commentary put it,
"to reveal the hand of the Almighty at work."76

In a manner of speaking, the park was an extension of the techniques and themes of the nature films. The wonders of technology, as a theme in Tomorrowland and an effect throughout the park, intersected with the exploration of the natural world in Adventureland and American history in Frontierland. The entire experience of the park was visually anchored, moreover, by the castle of Fantasyland, whence emanated the anthropomorphic creatures that serve as the park's ubiquitous hosts. Combining the best of animal appearance and human values, they consolidated and epitomized the evolutionary narrative out of which U.S. Cold War triumph was destined to emerge.

In the way it promoted the culture of containment, Disneyland's ethics and aesthetics were necessarily continuous with the American life they both idealized and proscribed. *Disneyland* was the conduit for those ethics and aesthetics, and television was the highway out of Disneyland—as, experimentally, it had been since the 1939 World's Fair—in the same way that the interstate was the highway in. In a tight cultural loop, these two thoroughfares took you to and from the same place—the fantasy version of your own Cold War life, facilitated by government policies intent on helping the United States win that war: federal policies such as defense spending, the interstate highway system, veterans' and Federal Housing Administration (FHA) mortgage reinsurance, all of which accelerated urban expansion.77

But this urban expansion, regardless of its specific locale, had the tone and character of a Western settlement. Between 1946 and 1957, the United States gained an average of almost 37,700 new subdivided lots each year, the vast majority going to owner-occupied, single-family, detached homes.78 The vast majority of these homes had structural and social similarities that superseded regional differences, so that a development in Orange County, California, and another in Nassau County, New York, shared more social and architectural similarities than the vast geographic and climatic differences would logically seem to encourage. Part of the common social bond came from the car-focused, highway-dependent existence that extracted these thousands of communities from what otherwise would have been their agrarian surroundings. The uniformity of construction and financing also created, out of a diversified urban class mix, coherent socioeconomic nodules with no enduring attachments to their land or its structures and traditions.

Even in the more upscale of these nodules, there could be no "old wealth" in the way that term has referred to the pillars of communities, or the estates, establishments, and structures with which they were identified. In a suburban development, the pillars of the community were usually built at the same time as all its other structures, and even if they weren't, the community by definition contained no members whose residential memory had meaningful heft. The pillars of these communities, like the real life they were supposed to epitomize, actually resided elsewhere, for example, in large defense plants, fifteen, twenty-five, forty miles away. These financial pillars were integral to the community's welfare but not to its space or history or infrastructure; the connection was an external apparatus, an interstate, authorized and funded by a distant and unseen power.

The specific income differences that might have distinguished one nodule from another were elided by the normatizing narratives they received with increasing frequency and abundance from the authoritative source of reality: their television sets. According to television, all these suburbanites were *really* the same, in the best, most patriotic, and middle-class sense of sameness. They were the bastion of the values that promised Cold War supremacy, and their behavior was a best-case-scenario manifestation of those values. In the evening, suburbia en masse watched the same shows, laughed at the same jokes, and reacted to the same news. Each community was united with the thousands of communities like it. The fact that members of these communities rarely saw their neighbors sharing this news and entertainment was not significant because citizenship after all was inferential, with television regularly confirming the inferences. Television in this sense, even more than the individual new suburban settlement, was the newest version of the frontier. For that reason, as Findlay so insightfully writes,

> in order to appreciate Disneyland fully, it is necessary to understand that its origins and influence also possessed a distinctly *Western* character. Above all else, Disneyland was a product of southern California's motion picture industry. It could not have appeared without the skills and marketing associated with feature filmmaking. At the same time when Americans spoke about the demise of motion pictures, Walt Disney insured that, through theme parks and through television, Hollywood and the West became not less influential but more so.79

The Racial Margins

This influence of the West, as the motion-picture version of itself, came at a huge cost—as did the entire entertainment industry—to those who did not conform to what the industry perceived as commodifiable images. In the pursuit of middle-class homogeneity, television, the interstate, suburbia, and Disneyland all attempted to erase the presence of the poor and, especially, of ethnic minorities.

In his chapter "White Roads through Black Bedrooms," Mowbray describes in detail how the rerouting of I-40 through a black neighborhood in Nashville was particularly destructive to the neighborhood and to black-owned businesses. This route typified the tendency of interstates to traffic members of the suburban white middle class to and from their sites of commerce and entertainment in a way that could make them oblivious to those who did not share their opportunities.[80] In the late 1940s, for example, highway construction tore up Detroit's most densely populated black neighborhoods. While carefully protecting middle-class residential neighborhoods from disruption, Detroit highway planners "blasted through the black [sections], wiping out many of the city's most prominent African American institutions, from jazz clubs to the Saint Antoine branch of the YMCA."[81] The announcement of highway projects years before actual construction exacerbated the problem. Thomas J. Sugrue points out, "Homeowners and shopkeepers were trapped, unable to sell property that would soon be condemned, unable to move without the money from a property sale. Building owners had no incentive to invest in improvements. An enormous number of buildings were leveled to make way for the new expressways."[82]

This type of destruction was not what President Eisenhower had envisioned when he pushed through legislation to create the interstate highway system. That legislation, the result of numerous compromises, resulted in a relatively autonomous Highway Trust Fund that would serve as a virtual "perpetual-motion machine" to funnel all revenues earmarked for highway construction back into the system, with little political accountability. When he discovered that the highways were going through rather than around cities, Eisenhower, according to Stephen B. Goddard, "recoiled in horror. . . . Amazingly he had been unaware during the lengthy congressional donnybrook that the only way the interstates could become a reality in this increasingly urban nation was to promise cities enough money to eviscerate themselves."[83]

The destruction of communities whose inhabitants relied on public transportation and, in many regions, lived in multiple-unit dwellings served multiple ends. It subordinated the needs of the weakest and the poorest to those of the more wealthy, and it helped guarantee that opportunities for upward mobility would be distributed along racial lines. The Federal Housing Administration encouraged bank loans for new suburban houses "while openly refusing to stake money on older city properties."[84] The suburban communities continued to increase in value by virtue of the ease with which suburbanites could reach the city. That ease, of course, entailed great difficulty for urban businesses and homes owned by minorities. Customers were separated from businesses, local economic bases deprived of their necessary profit thresholds, contiguous residential sectors fractured, local traffic patterns destroyed. Remaining residences, surrounded by unsightly obstructions and blanketed in noise and air pollution, declined in value, making it difficult if not impossible for homeowners to trade up to the suburbs—a move made even more unlikely by the discriminatory practices of banks and developers.[85]

The growth of suburbia as we know it, in other words, would have been impossible without countless uncompensated sacrifices by urban minorities. This historical context provides one more illumination of the enduring power of Ralph Ellison's 1952 novel, *Invisible Man*, about the conditions of black America. The social invisibility of black Americans from the end of Reconstruction until the 1960s both allowed and was exacerbated by the development of interstates and freeways. In this way, the interstates played the same role as Cold War television.

It is important to remember that another way to view 1950s homogeneity is to say it was achieved by separating the people more likely to *own* television sets from those more likely not to. The white, upwardly mobile middle class lived in neat, well-patterned communities. Viewed from a few thousand feet, they suggested a twentieth-century Garden of Versailles on a scale unimaginable even to someone as excessive as Louis XIV. A view of the urban pattern from the same distance, however, is apt to be dominated not by the dwellings but by the long, intersecting thoroughfares converging from every direction in an intricate design—three- and four-lane concrete ribbons, decorated by cloverleaf bows. Their purpose, like the neat suburban patterns, was to affirm domestic suburban life by allowing members of the white middle class who lived in suburbia to retain a notion of themselves as definitive Americans. To do so, they remained on a road with uniform standards from coast to coast, traversing space at a speed that rendered extraneous anything that the highway cut through. Theirs was a controlled-access road that allowed them to live in controlled-access communities, where they watched television shows that limited the access of

These three- and four-lane concrete ribbons, decorated by cloverleaf bows, served to affirm domestic suburban life by allowing white middle-class suburbanites to retain a notion of themselves as definitive Americans. *Library of Congress, Prints and Photographs Division* [LC-USZ62-108098].

minorities, on television sets to which, in mid-decade, disproportionately few blacks had access. In 1954, a huge number of those suburban people watched *Disneyland*, a television show named after a place soon to be completed that, at both mythic and quotidian levels, would complement the work of the interstates.

The park's project was to reassure white middle-class visitors that their lives had stature as representatives of the West. To that end, Disneyland worked equally hard at extolling the visitor's whiteness and his or her middle-class, Cold War values. It employed no black workers until 1963, and then only under pressure.[86] Not until the end of the 1960s did African Americans receive visible roles. By the park's own admission, it recruited employees who "possessed the 'Disney Look' and accepted the 'Disney way.'"[87] The "people specialists," as they were called, presented the 1950s patron with standardized appearance and demeanor, consistent with the

"Disney effect" noted earlier that rendered the design of the park reassuring through a carefully uniform color design. "The girls are generally blonde," Schickel writes,

> blue-eyed and self-effacing, all looking as if they stepped out of an ad for California sportswear and are heading for suburban motherhood. The boys, who pilot vehicles and help you on and off rides, are outdoorsy, All-American types, the kind of vacuously pleasant lad your mother was always telling you to imitate. . . . Even the cops at Disneyland are a new breed—generally moonlighting schoolteachers, with physical education instructors predominant among them.[88]

In this, as in everything, Disneyland engaged in the same purification process as did black-and-white television, available to roughly the same demographic group and roughly in tune with its needs, willfully oblivious to alternative (and by definition aberrant) aesthetic, social, or economic values. As Spigel points out, this quality also characterized suburbia. Suburban space, she explained, was "designed to purify communal spaces, to sweep away urban clutter, while at the same time preserving the populist ideal of good neighborliness that carried Americans through the Depression."[89] Television, Spigel makes clear, was a powerful instrument of that sanitational objective:

> In the postwar era, the fantasy of antiseptic electrical space was transposed onto television. Numerous commentators claimed that television allowed people to travel from their homes while remaining untouched by the actual social contexts to which they imaginatively traveled. . . .
>
> Television promised more than just practical benefits. Like previous communication technologies, it offered the possibility of an intellectual neighborhood, purified of social unrest and human misunderstanding.[90]

Disney's sanitized neighborhood, however, was less intellectual than historical in that its appeal was to people who could identify with turn-of-the-century America, if only imaginatively. Disneyland, in this regard, served the same ideological ends as Christmas and Thanksgiving, events that popularized standard icons for a nation of baby boomers. In the economic explosion of the postwar era, they could indeed imagine the bounty of a classic holiday turkey, of plentiful gifts and many celebrations. By providing a set of songs and drawings to these baby boomers—the first wave of whom entered kindergarten about the time that CBS broadcast Disney's first Christmas television specials—the schools and the media combined, by secularizing the holidays, to make Thanksgiving and Christmas the cornerstones of a national religion. In the 1950s, some stations even started the Christmas Eve practice of showing burning Yule logs on television screens.[91] The holidays ritualized by television represented neither the nation's shared beliefs nor its common history but rather a set of secular rituals that (white) Americans could imagine having performed.

There is no way of telling, of course, how much a half century of moviegoing facilitated the ability of first-, second-, or even third-generation children in Brooklyn, Shaker Heights, or West Hollywood to sing with conviction and pleasure, "Over the river and through the woods, to Grandmother's house we go; the horse knows the way to carry the sleigh. . . ." Nevertheless, this imaginary white grandmother, accessible only by horse and sleigh (with bells that jingle all the way) provides a common reference point to illustrate just how far the interstate has brought us, that is, to the point at which the imaginary horse-drawn trip is a theme ride we have all taken in that definitive Disneyland of the mind, for which the park is the logical validation.

But what of those for whom film and television did not provide an applicable fantasy, a seamless narrative that merged their identity with valorized projections of the American folk and historical past? For some, dreaming of a *white* Christmas—as the song and 1954 movie of the same name implied was obligatory—required a specific leap of racial as well as geographical imagination, without which they sacrificed a portion of their cultural citizenship. That sacrifice, however, was just a figurative version of the material sacrifice the interstate exacted from their communities in the process of establishing—in Cold War national interests—the suburban nuclear family as a national standard for domestic security. Noting that Disneyland's development depended on its convenient connection to "new freeways in the midst of the region's largest locus of population growth," and that it "redefined public space and culture, with its location and admission costs making it much more accessible to suburban white families than to ethnic minority residents of the inner city," George Lipsitz also points out that "its appeal depended on more than accessibility; as a new kind of public space Disneyland contrasted sharply with alternative experiences in the Los Angeles area."[92]

But if we are to believe the comments of Disney and his associates, the park was more than a contrast or alternative to contemporary (multiethnic) urban life. Disneyland was the remedy—America denuded of impurities. Perhaps most sadly, by lodging the park simultaneously and firmly in the past and the future, in the real and the fantastic, its designers provided narratives that precluded diversity. Since Main Street 1900 is a continuation of the interstate, and the park is shaped like a highway cloverleaf with all the spurs returning visitors to 1900, Disneyland's overall design precludes other versions of history, pathways to a different model of America, a different kind of reinvention. The perfect control in the park, the pleasingly uniform faces and sets, the absolute enforcement of norms, and finally the twenty-five-foot berm all deny the need for alternatives, for different national narratives, for a destiny that can be reached by a route that does not require controlled access.

In this regard, Disneyland, like television, was largely consistent with the national agenda. Although during World War II defense plants created an ethnically heterogeneous environment, and Los Angeles was developing richly diversified living spaces,

> the growth of the postwar suburbs (largely subsidized by tax spending on new highways and the extension of city services including water, gas, electric, and sewer lines), encouraged new forms of isolation and segregation. Racial discrimination by private realtors and developers denied most African-Americans and Mexican Americans access to the new suburbs, while the federal government's discriminatory home loan policies effectively subsidized the creation of all-white neighborhoods in the San Fernando Valley and Orange County. The newly dispersed population made public transit less efficient per mile and the numbers of automobiles driven by commuters further slowed the speed of trolleys and buses, thereby providing central city dwellers with even more reasons to move to the suburbs. In less than a decade, Los Angeles's diverse urban space became more segregated than ever, its effective rapid transit system collapsed, and the success of suburbs and freeways only contributed to ever-increasing fragmentation, segregation, and dispersal of the city's population."93

Television, Disneyland, and the interstate contributed to the racial segregation that the Supreme Court had outlawed from public schools just a few months before the premiere of *Disneyland*. The show and the park made white suburban values the figurative goal of interstate travel.

From Frontierland to the Adult Western

If Disneyland and Los Angeles became the places where the highway and the land of opportunity united, television made that land endless as a commercial reality, a point dramatically illustrated by Disney's December 1954 visit to Frontierland. Whatever the power of *Disneyland* or the potential of Disneyland, at the end of 1954 that power and that potential both took a quantum leap when viewers were first exposed to Davy Crockett. Three of *Disneyland*'s "Frontierland" episodes dealt with the legendary hero, the first focusing on his adventures in the Indian Wars, the second on his experience as a U.S. congressman, and the third on his death at the Alamo. When the Indian Wars episode aired in December, it set off a huge and unprecedented national craze. "In part, the craze reflected the powerful appeal of the new medium of television," Watts explains. "In part its roots lay in people's nostalgic yearning for an earlier, simpler age, before factories, bureaucracies, big government, labor unions, and other institutions of modern industrial society made it more difficult for individuals to confront and solve issues directly."94 In addition, the programs connected Crockett and Frontierland with the suburban social landscape, Marling points out:

> Frontierland embodied both the national past and the most popular
> recurring theme of the *Disneyland* program, thanks to the Davy Crockett
> mania of the 1954–55 season. Like Tomorrowland, Frontierland
> resonated to powerful themes in the suburban imagination. The ranch,
> the knotty-pine den, the outdoor barbecue, the search for an acre of
> crabgrass beyond the boundaries of urban civilization: these facts of
> American life in the 1950s helped explain why the Western genre
> accounted for more than a quarter of the movies produced in Hollywood
> and why the cowboy film of the period was so often domestic in
> flavor. . . . Disney's *Davy Crockett* episodes—the first one-hour, prime-time
> Westerns on network television—garnered the highest ratings of the
> decade . . . by validating suburban mobility in the person of the restless
> frontiersman who waxes nostalgic about home and family as he dies in
> the wilds of Texas.95

The Davy Crockett sensation marked the moment when television came of age as a cultural force, blending its technological, commercial, and social energies into one cogent and coherent phenomenon. Whatever financial and technological realities bankrolled the construction of Walt

Disney's dream, the blending of dream and reality, narrative as commercial promotion and as commercial product, exceeded Disney's greatest expectations when, on December 13, 1954, the Disney studio premiered the first of three "Frontierland" episodes based on the life of Davy Crockett.

Nothing to date had suggested the immense commercial potential of television, not only to deliver audiences to sponsors but also to create connected commercial products. In addition to helping ABC become a viable network and *Disneyland* become, according to a *TV Guide* poll of forty-five thousand readers, the most popular show of the 1954–1955 season (it was rated second by Nielsen), the Davy Crockett episodes set off a craze that gave television, in the words of *TV Guide*, its "first genuine overnight star"[96] and "provided the nation with a new hero and a new song hit, both named Davy Crockett."[97] In the first six months, seventeen versions of "The Ballad of Davy Crockett" sold seven million copies, and one version topped the record charts for five consecutive weeks.[98] The hero and the song, reciprocally, provided endorsements not only for *Disneyland* and Disneyland but also for countless products, such as t-shirts, lunch boxes, toy rifles, and the ubiquitous coonskin caps. By the summer of 1955, about $100 million had been made from sales of approximately two hundred separate retail items.[99]

If the "flow" that Raymond Williams identified as characterizing television[100] could be imagined as a Möbius strip in which the "inside" and the "outside" of American experience—the reality of consumerism and the reality that circumscribed the consumer's material life with informing narratives—became a seamless continuum, the case could be made that *Disneyland* in general and the Davy Crockett episodes in particular marked the moment when the ends of the strip were cemented together. One reason was that the show occurred when television was starting to occupy the attention of a majority of all Americans, making it perhaps the single most common experience of Cold War America. It created, in other words, a kind of public space heretofore inaccessible, given the spatial and temporal vastness and diversity of the United States. Within the parameters of that public space, moreover, it targeted that huge demographic bubble, the baby boomers, who throughout the second half of the twentieth century would critically inflect America's cultural norms. *Disneyland* provided this generation with a common past and with informing myths based on rereadings of a privileged set of fairy tales.[101]

The ubiquity of the coonskin hats popularized by the show *Davy Crock-ett* was proof positive of television's commercial power. *Library of Congress, Prints and Photographs Division [LC-USZ62-75888]. Reprinted with permission of Sunkist Growers, Inc. All Rights Reserved.*

It also, as TV *Guide* pointed out, supplied a national hero grounded in the allegedly "true" adventures of a real person who had lived on the American frontier. This frontiersman was particularly well suited at that moment to represent the quintessence of America. Like the parents of his chief audience, he was a recent war veteran (of the Indian Wars), and like the president he had moved from a military into a political career. The last episode, which recounted Crockett's journey to and death at the Alamo, constructed Crockett's memory in the image of the Cold Warrior, drawn to foreign soil by the cause of "freedom." "Crockett symbolized the American character in the death struggle with the Communist foe."[102]

Another factor that contributed to the Crockett craze was that well before the *Disneyland* episodes, American culture in general, and television in particular, had drawn its heroes from the frontier. The Western had been, without doubt or serious competition, the most prolific genre in American film history, especially when one includes "B" pictures, and because the studios were not selling new movies to television before the coaxial cable allowed national network shows, *TV Guide* explained,

> stations were forced to use old ones, just to have something to show. . . . They soon found that cowboy movies, no matter how ancient, invariably built a regular audience.
>
> A psychiatrist once accounted for the popularity of Westerns by saying that the hero represents a "father image," the incorruptible leader with whom all viewers want to identify themselves.[103]

The availability and popularity of Westerns made Hopalong Cassidy (William Boyd), Roy Rogers, and Gene Autry superstars among the children in the early television audience.[104] A *TV Guide* article in the summer of 1954 announced explicitly, "Children Made Roy King of the Cowboys."[105] But Davy Crockett moved the Western hero from the world of children's fantasy to that of adult nation-making. In replacing Roy Rogers, "King of the Cowboys," with Davy Crockett, "King of the Wild Frontier," *Disneyland* was providing the American public space of TV land with a "father image" who combined fantasy with history, adventure with manifest destiny. Although the product of Frontierland, Davy Crockett's mythic status, his heroic adventures, his concern with western expansion, and his final devotion to the cause of Texas and thus the future of American borders and influence made him equally well a representative of Fantasyland, Adventureland, and Tomorrowland. To the extent, therefore, that Crockett represented *Disneyland*, he helped *Disneyland* represent America. And from the perspective of the 1950s, representing the West was not only America's role in popular culture and its destiny in nineteenth-century history but also its charge in the Cold War.

Un-remembering the Alamo

In this context, the final episode of the Crockett trilogy, "Davy Crockett at the Alamo," is particularly interesting. Host Walt Disney introduced the episode, which aired on February 23, 1955, by drastically inflating Crockett's role in the siege of the Alamo: "If he had done nothing else in his brief, adventurous life, Davy Crockett's courage and daring during the immortal battle of the Alamo would have earned him an honored place in American history. In tribute to this frontier hero, we present another story based on Davy's own journal."

For several reasons, Disney was describing neither the episode that would follow nor the facts upon which it was based. In the episode, Crockett's behavior was not significantly different from that of anyone else at the Alamo, a situation that did not particularly allow for individual heroics. The Alamo, after all, was not a fort but an abandoned mission, ill equipped to withstand the onslaught of thousands of Mexican troops. The 182 people there simply defended the walls until they were overrun. Since all those who fought at the Alamo were killed, no one could record Crockett's "courage and daring," and hence we cannot possibly know whether his actions there would have "won him an honored place in American history." Nor, of course, could the story have come from "Davy's own journal." No doubt Disney was referring to "*Col. Crockett's Exploits and Adventures in Texas, Written by Himself*," published the summer after the Alamo fell. That book—one in a long array of increasingly outlandish (and racist!) publications about Crockett that proliferated throughout the nineteenth century— was bogus, as James Shackford has shown, a "long-lived hoax."[106]

Disney's introduction also implied that the battle of the Alamo was a significant part of American history, another questionable point. Jim Bowie had been sent to the Alamo with orders not to hold it but to destroy it. For reasons that remain unclear, he could not bring himself to do so. The Alamo could not have provided a practical site from which to forestall the Mexican troops' advance, and the revolutionary forces under Sam Houston's command at the time of the siege were neither sufficient nor sufficiently well organized to engage Santa Anna's army.[107] If anything, the Alamo had symbolic significance, providing a rallying cry for the emerging Texas army and for the press in the United States.

One needs to ask, as well, in what sense the event was part of "American" history. In 1836, when the Alamo fell, it was located on Mexican soil and was the site of a conflict between the Mexican army and *Mexican* citizens (of American origin). The Mexican government had, from the 1820s on, encouraged the settlement of Texas by making generous land offers— one-tenth the price of public land in the United States, in parcels nearly sixty times larger[108]—with the condition that the settlers become Mexican citizens and Catholics. American land agents (*empresarios*) commissioned by the Mexican government—the most successful being Stephen Austin—encouraged settlement by advertising widely throughout the United States. As a result, by the 1830s 75 percent of the Texas region's population was Anglo-American.

This Texas population, however, was by no means representative of the U.S. population as a whole but rather of a specific segment that was, as T. R. Fehrenbach reminds us, inordinately prone to aggression and violence: "No matter how many historians prefer to gloss over the fact, the first Trans-Appalachian-born or -bred generation was an extremely tough and violent race. Texas was where the action was."[109] The settlers included an array of opportunistic scoundrels, many of whom, such as Jim Bowie, Sam Houston, and William Travis, figured prominently in the Texas Revolution. Bowie, a broke slave runner, smuggler, and land scammer was, by 1834, severely alcoholic,[110] as was Houston, the former governor of Tennessee, who in the 1830s was living among the Arkansas Cherokee with a drinking problem so severe that the Cherokee dubbed him Oo-tse-tee Ar-de-tah-skee (Cherokee for "Big Drunk"). Travis, who had abandoned his son and pregnant wife to seek his fortune in Texas, there "conducted a thriving legal practice, gambled heavily, and bedded as many women as he could, making notes in Spanish in his diary of each conquest."[111] Travis became a leader among the Anglo settlers known as the War Dogs—almost all of them young Southern lawyers—who for financial reasons favored open rebellion from Mexico.

Hardly a cross-section of America, either demographically or philosophically, Austin's immigrants were inordinately dominated by Southerners.[112] "The great difference between Texas and the other regions of the West was that Texas had a planter class," Fehrenbach explains, "[that] stamped the lasting standards of conduct upon the Lone Star State. . . . Both because of early settlement and social financial prominence, the planter formed the apex of society in Texas."[113] Texas did not attract those governed by democratic principles or, given that they had to change nationality and religion, patriotism or theology. They wanted land and power.

So did Crockett. Like Houston, Crockett was a failed Tennessee politician; like Houston and Bowie, he had a serious drinking problem; and like Austin, Travis, Bowie, and Houston, he came to Texas for material gain. As Jeff Long succinctly puts it:

He was sick and tired of being broke. Texas seemed like a good
solution. . . .

Crockett didn't go to Texas to fight a revolution. He didn't go to sharp-
shoot tyrants or defend liberty. He went for himself.

He wanted land.

He wanted money.[114]

In the Disney episode, however, Crockett was drawn by a newspaper
headline:

Texas Independence Threatened
General Santa Anna Vows to Expel Settlers

Since at the time Texas independence did not exist, it could not, of
course, have been threatened. Nor was expulsion exactly the issue. Mexican
officials, concerned, as Mark Deer explains, "at what they saw as an American takeover . . . outlawed immigration from the United States *and banned
slavery in the province.* They also sought to break the settlers' monopoly on
shipping and levied taxes, in an attempt to pressure people into leaving.
The colonists ignored the new laws, and the Mexicans strengthened their
garrisons to enforce them"[115] (emphasis added). By the mid-1830s, as Long
puts it, "Texas was being radicalized by men who stood to gain fortunes if
they could cut it loose of the Mexican republic."[116] Hence, Mexico's attempt
to regain authority over the region and over the Mexican citizens (of American origin) who lived there led to the Texas Revolution.

When, in the Disney episode, Crockett's sidekick, George Russell
(Buddy Ebsen), accurately responded to the newspaper headline, "There's
nothing there but a mess o' trouble," Crockett reflected the tone of 1830s
propaganda when he tersely replied, "Americans in trouble." No doubt this
was the way that many Americans regarded the Texas expatriates, in that
their nationality had little to do with citizenship and everything to do with
race and national origin. "Americanness" was something the Texas colonizers in effect carried with them, the inalienable right to be Americans, regardless of their location or their citizenship. Texans thus extended the
borders of the nation simply by being American, by claiming the rights of
Americans, even when they technically were Mexicans. If they believed that
the quintessential right of the American was "freedom," in this case that
entailed freedom from obeying Mexican law; in other words, they regarded
the Mexican laws as local and American freedom as universal.

Even after the Texas Revolution neither the Alamo nor the rest of the Texas territory became part of the United States, instead functioning as an independent country, the Lone Star Republic, for nearly a decade. Only after the Mexican War of 1846 did Texas become part of the United States. The Alamo thus was a part of *American* history only in terms of the way in which it manifested the continental destiny of the United States.

"Manifest destiny," however, as Reginald Horsman has shown, was lodged from its beginnings in a notion of a superior "Anglo-Saxon race." This notion justified the subordination of non-Anglo-Saxons in the name of freedom, so that the American history of which the Alamo constituted a part was a history based not on nation but on race. "The Texas Revolution," Horsman writes, "was from its beginnings interpreted in the United States and among Americans in Texas as a racial clash, not simply a revolt against unjust government or tyranny."[117] The actual term "manifest destiny" first came into use in the 1840s in regard to the annexation of Mexico. Drawing as it did on early-nineteenth-century concepts of racial supremacy, the phrase quickly gained currency, evoking the sundry concerns felt to be implicit in the dangers of a racially mixed nation and focusing on what Horsman identified as the "general low regard in which the people of Mexico were held by the government and people of the United States. . . . Since the time of the Texas Revolution, the Mexicans had been repeatedly attacked in the United States as a degenerate, largely Indian race unable to control or improve the territories it owned."[118]

Manifest destiny held that inferior peoples would "naturally" be replaced by or subordinated to superior Anglo-Saxons. So the term "American," in the sense that the Disney episode employed it, described a political mandate arising out of genetic inevitability. The inevitability was proved through a temporal inversion that retrospectively extended America to the sites it was (historically? biologically? theologically?) "destined" to acquire. The successful annexation of Texas that followed ten years after the Anglos' successful expulsion of the Mexicans from the Texas territory, according to this logic, proved that the Alamo was American.

This fulfillment of racial "destiny" effectively freed the repatriated Americans from the restrictions of Mexican law, including the law abolishing slavery. If destiny declared that the Texans were fighting for freedom, that freedom was defined racially, and the issue of Texas annexation was linked from the outset to the struggle between proslavery and abolitionist forces over the potential expansion of slavery into western regions of the United States.

Thus, the Alamo was important to American history because history was the product of a destiny that was the function of race, and freedom represented the ability to distribute rights and define property along racial lines. To this concept of freedom the idea of the Alamo as a site in a civil war among Mexican citizens was anathema, for it precluded the narrative in which the Alamo signified the triumph, even in defeat, of America's racial destiny. Russell reflected this universalizing narrative of America's destiny in his reply to Crockett: "Yeah, a bunch of crazy fools that're trying to take on a whole army. They're so far away from the rest of the country that they know they ain't gonna get no help—a bunch of rock-headed idiots that won't quit because they think they're right. . . . How soon you reckon we'll be headed out that way?"

We can clearly see the Cold War narrative implicit in this interchange between Crockett and Russell, enacted through the bonding in danger and death of white men who are investing a small frontier community with the quintessence of America. Because America is not a place but a set of values, a dedication to the cause of freedom, Americans feel obliged to fight for freedom wherever its cry is heard. As this show aired, we should remember, American soldiers had just returned from a "police action" in Korea, and Vietnam was being divided, with American support and blessing, into North and South zones in concurrence with the 1954 Geneva Accord. The episode's final image—Davy Crockett swinging his rifle against an onslaught of Mexican soldiers dissolving into a Lone Star Republic flag—blended the defeat at the Alamo into the long-term triumph of manifest destiny, at the same time obscuring the gap between the sign of freedom and the expansion of slavery that the history surrounding the Alamo entailed. This image indeed captured the spirit in which Lyndon Johnson is believed to have equated the Alamo with Vietnam[119] and also suggested how the Alamo signified television itself, that emerging public space of the 1950s that replaced regional interests with national narratives.

The frontier, the "real" West, Davy Crockett, *Disneyland*, the effectiveness of telefilm, the power of television, were all consolidated vividly at the Alamo. With the advent of *Disneyland* and, as its most consumable image, Davy Crockett, Walt Disney had found his métier. The show identified the frontier—imagined through the relentless and relentlessly anachronistic middle-classism of Walt Disney—as connecting the hero of the baby boomers with the hero of their parents, America as fantasy land with

America as tomorrow land, television as source of real life with television as producer of filmed fantasy.

Integration

For this reason, Marling is correct when she states that since "World War II an unprecedented increase in middle-class affluence and leisure time had combined with a booming automobile industry and a nationwide freeway system to make possible—even obligatory—for Americans, adults and children, at least one pilgrimage to Disney Land or World as a popular culture 'mecca' of nearly religious importance."[120]

At the same time, the "Magic Lands"—those postwar Western cities for which in some ways Disneyland was a prototype—did not "solve" most of the problems of the urban city. Findlay reminds us,

> In fact, something like the opposite may have occurred. Many of the Westerners arrived at some sort of understanding of the metropolis only by simplifying it through mental maps, by designing away contradictions in the cultural landscape, and by walling themselves off from the complications of city life. Magic kingdoms attempted to exclude diversity and misery from their idealized settings, substituting in their stead a world indexed to the middle-class standards of an affluent society.[121]

Western cities, in other words, following the lead of Disneyland, idealized American life through exclusionary tactics in exactly the same way that television did. As part of a Cold War agenda, television represented the West as problem-free, and the West mirrored the televisual image, for both of which Disney set the "real" norm. "In a profound way," Watts points out, "television dramatically connected the various fiefdoms in the growing Disney empire. It was, however, only the most obvious manifestation of the much larger principle that fueled expansion of the postwar Disney enterprise. 'Integration,' a sacred word in the Disney lexicon, became the heart and soul of this culture-industry behemoth in the 1950s."[122]

"This culture-industry behemoth" was, I have been arguing, America itself. Walt Disney understood the need to cluster the nation's knowledge, history, imagery, iconography, and commercial enterprise around Disneyland. His implicit objective was to turn the notion of Disneyland as the common place of America into a national commonplace. To say that his objective was commercial is simply to rephrase the cliché that "the business of America is business." In that sense, if Disneyland was America, *Disneyland* was America's TV commercial, and "Disney" was the trademark for its consolidated national interests. "Integration" thus referred to media, to narratives, and to ventures, but not to races. If Disneyland was the common place—the town square—where America integrated its history and destiny, its technology and geography, its family and industry—it was also the place where all the significant elements of that unprecedented integration were white.

During the months when *Disneyland* was preparing to air and Disneyland was being planned, the Supreme Court issued perhaps its most significant decision of the twentieth century, declaring on May 17, 1954, in the case of *Brown v. Board of Education of Topeka*, that racially segregated schools were unconstitutional. As the schools (and other institutions) of America moved—however slowly, painfully, and incompletely—toward racial integration, *Disneyland* and Disney Enterprises would provide a relentless commercial for an alternative integration of American values. In this way Disney would encapsulate the work of black-and-white television in general, as it provided the electronic avenue to the ultimate destination of the interstate highway: the West, that apotheosis of Cold War values that vouchsafed (white) America's global victory. As Disney so vigilantly asserted and television so relentlessly affirmed, this was the real America, the truths we "all" had in common.

In many senses, as we have seen, Davy Crockett was a genuine Western pioneer. Metaphorically, he was a prominent reference point in the landscape of American mythology, a figure of heroic status in the cluster of legends that made a composite narrative of national destiny. The name "Davy Crockett" helped expand the story of the frontier. The man, Davy Crockett, could also be counted among the literal throng of anonymous Anglo settlers whose activities continued to unsettle the space beyond the westernmost limits of quotidian Eastern economy, social influence, and national allegiance. And to the extent that his literal role was representative of numerous other settlers, his pioneering was exemplary as well as symbolic.

Over one hundred years after his death, he took part in pioneering a new, monumental national activity: the creation of a televisual nation. Demonstrating beyond question the power of television to control national imagery and, through it, national commerce, Davy Crockett—the Disney presentation and Disney trademark item—pioneered the merger of film and television, helping to unsettle and resettle the boundaries of mass media and, with them, the conception of national space. In so doing, the Disney Crockett resembled his nineteenth-century namesake. Both Crocketts helped to construct a new sense of nation, one associated, in both cases, with the West. Both Crocketts represented the expansion of commercial interests, based on legends that unified an Anglo-Saxon nation as a place to be traversed with ease and to be universally domesticated.

4 The Adult Western and the Western Bloc

In addition to leading the migration of television to film, Disney's Crockett led the migration of the Western genre to prime-time television production. From the mid-nineteenth century through the 1950s the most prolific narrative genre in American popular culture was the Western. As serious, dramatic film it peaked in the decade following World War II, reaching a pinnacle in 1955, when two of the three initial Crockett episodes aired. "Long before the so-called adult Westerns premiered in the fall of 1955," J. Fred MacDonald points out, "the *Davy Crockett* features illustrated the potential impact of mature Westerns on viewers."[1]

Starting in 1955 with the shows *Gunsmoke* and *The Life and Legend of Wyatt Earp*, adult Westerns came by the end of the decade to dominate prime time and the Nielsen ratings. These series differentiated themselves from children's Westerns (such as those featuring Roy Rogers, Hopalong Cassidy, Gene Autry, and Annie Oakley) by claiming to be grounded in realistic, even true stories about heroes such as Davy Crockett. In the second half of the decade, while film production of Westerns declined rapidly, television Westerns proliferated, so that in 1957 there were twenty adult Westerns per week on prime-time network television, in 1958 twenty-six (with many more in syndication), and in 1959 thirty, covering just about one-quarter of all prime-time network programming. In that 1959–1960 television season, in some months eight of the top ten shows in the country were "adult Westerns," and for a three-year period, culminating in that 1959–1960 season, roughly half of the top ten shows and half of the top twenty shows were adult Westerns.

The character of Davy Crockett might be seen as having "inspired" the adult Western trend, a Disney spokesman contended in 1956. Like the Crockett series, *TV Guide* pointed out, the adult Westerns had a "relative absence of 'bad men' and [an] emphasis on historic atmosphere."[2] They also emphasized psychology over action and shunned the use of chases and shootouts for their own sake. Particularly, they were united by at least an ostensible commitment to "realism," that is, to the idea that the West was a real place, populated by more or less ordinary people (who nevertheless often did extraordinary things). This new genre, the adult Western television show, grounded its value, in other words, on the notion that television had a monopoly on reality, a notion its advocates had worked so tenaciously to establish in its earliest inceptions.

According to a review of *Wyatt Earp*, "Earp's exploits as a frontier marshal were so crammed with gun-slinging action, suspense and excitement that a producer could hardly go wrong basing a show on his life. . . . The scripts . . . adhere to reality with only an occasional foray into fiction."3 In January 1956, Hugh O'Brien, the real star of *Wyatt Earp*, wrote an article on the real Earp indicating that the series used Stuart Lake's biography of Earp as its guide.4 That article was paired with "My Cousin Wyatt," an article by a distant relative of Earp's who happened to be on *TV Guide*'s staff.5

Articles frequently emphasized that adult Westerns depicted real history. A *TV Guide* description for the premiere episode of *Bat Masterson* indicated: "Reports differ on how this actual incident ended. Tonight's show offers dramatizations of two different versions of the windup."6 And in February 1959, the producer of *Bat Masterson*, in an article titled "The Facts Are Enough," indicated that the show wanted to be as accurate as possible.7

Adult Westerns in Black-and-White

If television, as we have seen, viewed itself as the medium both of reality and of normativity, of the descriptive and of the proscriptive, then it was ill suited to explore the ideological gap between history and mythology. It could be argued, in fact, that television's conditions of production required it to disguise rather than expose or interrogate that gap. In any case, if Cold War television had other options, it did not exercise them. Instead it created by the end of the 1950s an extensive and extensively consistent viewing experience that merged past and present in such a way as to suggest that the settlement of the West was a version of contemporary (Cold War) life and values. The remarkable character of Western heroes and Western settlers was, first and foremost, how much and how often they resembled the contemporary television audience.

In the same way that the interstate created a consistent notion of America by converting distance into time, so did the networks' network of adult Western narratives create versions of past and present uncannily consistent with one another by conflating historical time and geographical space. The

Old West was a time as much as it was a place, and therefore the adult Westerns provided viewers with the same easy and controlled access to national history that the interstate provided to urban centers. This facile conflation of history and mythology, no doubt, invested the adult Western with the quality of destiny, for destiny is the narrative in which history realizes, with a sense of entitlement, its mythic proportions.

Because the genre had so much invested in its connection to an identifiable American reality, adult Westerns employed several rhetorical strategies that typified early television's extensive attempts to assert its veracity. An article accounting for *Gunsmoke*'s success, for example, explained that the concept for the show was that "everyone would behave more or less as human beings behave in real life, where characters would resemble the real articles. . . . The show would operate on the revolutionary but entirely valid principle that in the early West the most hated man in town was usually the marshal."[8] James Arness, the series star, said in 1958 that "people like Westerns because they represent a time of freedom. A cowboy wasn't tied down to one place or to one woman. When he got mad he hauled off and slugged someone. When he drank he got good and drunk."[9]

Gunsmoke was based on a radio series by the same name that had premiered in 1952 and that, like the subsequent television show, dedicated itself to a realistic depiction of the West. John Meston, one of the show's creators, explained that

> homicidal psychopaths gathered along the frontier and had themselves a real circus with little or nothing to stop them from happily mowing one another down. . . . It ended finally. The murderers killed one another off and gradually disappeared from this section of the American scene. But the end was partly hastened by a few strangers who happened to get their satisfaction from killing on the side of the law—sheriffs, marshals and the like. . . . Matt Dillon, because of obvious reasons, is a cut above the lawman I've described. But he's not, I trust, so far above the real thing to be pure fiction.[10]

The "cut above" that Meston sought to portray captures the spirit of the adult Western as a cultural phenomenon. At the same time that it claimed to be based on authentic American history, it also gave us an idealistic vision of the West, one that was a cut above. Meston, in effect, was merging a sense of manifest destiny with a version of social Darwinism. In a process of natural selection, "the murderers killed one another off and gradually disappeared," although the disappearance was less gradual because of a modification in the environment: killers on the side of the law. These killers helped rid the West of killers. By being both of their ilk and a cut above, Marshal Dillon bridged the gap between the mythology of Western ideals—so important to justifying Cold War policy—and the practice of settling the West. Dillon's ethical superiority thus became the linchpin connecting American history to the idealist vision of itself as both mythology and destiny. As such, Dillon, in the way Meston conceived him for radio, was the perfect hero to bring adult Westerns to television.[11] With the advent of Matt Dillon, the days in which the Western hero shot the gun out of the villain's hand were dead and buried. If not graphic, the violence was often lethal and always potentially so, a point emphasized by the fact that in the initial season, Dillon began each episode speaking to the audience from the town's graveyard, Boot Hill.

If Marshal Dillon was the ideal lawman to affirm the connection between the mythic truth of the American West and the authoritative truth of televisual representation, Dodge City, apparently, was the ideal city. The two shows most credited with starting the adult Western craze, *Gunsmoke* and *Wyatt Earp*, both featured heroes who were the marshals of Dodge City, Kansas. ("The two lawmen," as Alex McNeil points out, "never met, as their shows were on different networks."[12]) Although the names of the marshals and of the networks differed, the imprimatur of Dodge City remained the same. "Dodge City," according to Meston, "at that time was the wildest town in America,"[13] and thus both the fictional Dillon and the real Wyatt Earp accrued from their peacekeeping activities there a level of authenticity.

Significantly, the first episode of *Gunsmoke* was introduced by John Wayne, whose credibility as a Western hero lent veracity to the series. Each subsequent episode the first season was introduced by star James Arness in the persona of Marshal Matt Dillon. The setting and the direct address created an aura of historical facticity, as though the episode were going to perform the historical act of bringing the past to life. The *Zane Grey Theater*, a Western anthology series hosted by Dick Powell, spoke on behalf of the past by evoking the authority of the museum. Powell, who assumed in his introductions the persona of a museum curator, began each show with a discussion of facts about the Old West. Walking through a replica set or displaying an assortment of artifacts, Powell provided details and anecdotes in some way related to the dramatization that was to follow, so that the fictional episodes of *Zane Grey Theater* served to exemplify the historical details that preceded them. They were much like the dramas that urban baby boomers frequently encountered as part of school trips to museums or in the education films and performances they saw on "auditorium days" (as they were known in my school district). The fact that Powell was dressed in Western garb and periodically appeared in the dramas enhanced his credibility as historian and curator, suggesting, at least subliminally, that somehow his knowledge was based on experience. *Death Valley Days*, a syndicated anthology series that actually anticipated by three years the network development of adult Westerns, took a similar approach, employing the persona of "the Old Ranger," a costumed spokesman who explained in a combination of folk idiom and teacherly expertise the true historical contexts surrounding that week's episode. Like Powell, the Old Ranger looked and spoke as though he were conveying firsthand knowledge.

Tombstone Territory, presenting the adventures of the newspaper editor and the sheriff of 1880s Tombstone, Arizona, similarly claimed archival veracity, with the Editor announcing at the outset of each episode that it was "an actual account from the pages of my newspaper, the *Tombstone Epitaph*. This is the way it happened in the town too tough to die." Gil Favor, the trail boss of *Rawhide*, while not claiming to present "true" stories, nevertheless began each episode of *Rawhide* by sharing trail wisdom and historical details about herding cattle out of Texas.

The unmediated address by these fictional characters speaking directly to the television audience functioned, as Dick Powell's and the Old Ranger's curatorial personae did, to situate the host of the fictional drama not only at the site of truth—the museum or the classroom—but also in the real televisual time that conflated past and present, demonstrating how, even on film, television continued to fulfill the promise Pat Weaver saw in the live medium: "being exposed to the whole range of diversity of mankind's past, present, and the aspirations for mankind's future."

This combination of the museum and the movie set, of direct address and transtemporal voyeurism, as we have seen, was an important dimension of Disney's park and television show, both using the newly created national space of television to forge a national destiny out of cinematic representation. This hybrid technique was widely echoed. Dick Powell, the Old Ranger, the Editor of the *Tombstone Epitaph*, and numerous other Western characters and hosts replicated the living museum qualities of Disney's park and of his show. Disney maintained unflinching belief that his park

"The Old Ranger," *Death Valley Days*' costumed spokesman, who explained in a combination of folk idiom and teacherly expertise the true historical contexts surrounding each week's episode. *Photofest.*

was the true site of reality, as the show that continually advertised it was the voice of that reality. No doubt this faith was contagious and contributed greatly to the lasting grip that Davy Crockett has had on the American imaginary, such that any historian presenting credible evidence that Crockett did not die at the Alamo swinging his trusty rifle encounters an assault that runs the gamut from hostility to outright threat. In 1978, when Dan Kilgore, a former president of the Texas State Historical Association, published a book arguing that Crockett had surrendered at the Alamo and had subsequently been executed, "outraged Crockettophiles fiercely attacked him and suggested that he and others who agreed with him were probably atheists, Communists, or intellectuals, or maybe all three."[14]

In this context, "Walt Disney Presents" (the first of many name changes that *Disneyland* underwent from 1958 on) continued the practice begun by *The Adventures of Davy Crockett* of using—and thus affirming—the credibility of television by conflating history, geography, and fiction into the immutable truths of the West. The *Texas John Slaughter* series (1958–1961) shown as episodes of the Disney television show, was meant to be both the historical and commercial successor to Davy Crockett. It employed the themes and techniques associated with the veracity of adult Westerns. Like several other shows, the John Slaughter episodes began with a direct address to the audience. At the outset of each episode, Walt Disney, as the patriarch of Disneyland, whose reassuring presence had come to stand for sincerity, assumed the role of Western historian and Slaughter biographer. He spoke directly to the audience in a manner that confirmed the truth of the fictional episode and also linked it to the popular motifs of the West. Via Disney's introduction, the episodes comprised a living museum, an illustration of how the facts and artifacts presented by Disney functioned in the real life of Slaughter and, by (often explicit) extension, in the real history of the West.

Prefacing the first Slaughter episode, for example, Disney began: "Historians tell us the West would have never been settled without the cow pony, the frontiersman's axe, the six shooter and the Texas Rangers." In thus equating "the West" with Texas, Disney evoked the same connection he had made four seasons earlier, treating the liberation of Texas and the stand at the Alamo as the quintessential sign of American values. Since Crockett had died at the Alamo fighting for American freedom, Slaughter as a Texas Ranger became the logical extension of Crockett and of the West. He took responsibility for settling the land that Crockett helped liberate. If Crockett as frontiersman wielded the axe, Slaughter as Ranger, gunman, and cowman was Crockett's heir apparent, bringing to the West all the elements vital to its settlement (as the "historians tell us," according to Disney). "Originally the Texas Rangers were organized," Disney explained, "to protect the settlers from Indian raids." Just as Crockett began his career (as frontier hero) by fighting Indians, Slaughter began his protecting the post–Civil War West from Indian raids.

But Slaughter's task, for which Crockett paved the way, entailed not only fighting the savage elements but also bringing law, order, commerce, and civility to that Western space, that is, turning the West into the kind of place suitable for the erection of Disneyland and congenial to the lifestyles of the families that would visit it. The Rangers, therefore, later

> became law enforcement officers, fighting outlaws and rustlers from the Red River to the Rio Grande. But it was here, in this corner of southwest Texas that the outlaws were the boldest, operating in open defiance of the law. They knew that the Rio Grande was the international boundary and

that the Rangers' authority ended there. So, at the first sign of trouble they could hightail it across the border and find sanctuary in Mexico. It was here, in this lawless, brawling border area that John Slaughter began his fabulous career as a law officer.

These beginnings take us through a set of adventures that moved Slaughter from Ranger to rancher to sheriff. If Davy Crockett's guiding principle was "make sure you're right, then go ahead," Slaughter's, at least according to Disney, could be summed up in the theme song: "Texas John Slaughter made men do what they oughtta, 'cause if they didn't they died." As a transition from the song to the episode, Disney once again reiterated the unifying motif: "This program, based on the adventures of our true hero of the West, shows that even the Rangers had to ignore the strict letter of the law to preserve the law itself."

"The law itself," that is, the essence of the law, the *real* law, is at odds with the letter of the law, just as the essence of reality, the *real* reality that Disneyland stood for, as Disney had told Billy Graham, is at odds with the world of social problems. Reality, meaning things as they ought be, trumped letters, that is, reality as it was recorded. This was Disney's view of history as well as of amusement parks. Everywhere Disney affirmed reality by having men "do what they oughtta" ('cause if they didn't—in that era when the nuclear family was seen as the first line of defense against nuclear annihilation—they could die).

In the second Slaughter episode, "Killer from Kansas," Disney again emphasized the connection between Slaughter and Crockett, this time in terms of weaponry. Using a museum-like setting and the persona of historian/curator to lend authority to the connection, Disney intoned, "This is a collector's item from the Santa Anna gun room. It is one of the rarest guns in existence, the Walker Colt." To show how this pistol united the elements that tamed the West, Disney explained that it "was named after Captain Sam Walker of the Texas Rangers, who tested the original model and suggested a number of improvements including this trigger guide. Originally, the Rangers' only weapons were long rifles like this, or heavy single shot horse pistols like this." Disney intentionally displayed weapons fused in the American imagination with Crockett. The consumer craze that had flooded the nation with their toy replicas had led millions of baby boomers to don coonskin caps and imitate Crockett; they knew the gun. The Rangers inherited not only Crockett's charge to tame the West but also his tools for doing so.

However, Disney explained, neither of these Crockett-style weapons "was very effective for men who did most of their fighting on galloping horses. Indeed the history of the Rangers might have been different but for the invention of the revolver. As a matter of fact it was the Rangers who gave it the name we know it by today, the six-shooter." The Rangers thus proved themselves worthy of Crockett's tools by improving upon them. The theme of progress, therefore, describes equally the conquest of the West and the development of the tools facilitating that conquest. For both of these tasks, the Texas Rangers were vital. In yet one more way they helped us remember the Alamo, in the sense that remembering meant avenging. The rare—albeit exemplary—pistol came, after all, from the *Santa Anna* gun room. The Alamo that created Texas led to the Texas Rangers who created the gun that created the American West.

This creation, importantly, was effected by superior weaponry. If the story of the Alamo, in other words, encapsulated the narrative of Cold War foreign policy—Americans rushing to foreign soil to take the stand for freedom—the emphasis on better guns evoked the narrative of Cold War deterrence, in which superior weapons were supposed to inhibit rather than provoke conflict.

Weaponry was at the heart of a number of the adult Westerns. *The Rifleman*, as the title suggests, featured a hero whose rifle was superior to his foes' pistols. Wyatt Earp carried a Buntline Special that had an extra-long barrel, and Josh Randall, the bounty-hunter hero of *Wanted Dead or Alive*, used a sawed-off shotgun as a sidearm. No adult Western, however, made the technologically superior weapon so central a theme as did *Colt .45*. On October 18, 1957, the half-hour adult Western premiered on ABC with an episode titled "The Judgment Day." The series premise was that Christopher Colt (Wayde Preston) traveled the West in the guise of a gun salesman, demonstrating the new Colt .45 (which he described as "the deadliest, most powerful handgun in the world") while actually working as a federal undercover agent.

"The Judgment Day" begins with a public demonstration of the new Colt .45 revolver, showing not only its speed and accuracy but also its "penetration" (according to the script, more than eight inches). After the demonstration, a young woman (Erin O'Brien) stops Colt and asks him, "Don't the old guns kill people well enough?" to which he responds,

"Ma'am, guns don't kill people; people kill people. . . ."
"With guns. That's the most destructive thing I've ever seen."
"This, ma'am? We call this 'the Peacemaker.'"

The Rifleman with his special rifle—weaponry was at the heart of a number of the adult westerns. *Photofest.*

The woman with whom Colt discusses arms and deterrence, it turns out, is a sister in an educational society of missionaries whose goal is to teach the Apaches how to read (English) so that they can be brought into the (Christian) faith and thus learn the ways of peace. She later tells Colt that she was about to give up her calling because "it didn't make sense—teaching the Indians a philosophy we don't follow ourselves." Inspired by Colt's restraint, however, in not killing Jim Rexford (Andrew Duggan), the town bully, her faith is renewed (by the gun salesman tellingly named Christopher). At the end of the episode, Rexford refuses to let Colt leave town peacefully unless he crawls down the street. Seeing the sister, Colt doesn't know whether he should destroy her faith in his Christian nonviolence or allow Rexford to humiliate him. She solves his dilemma by quoting from the scriptures: "Mr. Colt, the Bible says the evil shall fall down before the good and the wicked before the gates of the just. I don't think the Lord intended you to live on your knees." Thus, the same faith that validates Christian restraint also provides the mandate to kill Rexford, a mandate supported, like American foreign policy in the Cold War and since, by superior technology: "I'll be walking to the hotel," Colt tells Rexford, "and if you've got any sense at all you'll remember one thing: This gun I'm carrying is a Colt .45." These were, of course, the last words the heedless Rexford ever hears.

The "Judgment Day" of the title thus refers to a meaningless gunfight. Our manly Western hero—especially when armed with a loaded, rapid-fire gun—would have killed Rexford before the first commercial were he not under secret orders to make sure nothing happens to the other man because Rexford was supposed to meet an archvillain whom the army wanted to capture. Thus, Colt endures Rexford's taunts and abuses through the bulk of the episode until, in the final minutes, he discovers that the villain has been apprehended and that he is therefore no longer obliged to keep Rexford alive. By this point, however, Colt has become a model of temperance who has renewed the faith of the missionary sister in her quest to "civilize" the Third World (so to speak). Because she conveniently witnesses the showdown between Rexford and Colt, she reconciles Colt's religious and martial impulses, allowing her peacemaker to use his "Peacemaker" in such a way that killing Rexford amounts to following the Lord's intentions. Since the shooting ends the episode, we can only wonder whether she will deliver the same message to the Indians that she did to Colt—that the Lord did not intend them to live on their knees. Although that judgment falls outside the range of the story, we still have to decide what kind of judgment is referred to by the episode's title, which, like its hero's name, seems to connect religion and weaponry.

Only in a metonymic sense, of course, can this be called a "Judgment Day" drama, in that it represents but one small affront in a world, as the missionary sister pointed out, replete with violence, and the only judgment rendered is that the Lord intended the goals of peace sometimes to be pursued with a Colt .45. Although I have no idea if this was sound theology, it does provide a virtual template for American foreign policy in the 1950s.

The strategy of "containment" authorized America to champion the cause of (Judeo-)Christian, capitalist individualism against the forces of atheistic, communist collectivism, by overt and covert means, at any point, no matter how ostensibly small or trivial, lest there be a perceived weakness in the containment of communism, for that weakness could turn into an actual weak spot—a leak in the dike, so to speak—that would precipitate a flood.[15] Thus, the full heft of American high-tech weaponry, up to and implicitly including nuclear strikes, was pledged to the arresting of communist "infiltration" at any spot on the globe. The linchpin of the policy, in fact, was America's nuclear capacity and the avowed willingness to use it, if deemed necessary, in any conflict that might lead to the spread of communism. This policy formed the foundation for the NATO and Southeast Asia Treaty Organization (SEATO) pacts, explained America's taking over for the French in Vietnam in 1954, and led to numerous covert activities throughout the world as well as the support of sundry dictators in Africa, Asia, the Middle East, and Latin America. The objective of containment was to win the Cold War by containing communism while demonstrating that "democracy," "free enterprise," and the American industrial model were more productive, more beneficial, and more consistent with the Lord's desires than state-owned and -regulated social and production systems.

The Judgment Day that Christopher Colt faced, therefore, was just a tactical fight in part of an overreaching strategy, overtly undertaken by an agent of industry and technology and covertly by an agent of the federal government, supported in both cases by the most potent weaponry in man's world (the gun) and in God's (the word). At stake was the future of the West, which by 1957 was history; because it was history, the Western genre could provide a scaffold for dramatizing contemporary history, that is, the future of the Western bloc, which it did through the most pervasive dramatic mechanism ever invented—a mechanism unique to the atomic age: broadcast television. The dozens upon dozens of "adult Western" series of the late 1950s daily effected innumerable judgments about the future of the West by dramatizing the history of the West.

Whereas imperialism in the nineteenth century was leveraged crucially by naval supremacy, in the second half of the twentieth century it was determined by nuclear supremacy. At the end of World War II, having won the war with an intimidating display of technological prowess but without incurring significant damage on its own soil, America was alone in its capacity for immediate economic, industrial, commercial, social, and technological

expansion, while in Europe and Asia victors and vanquished alike had to re-
build their industrial and commercial capacities. The vertical sphere of influence that the United States had claimed since Monroe, embracing the
Latin American nations, thus acquired a horizontal dimension extending to
the most industrially advanced nations in Europe and Asia. The war also
helped the United States develop a huge and complex spy, military, and para-
military system, capable of integrating globally a multiplicity of overt and
covert "actions" in the interest of maintaining that influence.

This unprecedented opportunity to construct a twentieth-century empire, however, coincided with a worldwide denunciation of colonialism,
necessarily contorting the form of the Cold War American global influence
into intricate economic, political, and military relationships with ostensibly "free" nations (e.g., Mexico, Iran, Guatemala, Turkey, South Korea,
South Vietnam, Batista's Cuba, Peron's Argentina, etc.). The visible sway of
America in the internal politics of these "free" nations was mediated by an
array of narratives that coalesced under the rubric of "democracy," a term
that, in these narratives, named something America was obliged, by supreme ordination, to "spread."[16] The spreading of democracy was as much
a task of public performance as of political intrigue in that it privileged narratives constructed in the public imaginary, especially domestically,
through which imperialism could be read as democracy.

In this light, the performative aspects of public history were an essential
aspect of American influence and policy in the postcolonial world. The
more pervasively and prolifically the story of democracy was linked to every
aspect of American past, present, and future actions, the more acceptably
the past seemed to enfold the future in such a way that the cause of "freedom" created a privileged conceptual space where the past and the future—
history and destiny—merged. The cause of freedom, in other words, would
cause freedom; (American) freedom was both the cause and the effect. The
cause of freedom thus linked numerous sites—domestic and foreign,
friendly and hostile, self-sufficient and dependent—with the destiny of the
West. If nuclear technology underwrote that destiny, televisual technology
proliferated the performance of its informing narratives.

My point is that television drama in the late 1950s was more than a reflection of America's global policies. Especially domestically, it was a performative aspect of those policies. The crucial shift marked by the advent of
televisual communication was the unprecedented capacity to integrate nar-

ratives and normalize them as integral to daily life. As Raymond Williams cogently notes,

> it seems probable that in societies like Britain and the United States more drama is watched in a week or weekend, by the majority of viewers, than would have been watched in a year or in some cases a lifetime in any previous historical period. . . . The implications of this have scarcely begun to be considered. . . . It is clear that watching dramatic simulations of a wide range of experiences is now an essential part of our modern cultural pattern. Or to put it categorically, most spend more time watching various kinds of drama than in preparing and eating food.[17]

By the end of the 1950s, American consumption of televisual drama reached a point of virtual saturation, as over 90 percent of all American households had at least one television set. During that period when television was saturating American living rooms, the people inhabiting those living rooms were being saturated with messages about representing the West in a global struggle. And if television viewed the undomesticated West as a simulation of America, it also represented that West as always already domesticated, the site of morality dramas that affirmed the religious, patriarchal, nuclear family idealized by American Cold War values. The wagonmaster of *Wagon Train*, the trail boss of *Rawhide*, Marshal Dillon, Ben Cartwright, and the Rifleman—to cite a very few—seem modeled more on Jim Anderson, the father in the very popular *Father Knows Best*, than on any real or fictional hero of the Old West. Television adult Westerns conflated the domestic interests of America and its global expansionist desires and reiterated Cold War rhetoric in patriarchal morality dramas, urging peaceful conflict resolution, always supported by the superior use of arms.

America, these Westerns told us, was an extension of the anecdotal small town.[18] The nation emerged from exactly those communities both remembered and anticipated by Disneyland, a theme repeatedly emphasized, for example, in Walt Disney's introductions to the John Slaughter episodes. Marking Slaughter's emigration from Texas to Arizona, Disney explained that Slaughter's goals were always domestic rather than martial: "John Slaughter had to join the Texas Rangers to fight for law and order before he could realize his life's ambition, to marry, settle down, and become a peaceful cattleman." It was almost as though Slaughter's legitimacy as the heir to Davy Crockett and the wild frontier derived from his role as model for the suburban husbands who would inhabit the postwar developments on the land that Slaughter had helped tame. The suburbs that fed the interstates thus composed the legacy of the West; they were the communities that provided Slaughter (and those like him) a raison d'être.

If Slaughter's restlessness was motivated by his desire to settle down, it was further stimulated, like Crockett's, by the death of his wife. Disney makes this clear: "But when [Slaughter's] wife, Addie, died, anxious to put his unhappy memories behind him, he gave up everything he had built in Texas and headed west. His destination was the untamed Arizona territory. Here in the new land he would build a new life." That new life, in merging commerce, domesticity, and law enforcement, exemplified Western Cold War values. Civilizing the West represented winning the Cold War as defined by securing for the (less completely civilized) nonaligned states the American way of life: families in safe secure homes, supported by access to free markets.

Despite the shots of visual expanse, therefore—a wagon train or cattle drive traversing a valley, horses galloping on the open stretches of the Ponderosa—for the most part these Westerns took place in confined spaces, the drama unfolding in Matt Dillon's jailhouse or Kitty's saloon, in front of a campfire or in the back seat of a covered wagon. Even the classic gunfight usually took place in towns possessing one short main street, such as the one in the "Judgment Day" episode of Colt .45. As in that episode, the dramas often reflected the quasi-religious ideology of the 1950s, the decade whose ten-second televised public service announcements told us that "the family that prays together stays together."[19] The West was thus the site wherein (Judeo-)Christian values could reach their anecdotal plenitude in that it occasioned repeated tests—such as Christopher Colt's—of the (Judeo-)Christian ethic upon which the West in the Cold War grounded its global mandate. The American empire, in other words, was a media empire marked by its capacity to dramatize its informing narratives and deploy those dramatizations. TV adult Westerns, therefore, despite their common iconography—horses, guns, saloons, Indians, sheriffs, stagecoaches— were united less by temporal or geographical coherence than by a set of common themes that anchored their symbolic capital.

One particularly pervasive theme of these Westerns—linking the most popular TV genre of the late 1950s to the most popular film genre, the biblical epic[20]—was, as I've noted, religion. If the Western bloc of nations supported God and capitalism, as exemplified by America (the land that be-

An episode of *Wagon Train*. For the most part these westerns took place in confined spaces, the drama unfolding in Matt Dillon's jailhouse or Kitty's saloon, in front of a campfire or in the back seat of a covered wagon. *Photofest.*

lieved like no other in the collaboration of prophets and profits), then episodes of numerous adult Western series represented the West as the place of spiritual redemption. On *Wagon Train*, for example, while moving west, into the future, the wagon train repeatedly became the venue for undoing the past. The tone was set in the premiere episode, "The Willie Moran Story" (broadcast exactly one month before the *Colt .45* premiere).[21] In that episode, Ernest Borgnine, playing the titular former heavyweight fighter ruined by alcoholism, gets a chance to save himself by saving the wagon train, thereby taking advantage of the second chance offered him by the wagonmaster, Major Adams (Ward Bond). As both the kind shepherd and the vengeful father, Major Adams does the Lord's work, enforcing strict rules and harsh ultimatums, always in the interest of giving people the opportunity to redeem themselves. In many ways, from Major Adams's military title to the tone of the widow, Mrs. Palmer (Marjorie Lord), who gives Willy coffee, sympathy, and a second chance ("You're a good man, Willy Moran. Don't let anyone rob you of that"), this episode gives the wagon train the quality of the Salvation Army. (At one point Willy even gets the donation of used clothing; at another, one of Mrs. Palmer's children says he looked like Santa Claus.)

This Salvation Army, however, serves not only spiritual but also national interests in that it creates a united nation out of the individual interests of disparate settlers from varied backgrounds. Most significant is the specter of the Civil War, which creates tension throughout the episode. Willy, we discover in the first moments, fought well for the North at Gettysburg under Major Adams's command, and Mrs. Palmer lost her husband, who fought for the South, in the first days of the war. The enemies from whom, in the end, Willie helps save the wagon train are Quantrill's Raiders, the renegade Southerners. The episode thus makes the wagon train the mechanism for settling the West by healing divisions, overcoming weaknesses, and repelling evil. Because they are redeemed on their way to settle the West, the members of the wagon train can, in turn, redeem the West itself. The future, the land before the settlers, will not redeem them; they will redeem it by incorporating it into the sphere of (Judeo-)Christian Western values, a task for which the journey west apparently serves to prepare them.

"The Orly French Story,"[22] a later episode in the series, is even more explicit about the role of spiritual redemption in the settlement of the West. It begins with a lawman named Jason Hartman (John Doucette) capturing and wounding a young outlaw, Orly French (Peter Fonda). Immediately after wounding French, Hartman prays: "Well, Lord, looks like we've halted another sinner on his downward path. Thank you for keeping my hand quick and steady. Thank you for providing me with another opportunity to do your good work, another lost soul for me to redeem in your name. Amen." Hartman meets up with the wagon train, and the settlers offer him space in a wagon to bring his injured captive back to civilization and trial.

During this trip, Hartman has two interrelated objectives: to get Orly to tell him where he'd hidden $50,000 in stolen money, and thus to help Orly repent. In frustration, Orly at one point asks, "Can't you make up your mind whether you're a marshal, a preacher, or a gunslinger?" "I'm a little of all three," Hartman replies, "and I got to warn you that's a combination that's gonna be hard to beat." Hartman reads to Orly from the Bible constantly and also introduces Orly to a young woman traveling on the wagon train, with whom Orly falls in love. Because, unbeknownst to Orly, she is terminally ill, she rejects his profession of love. He rebels against his redemption and seduces Hartman to sin by offering to share the stolen money with him. In a moment of weakness, however, Hartman runs off with all the money. He is subsequently caught and killed in a gunfight; only after the fight, instigated by Hartman, do they discover that he has removed the bullets from his gun. In addition to the stolen money, they also recover Hartman's Bible, open to a passage on the sin of temptation, and the episode ends with Orly reading it aloud. Although the viewers are set up to see Hartman as a hypocrite, the episode makes clear that his lapse into theft—the sign of his human frailty—is the aberration that tests his true commitment to God. In the end, under the auspices of the redemptive wagon train, full of good and forgiving people, Orly and Hartman share the same scripture and belief.

A similar process occurs in an episode of Rawhide (a series about a cattle drive that was Wagon Train sans wheels or women) titled "Incident of the Golden Calf."[23] The cattle drive, led by trail boss Gil Favor (Eric Fleming), comes across an abandoned preacher, Brother Bent (MacDonald Carey), in the middle of an open range. As it turns out, he is an able cowboy as well, so he is invited to join the cattle drive. Once a part of the company, Brother Bent becomes a corrupting force, preaching Christian doctrine that urges the men not to be corrupted by greed. "My text for today," he says at one point, "is the parable of the Golden Calf—and so it happened in the town I've already told you of." Combining his preaching about the dangers of gold, and of greed in general, with visible evidence in the form of rocks containing gold ore, he successfully undermines his own message and makes the cowboys more and more insistent that he tell them where the gold was found. The cowboys even start fighting among themselves. Eventually, when they get Brother Bent drunk, he reveals the exact location of the town, and they quit the cattle drive to find the gold. Brother Bent, however, is actually a decoy for another group of cattle herders who have lost their own herd and want to buy Favor's cattle. Without his men, and thus without hope of getting the herd to market, Favor is forced to sell his cattle to the other group for an unreasonably low price.

The episode seems subtly to pit religion against capitalism in that the scriptures are used to direct the energy of the cowhands away from their tasks. Brother Bent's chronic preaching creates a disruptive force on the cattle drive because he constantly invokes an authority that challenges the trail boss, whose authority, like that of *Wagon Train*'s wagonmaster, is supposed to be absolute. Favor's power has to be absolute, the series makes clear, not only because of his financial responsibilities to his bosses, the cattle owners, and to his employees, the cattle herders, but also because of his social and moral responsibility to his men. Near the beginning of this episode, the cook, Wishbone (Paul Brinager), makes Favor's role clear when he says, "Start out with men, half of them green, half of them rusty, and you turn them into an outfit—don't know how you do it." Favor responds in terms not of his management technique but of his faith in the innate character of the men: "They're good men to begin with." Favor thus constructs an equation between good men and good work—between character and economics—for which he has to be the mediating force, a kind of Protestant-ethic miracle worker. The miracle he works, moreover, is not just organizing and focusing the positive energies of his men; it is blending the old and the new—the "rusty" and the "green"—into the destiny of the present, the destiny of the rewards at the end of the trail. As the show's theme song explains, the cowboys will be living high and wide at the end of their ride. The way to make sure that the men get their rewards at trail's end is also suggested by the song: "Keep movin' movin' movin' / though they're disapprovin'." By suggesting an alternative road to heaven, Brother Bent casts in doubt Favor's ability to perform his industrial miracle.

Brother Bent also undermines Favor's capacity to provide material rewards by suggesting that he can show the men the way to far greater wealth than Favor can promise, and that he can give it to them sooner, as the town with gold is nearby, in distinct contrast to the distant end of the trail. The title of the episode, "Incident of the Golden Calf," further suggests the religious significance of Favor's job by casting him as Moses, a point underscored by Brother Bent's first words when Favor finds him alone: "The Lord bless you, son. What are you doing out here in the wilderness?" an allusion that not only equates Favor with Moses but equates the end of the cattle drive with the promised land. The allegorical status of the cattle drive is thus foregrounded because in no literal sense is the cattle trail a wilderness; it does not traverse new unsettled land but rather travels an established trail from the ranches to the more developed centers that link the cattle range to the meat markets.

The connection between the validity of Brother Bent's words, national interests, and the work ethic are articulated explicitly by Brother Bent at the conclusion of his sermon on the golden calf: "O you who are the lifeline of this great and growing nation, close your eyes to the sins of the golden calf. Let your rewards be your own accomplishments. Amen." This puts a very interesting spin on the biblical story, since the story of the golden calf is not about opting for gold instead of work but about losing faith in Moses and in God. Although in the Bible the Israelites gave up gold to create a false idol, in Brother Bent's version they give up their work ethic to get gold. The interests served by his reinterpretation, the sermon makes clear, are those of the "great and growing nation." Like Favor's shepherding, Brother Bent's preaching commodifies labor in the interest of God and nation.

Instead of Brother Bent's actions undermining his preaching, therefore, the reverse occurs. In the final moments, Favor—whose men, chastened by the error of their ways, have returned to him—confront the corrupt herders. Bent, now in a regular Western outfit rather than his black preacher's jacket, has taken his place among the dishonest cowboys. But when one of that group attempts to kill Favor, Bent intervenes, telling the corrupt cowboys that although he has gone along with getting the herd from Favor and, subsequently, stealing back the money: "I draw the line with murder." By throwing a stone (David-and-Goliath style?) at the man about to shoot Favor, he enables Favor instead to kill his would-be murderer as well as regain his herd.

At the end of the episode, Favor invites Bent to rejoin the cattle drive: "We'd be glad to have you with the herd." But Bent declines, opting instead to become the preacher he had pretended to be. "It seems," he explains, "all my preaching has got me one convert, myself." The power of the word was greater than the character of the speaker or, perhaps, it brought out the true character latent within that speaker. Like the other members of Favor's band, the episode proves, he was a good man to begin with. Bent parts with the explanation that "what I've done makes me feel I'd rather be with the Good Lord than agen' him." Unlike the other cowboys, Bent is thus able to do the Good Lord's work without Favor's assistance, instruction, or protection.

The fraudulence of Brother Bent's preaching thus comes dangerously close to making a sham of Favor's judgment by articulating exactly what is at stake in his role, that is, that he has to moderate his men's greed and intemperance in the interest of meeting the commercial and very temporal goals of the cattle drive. So long, however, as the mediations between the commercial and moral spheres remain Favor's internalized deliberations, his decisions have the authority of monologic truth, deriving from an economy of paternalism: In exchange for being overworked and underpaid, the men are cared for; their opportunity to err is diminished while their character is enhanced. Brother Bent offers them better pay with less work, but the cost is that they have to make their own moral and tactical choices, something they are ill equipped to do. Because they are, in other words, laborers who have to be made ready for prosperity, the cattle drive teaches them deferred gratification, allowing the green to grow up and the rusty to shine. Thus, Favor's Christian doctrine—taught through quotidian parables, in a celibate setting, by if not a good shepherd then at least a good herdsman—becomes a form of capital investment that will yield everything at the end of the drive.

They end the drive, of course (north)east of where they started, so that if the West represents the future, and hence America's potential, the East provides the authority to use the resources of the West to realize that potential. The raw spiritual and physical materials provide, under the auspices of (Judeo-)Christian redemption, the purchase power that allows the West to produce the cultural capital of the Protestant ethic.

In the Texas John Slaughter episodes, Disney similarly uses the idea of "productivity" to reconcile Slaughter's Western adventurism with his stability as 1950s patriarch:

> All his life John Slaughter was a man who seemed to go out of his way to find danger and excitement, so it is probably no accident that when he moved to the Arizona territory he decided to make his home in the wildest and toughest area in the old south west—Cochise County—where Indians and outlaws still prowled the hills and passes, where the only semblance of civilization was the roaring, brawling community of Tombstone. This is the land John Slaughter was determined *to tame and make productive* [emphasis added].

Despite his lifetime yen for adventure, in other words, Slaughter never sought excitement for its own sake. Slaughter's goal, like that of American covert and overt actions around the globe in the 1950s, was "to tame and make productive." And since the "product" of the West was cattle—hence the crucial role, as noted by Disney in the first Slaughter episode, of the cow pony in settling the West—Slaughter's entrepreneurial prowess is exemplified not only by his ranching and herding cattle but also by his building the better mousetrap of the cattle industry, the Slaughter Trail. A quintessential capitalist, he devises a more effective way to open up markets. "Cattlemen today have no trouble getting their beef to the market," Disney points out,

> at any of the conveniently located stock yards in Chicago, Kansas City, and on either coast. But back in the days of the Old West, getting cattle to the market was a perilous, bold, tiring job, often lasting for months. Usually several neighboring ranchers would combine their herds and drive over land to the nearest rail head. These drives were over well-established cattle trails that had plenty of grass and water. The famous Chisolm trail from San Antonio to Abilene, the Western Cattle Trail to Dodge City, and yet another Chisolm trail from Fort Davis through southwestern Texas to Fort Wilplain in northern Arizona. One of the most famous cattle trails was the John Slaughter cattle trail, starting here at Fort Youle in Laredo. Then it went up through the wild Indian country of southern New Mexico and ended here at Fort Witchuka.

In John Slaughter, the expansion of commerce and the consolidation of lawful communities found a common matrix. If Gil Favor's cattle drive merges the patriarch with the good shepherd, Slaughter's merges the patriarch with the community man. If Favor is the ideal corporate manager, Slaughter was the quintessential entrepreneur. According to an interview with the star Tom Tryon, "Slaughter's violent defense of Western ranchers stemmed from 'a psychological hatred of those who don't respect private property.'"[24]

Using maps to illustrate Slaughter's accomplishment, Disney combined the authority of a high school teacher with the self-assurance of a real estate broker selling plots in a new development, comparing the Slaughter property to the Chisholm (or the Levittown) land. He demonstrated Slaughter's importance by associating him with the subdivisions that would ultimately unite the East and the West into a like community. In this way, the cattle trail, like the wagon train, became one more prototype for the network of interstate highway systems and the networks of national broadcasters.

Disney even went so far, in one introduction, as to connect this pioneer spirit directly to Disneyland: "Well, I have a personal interest in John Slaughter, too. Our research department discovered that when Mrs. Slaughter died in 1942, among her personal effects were 100 shares of Walt Disney Production stocks. That just goes to show that this old West that we talk about is not so old after all. It's only yesterday in this young country of ours. Yes, John Slaughter was quite a man." He was the precursor of today because he linked the Old West to Disney Productions. If taming the frontier can be seen as investing simultaneously in America's future and past, the same tight loop connected history and destiny that connected the interstate cloverleaf to Disneyland's turn-of-the-century Main Street. Stock in Disney Productions thus became stock in America, and by suggestion, America became a Disney production.

The Western frontier was always the frontier of industry and science. It was, after all, a space mastered by means of technological supremacy. New, more accurate and efficient weapons continued to leverage the advantage of the settlers over the elements and the indigenous people. Architecture, engineering, mining, via ever more efficient modes of transportation and communication, all connected the world of raw products with the world of manufactured goods. Every settlement or homestead thus became a small local monument to free enterprise, unequivocally equated in American history and lore with "civilization."

The premiere episode of *Maverick*, "The War of the Silver Kings" (broadcast just five days after *Wagon Train*'s "The Willy Moran Story" and twenty-six days before *Colt .45*'s "Judgment Day"),[25] dramatized this relationship vividly, showing how cunning individualism could unite the interests of labor and big business, large and small corporations, corrupt and honest politicians. Maverick (James Garner), a professional gambler (with a touch of the con man in him), establishes credit in the Western town of Echo Springs by outsmarting Phineas King (Edmund Lowe), the owner of the town's prosperous silver mine, in a poker game that King regularly won by cheating. Maverick also uses his ingenuity to thwart King's attempts to run him out of town and to have him killed. In addition, he tricks people into electing the town drunk as judge, thereby defeating the corrupt judge in King's control and giving the drunk the motivation to sober up. Maverick, in other words, is a reformer disguised as a con man. In the trickster tradition, he uses wit and initiative to expose and undermine corrupt authority so that in many ways he epitomized the spirit of rugged individualism so privileged by Cold War rhetoric as defining the West.

The plot of this episode takes an interesting twist, therefore, when Maverick uses this rugged individualism to organize the silver miners who are being exploited by King. First he gets all the small silver mine owners to unite in one cooperative company, the New Hope Mining Company, and then, using a loophole created by an outdated mining law, he shows them how they can actually mine the silver in King's claim. To handle this huge increase in productivity, they hire away King's miners by offering higher wages, shorter hours, and more humane conditions. In this way, Maverick seemed tantamount to a union organizer who has successfully undermined a ruthless monopoly through cooperative efforts and profit-sharing. Maverick knows, however, the prosperity of the New Hope Mining Company will be short-lived because he is sure the favorable court ruling will be overturned. In order to prevent the cooperative from mining the silver while the appeal is pending, King floods his own and New Hope's shafts. Thus, there is no work for anyone, so the organizing of miners becomes a virtual lockout, which Maverick then settles by getting King to accept all the miners' demands. He explains this to the townspeople in a speech conflating the workers with the owners of New Hope: "Phineas King and the New Hope mines are about to merge. . . . And that's not all; at Mr. King's insistence, all the reforms including the ten-cents-an-hour-raise and the shorter hours are to be included in the agreement." Maverick then argues to King that it is not "worth it to see men out of work, families going hungry. Your fortune is built on their discoveries [sic]. They're entitled to some consideration." Maverick assures King, moreover, that "all they ask for in this contract is just enough to get along—5 percent of the future profit of the combined companies." Just as the workers were unrepresented when New Hope was created, the owners of New Hope became invisible when King agrees to the merger and the contract. But if 5 percent of the combined profits would go to the workers, then the unstated truth is that 95 percent will go to the combined owners.

The story thus engages in a sleight-of-hand, shifting from the small businessmen to the workers as though there were no difference between organizing a corporation and organizing the labor employed by that corporation. The laborers, in fact, are never organized, and the only time we see them is at the end, when they are represented as an angry mob. All the organization is top-down, and the benefits that the laborers gain are not the result of their own efforts but of an alternative corporate structure. Because of this new structure, they realize a $.10-an-hour raise (perhaps $5 a week), while the partners in the New Hope Mining Company in a few months had already made a total of $600,000. While the story thus represented Maverick's efforts as benefiting equally the small businessmen and those who worked for them, in fact the benefits were clearly unequal. Maverick had, in other words, made some people rich by making sure that most had "enough to get along."

In this way, the drama employs Maverick's rugged individualism to the end of making the corporation more benign. The unspoken assumption is that anyone who owns and invests is entitled to a disproportionate share of the profits and, moreover, that this arrangement is beneficial to workers. This assumption differentiated the community composed of "individuals,"—i.e., people always potentially capable of starting their own businesses—from the collectivist community model of communist countries. For this reason, as the show's theme song reminded us, "Maverick is the legend of the West."

More than blurring the distinctions between classes and class interests, the Maverick episode also obscured the boundaries between the world of the fictional Echo Springs and the world of American industry, as represented by Kaiser Industries, the show's sponsor. In fact, the voice-over for one Kaiser Industries commercial during this episode was a virtual gloss of the story's resolution: "People, products, private investment capital—these are the foundations of the Kaiser Industries, a growing family of growing companies, building together for a better world." The productivity of the New Hope Mines was represented in the episode by a visual collage that, through a series of dissolves, blended together scenes from the mining industry: men digging, carts of ore being pushed on tracks, molten ore being poured, etc. In a commercial for the Kaiser Industries that appeared about halfway through the show, a detailed overview of Kaiser surveyed an array of its subsidiaries: "mountains of ore, a million tons of coal, men, machines, and modern science working together for a better world. Meet Kaiser Aluminum," a voice-over announced to narrate shots that uncannily resembled the collage chronicling the rise of the New Hope Mines. The equation between the New Hope Mines and Kaiser Industries was further underscored by the way in which they both were set in the context of representing the interests and spirit of the West. "Now meet Kaiser Steel," the voice-over continued, "another growing company now being expanded to become the largest steel-maker west of the Mississippi, and the West is the land of tomorrow. It grows like a mushroom, and Kaiser Steel grows with it. Mining iron ore from the vast resources of Eagle Mountain, owned by Kaiser Steel, converting this ore into more steel to build the framework of our better world." In this Western, Echo Springs echoes the Kaiser Industries, which echoes the interests of the West, dramatized as the legend of the West.

In the second half of the decade, in other words, on television the *history* of the American West was merging thematically with both the Cold War West and the desired *future* of the American West. Western history and Western destiny consolidated around a body of themes and practices that gave the Western its identifiable oppositions, well summarized by Richard Slotkin, who explains that the frontier "is nearly always understood as a border between an 'old world' which is seen as known, oppressive, and limiting, and a 'new world' which is rich in potential or mystery, liberating and full of opportunity."[26] The conflict between the archetypal aspects of the oppositions and their historical aspects, as Slotkin points out, gives the Western its ideological dimension, a point that becomes particularly cogent in light of the cultural conditions circumscribing television production in the 1950s.

The premiere episode of *Maverick* in combination with its commercials tells us that the West is the land of tomorrow as well as the land of yesterday; it comprises both America's history and its destiny. That destiny, moreover, is connected to the cloud of the technology that "grows like a mushroom," is "the deadliest, most powerful [weapon] in the world," and with the Lord's blessing, we can assume, provides even more than eight inches of penetration.

5 Rebel Integrity, Southern Injustice, and Civil Rights

Since television, as we have seen, touted its capacity for presenting unmediated reality, in many ways by the mid-1950s it started to make up the common space that defined America's everyday life in the same way that the Western constituted the space of the country's mythic life. In 1956, at the beginning of the adult Western craze, *TV Guide* indicated the connections to Disney's Crockett: "The adult Western has more in common with 'Crockett' than man-sized budgets. As producer Walt Disney points out: 'The "Crockett" show was based on historical frontier stories. It's not a story about bad men. Rather, Davy Crockett sets himself toward constructive causes.'"[1]

The "constructive" cause for which Crockett gave his life, however, was tainted heavily by proslavery interests and the notion of racial superiority underpinning the idea of manifest destiny. In reinventing the Alamo as a Cold War icon, Disney deracialized its history, suggesting that real Americans were defined by their willingness to fight for the freedom of others. In this Cold War narrative, the cause of slavery was replaced by a national cause, something that evoked transcendent American idealism, regardless of one's regional affiliation.

Desegregation and the Cold War

The migration of prime-time television to the West, between 1954 and 1960, was not marked by commensurate racial integration of the space delimited by that westward expansion. While courts, legislatures, and attorneys general throughout the nation, even some U.S. marshals, were abolishing the principle of "separate but equal," the television networks continued to remember the Alamo and the unfinished work Disney had started there. "The Disney Company," as Henry Giroux perceptively notes, "has become synonymous with a notion of innocence that aggressively rewrites the historical and collective identity of the American past. . . . The strategies of entertainment, escapism, historical forgetting and repressive pedagogy . . . produce a series of identifications that relentlessly define America as white and middle class."[2]

It is important to remember, therefore, that another dramatic event, simultaneous with the development of *Disneyland* and the production of the Crockett episodes, had profound national and international impact. Four months before the premiere of *Disneyland* (and fourteen months before the opening of Disneyland), the Supreme Court delivered its historic decision in the case of *Brown v. Board of Education of Topeka* overturning the principle of "separate but equal" racial treatment established by the 1896 *Plessy v. Ferguson* decision.[3] The unanimous 1954 court decision not only mandated drastic alterations in educational policy for large segments of the country but also opened the door to changes in myriad aspects of racial discrimination. The decision also had important international implications, as *Newsweek* was quick to note: "Over the years, segregation in the public schools has become a symbol of inequality, not only to Negroes in the United States but to colored peoples elsewhere in the world. It has also been a weapon of world communism. Now that symbol lies shattered."[4]

So important was the Cold War symbolism of *Brown v. Board of Education of Topeka* that "within an hour after the Supreme Court decision," the *New York Times* indicated, "the Voice of America sent a news broadcast by shortwave radio"[5] in thirty-four languages. Lost neither on *Newsweek* nor on the Voice of America was the decision's role in representing the West given that America, strategically and paradigmatically, was synonymous with the West in the geopolitical organization of the Cold War. One fact that could neither be ignored nor denied was that between 1945 and 1960 nearly thirty black African states gained independence from white colonial rule.

Mary Dudziak has extensively documented the role that foreign policy played in the court's decision. The U.S. Justice Department, she points out, filed an amicus brief arguing that desegregation served the national interest because, in part, of foreign policy: "The United States is trying to prove to the people of the world, of every nationality, race and color, that a free democracy is the most civilized, and most secure form of government yet devised by man."[6] That brief quoted at length Secretary of State Dean Acheson on the increasing damage that racial discrimination was doing to American foreign policy, pointing out that the "United States is under constant attack in the foreign press, over foreign radio, and in such international bodies as the United Nations because of various practices of discrimination against minority groups in this country."[7]

Of particular concern to the State Department, Dudziak explains, "was coverage of U.S. racism in the Soviet media."[8] "By 1949, according to the U.S. Embassy in Moscow, 'the "Negro question" [was] one of the principle Soviet propaganda themes regarding the United States.'"[9] In 1950, a member of the Dutch foreign ministry indicated to a member of the U.S. Embassy in The Hague that although he was not receptive to anti-American propaganda, the one theme that was extremely effective throughout Europe and even more so in Asia was criticism of American racial attitudes.[10] In a petition called *An Appeal to the World* prepared by W. E. B. Du Bois, the NAACP in 1947 told the United Nations that "it is not Russia that threatens the United States so much as Mississippi. . . . The disenfranchisement of the American Negro makes the functioning of all democracy in the nation difficult; and as democracy fails to function in the leading democracy in the world, it fails the world."[11] Justice William O. Douglas noted that the question of segregation was a prominent topic during his 1950 visit to India, concluding that "the attitude of the United States toward its colored minorities is a powerful factor in our relations with India."[12]

This Cold War imperative may shed light on the arguments made in the court's decision, arguments lodged not in legal precedent but in perceived social realities. "Relying more on the social scientists," James Reston explains, "than on legal practices—a procedure often in controversy in the past—the court insisted on equality of the mind and heart rather than on equal school facilities."[13]

In achieving unanimity, the Court constructed a liberal consensus by rejecting both conservative and progressive arguments. Noting that the state of public education at the time that the Fourteenth Amendment was passed was so rudimentary as to bear no resemblance to the issue at hand, the Court discounted as irrelevant all arguments emanating from the principle of original intent and similarly all those derived from the precedent of "separate but equal" established in *Plessy v. Ferguson*. "We must consider public education in the light of its full development and its present place in American life throughout the nation," the decision declared. "Only in this way can it be determined if segregation in public schools deprived these plaintiffs of the equal protection of the laws."[14]

Nor could the decision "turn on merely a comparison" of "tangible factors in Negro and white schools."[15] The kind of material fundamental to Marxist critique was found to be inappropriate in this case. So were the

principles of precedent and original intent, the linchpins of conservative
jurisprudence. Instead, the Court based its decision on a Cold War value
that was already a commonplace on television, typical in suburban architecture, exemplified by the civil engineering of the interstate highways, and
epitomized by Disneyland—normality: "Today, [public education] is a principal instrument in awakening the child to cultural values, in preparing him
for later professional training, and in helping him to adjust normally to his
environment" (emphasis added).[16]

The decision is striking, in other words, in its subordination of statutory
precedent to social necessity and its substituting of psychological concerns
for material consequences. To put it another way, the decision represented
the West as privileging what were ultimately spiritual and individualistic
interests in its citizens over a general concern with their material conditions. The Court's rationale was consistent with the anti-Marxist logic of
American Cold War culture in that it located class in the state of mind of the
individual rather than the economic structure of the state. Noting that "the
policy of separating the races is usually interpreted as denoting the inferiority of the Negro group," the decision stated, "A sense of inferiority af-
fects the motivation of the child to learn. Segregation with the sanction of
law, therefore, has a tendency to retard the educational and mental development of Negro children."[17]

While statistical and anecdotal evidence demonstrated clearly and in-
controvertibly that black schools were on the average grossly inferior to
white schools, the "real" problem with segregation, the decision indicated,
could be found in mental rather than material consequences. The decision,
in fact, made a fundamental connection between a pupil's state of mind
(and its concomitant educational consequences) and being a citizen: "[Ed-
ucation] is the very foundation of good citizenship."[18] The good citizen of
the West, the decision assumed, could not be marked by a sense of inferiority. An inequality inherent to segregation, then, was that it fostered a state
of mind incompatible with being a citizen of the nation that considered itself leader of the Free World.

To put it simply, in terms that any American in the 1950s—especially any
American who watched television regularly—would understand, segregation was wrong because it deprived Negro children of the opportunity to
learn how to be normal. In this sense, the case was prima facie: television
was the place where one found definitively normal families, and no black
children were to be found in that excessively normal world.

Representing the Interests of the Televisual West

To the extent, then, that the televisual West continued to represent both the history and the ethos of the United States, it solved the nation's twentieth-century race problems in the same way that "manifest destiny" solved its nineteenth-century land problems—by accepting as fact the inevitability of Anglo-Saxon domination. Although blacks, Hispanics, and Native Americans composed a significant percentage of actual cowboys, with some historians putting the figure at over 25 percent,[19] one rarely if ever found a black face in a prominent television cattle town.

No doubt the producers thought that black cowboys would undermine a show's claim to authenticity, which was the privileged commodity of both Cold War television as a medium and the adult Western as a genre. "When the West became a myth or game of 'let's pretend,' the Negro became an invisible man, or at best an Uncle Tom. There was no place for him in these community theatricals. He had been a real cowboy but could not easily pretend to be one."[20] Although this "'whitening' of the cowboy," as Quintard Taylor calls it, owed much to the Wild West shows that transformed the West from history to myth, as well as to the "dime novels, and later more substantive literature, such as Owen Wister's 1902 novel, The Virginian, [which] established the white Anglo-Saxon as the cowboy archetype of the imagined West," the racial manipulation of the cowboy image began much earlier.[21] "Despite the considerable skill, dedication, and innovation they brought to the range cattle industry, it was increasingly clear, even in the 1870s and 1880s, that the racial dynamics of the period precluded entry of black, brown, or red drovers into the pantheon of cowboy heroes."[22]

Although television thus rendered race invisible in the West, the medium's eclectic mode of presentation necessarily juxtaposed adult Westerns with reportage of civil rights conflicts. Those conflicts operated in the same rhythm as the television season, with most of the major events occurring in September, things winding down as summer approached, and late summer providing previews of the coming season.

For two well-publicized years—from the fall of 1957 to the fall of 1959—Arkansas governor Orval Faubus waged a war with federal authorities over the integration of Little Rock Central High School. By the 1956–1957 school year, some meaningful inroads had been made in Southern school desegregation, with 300,000 black children attending school in 723 desegregated districts. "Despite these gains," Manning Marable reminds us, "2.4 million black Southern children still [were] enrolled in Jim Crow schools, and 3,000 white school boards expressed every intention of maintaining the colour line in spite of the Supreme Court's mandates."[23] Throughout the South, in other words, the attitude toward desegregation was more often than not similar to Little Rock's, but the high visibility of Faubus's opposition to desegregation came to represent and consolidate many issues surrounding implementation of the Supreme Court decision.

That high visibility owed much to the age of television, as there can be no doubt that national reportage turned segregation from a regional issue to a national and international event. The national television news broadcasts not only exposed unsettling scenes of children being persecuted and police dogs being set loose but also made those images guests in the nation's living rooms. The broadcasts also presented images otherwise almost never seen on the 1950s television screen—black faces. And those faces belonged to ordinary citizens, not athletes and entertainers. In the 1950s and 1960s, Sean Dennis Cashman explains,

> civil rights demonstrations provided ideal media copy with their dramatic contrasts between nonviolent tactics and gestures of brotherhood on one side and profane displays of malice, discrimination, and violence by racist mobs on the other. Thus an NBC correspondent could claim with some exaggeration but essential truth, "Before television the American public had no idea of the abuses blacks suffered in the South. . . . " Thus by its civil rights demonstrations, television suggested that a political dialogue was taking place between civil rights activists and diehard segregationists—a dialogue in which television was giving the demonstrators the winning hand.[24]

Although Cashman is unquestionably correct when he stated that "the significance of television in the dramatic power play of civil rights can hardly be overemphasized,"[25] the heft of television's effect on civil rights was felt primarily in the 1960s in regard to the Freedom Riders, James Meredith's entrance into the University of Mississippi, Governor George Wallace's blocking the door of the University of Alabama, and dogs being set loose on peace protestors in Birmingham, Alabama. The televising of these events had an immeasurable impact on the Kennedy administration. "While John Kennedy was pushed by the force of events and the passion of his brother to champion the cause of black citizens, the American public was pushed by the force of television to acknowledge the civil rights movement as a struggle of consequence to the very nature of the republic."[26]

Governor Faubus, as the first television segregationist governor, was a pioneer. So was the coverage of Little Rock. Although spotty and uneven, nevertheless, day by day, it made the nation aware through the morning newspapers and the nightly newscasts that a new test was under way: a test of the U.S. Constitution and a test of the constitution of the West. Strong, deep, and numerous were the national rifts evoked by the civil rights movement in general and, in particular, by the confrontations between Southern elected officials and federal desegregation orders. These public rifts threatened equally the international credibility earned by the unanimous *Brown* decision and the national solidarity perceived as crucial to winning the Cold War.

The burden on television therefore was large and multifarious. By the time that the Little Rock confrontation began, television had become, as we have seen, a definitive apparatus of national norms. Enabling countless suburban communities to share visual experiences that unified and ritualized cultural values, it spoke with the authority of technology on behalf of the past and in the interest of the future. In this authoritative position, it fulfilled a virtual obligation to support American ideals by promoting an idealized version of America. It attempted to do so, furthermore, without alienating any significant portion of the viewing public, a role virtually assured by the legislation that enabled a small number of networks (initially two) to monopolize the airwaves. A more fragmented market, after all, could rely more easily on niche audiences. Since network programs, however, had to attract between 25 and 40 percent of the viewing public, alienating a bloc as large as the (white) South was not economically feasible. And even if a network were willing to risk in the interest of news what it was not willing to risk in the realm of entertainment, could it polarize the audience and still maintain its normative authority?

These problems grow in complexity when one considers that a network is not a tightly organized ideological mechanism, focused on a specific, agreed-upon agenda, explicitly articulated and widely disseminated among the decision makers. Rather, the cultural work performed by Cold War television comprised a symptom as much as a source of assumptions that passed for "natural" at the time of its inception and development. Those assumptions included the idea that television had a role in unifying the nation. They included that nation's near-utopian faith in technology as the cornerstone of progress and the broader media's acceptance of pervasive self-censorship, especially after the 1930s. These premises all coagulated around the fuzzy but fundamental notion of exceptionalism, that is, America as a special place, different in kind from any other nation. Individual producers, sponsors, writers, and executives, all fulfilling their roles rather than adhering to an explicit party line, represented the American South in news coverage, in a "balanced" set of interviews with a spectrum of elected officials, in public affairs specials, and in an array of prime-time dramas.

In the late 1950s, these dramas, in huge disproportion, took the form of adult Westerns,[27] a genre at the time particularly influential in articulating "real" American values, functioning both to normalize and idealize a national ethos. The fictional mode of these Westerns allowed far more latitude in representing the South favorably than, for example, news footage of federal marshals escorting children to school amid mobs of angry white protestors, or reports of a public school board's closing the schools rather than admitting blacks. In this way, prime-time programming inverted the news/drama relationship so that the news coverage (and, at that, only a portion of the coverage) could be seen as the anomaly, no more typifying normal American life than a tornado typified normal American weather.

A Bad Day at Little Rock

The Little Rock incidents were marked by outbreaks of violence and school closings. On some occasions, state and national troops were used to prevent black students from attending Central High, and at other times to permit them to attend. Particularly striking was the way in which Faubus constantly cast himself as the aggrieved victim. In his narrative, blacks were treated well by Arkansas whites and Southerners were treated unfairly by the federal government. Under the rubric of "states' rights," in other words, Faubus claimed the same privileges as had the Anglo-Americans at the Alamo.

These were the rights of Americans to self-determination in sovereign— lone star, so to speak—states. Invoking the Ninth ("states' rights") Amendment of the U.S. Constitution, Faubus positioned himself as the guardian of American principles that had nothing inherently to do with race. In this sense, Little Rock Central High was his Alamo, his rallying cry to the nation, his struggle to buy time until his forces—led by Southern whites— could regroup.

In August 1957, federal judge Ronald Davies ordered integration of Little Rock Central High School. On Labor Day, September 2, 1957, Governor Faubus ordered the National Guard to stop the black students from entering, announcing the next morning at 6 A.M. that "because of the harm that may occur tomorrow, the troops would not act as segregationists or integrationists. But order and peace could not be maintained if forcible integration went ahead."[28] Here, as throughout the struggle for desegregation, Southern authority emphasized self-defense, identifying a danger to the public welfare perpetrated upon the South by outside intervention, in this case legal and later physical.

Again and again, Southern leaders—often even moderate and progressive ones—would identify themselves as the victims rather than the perpetrators of injustice. This theme's credibility, at least for significant portions of the white Southern electorate, drew on a cogent mythology surrounding a noble Southern aristocracy and a fruitful social ecology that had both been destroyed by Union armies, Yankee manners, Northern greed, carpetbaggers, and unsupervised blacks. The book and, especially, the film *Gone with the Wind* drew on national inclinations to accept this myth as part of a post–Civil War reconciliation, one that would cast the Southern system not as racist but merely as engaging in a unique set of practices that worked for a unique region, a region that had suffered irrevocable harm during the Civil War and Reconstruction.

The perpetuation of this myth helped insure one-party supremacy in the South and, as David Goldenfield points out, efficiently served the needs of white Southern leaders:

> Segregation and the white supremacist ideals that framed it solved the political problems of white leaders. White supremacy became the common bond between whites of all social classes; to disrupt the bond implied the end of white supremacy and the beginning of Negro rule. To lend credence to this view, southern textbooks, movies, and popular literature created a historical fiction, depicting Reconstruction as an era of Yankee thuggery and black terror.[29]

In his rationale for calling out the guards and, the next day, for turning the black students away, Faubus once more foregrounded the neutrality of the South in the face of Northern aggression that, once again, threatened the safety of all Southerners. Echoing the claims of the patriarchal slaveholder, this Arkansas public servant cast himself as the guardian of black safety, which was threatened by Northern intrusion. Declaring in a televised address on the evening of September 2, 1957, that "the community opposed integration and bloodshed might break out if Negroes were permitted to attend school with white students,"[30] Faubus rejected the court order to integrate the school on the grounds of public welfare. He ostensibly was concerned about the welfare of the black students in that, of course, they, not the white community, were the presumed objects of that violence.

Faubus was articulating a well-established Southern narrative that had, even after the Civil War, been given credibility on the national level as a pattern of Supreme Court decisions arose to limit the effect of the Thirteenth, Fourteenth, and Fifteenth Amendments. In *Hall v. De Cuir*, for example, the Court held that a state law *forbidding* discrimination on public conveyances was unconstitutional (although later, in *Plessy v. Ferguson*, it would hold that state laws *enforcing* segregation were constitutional).[31] In a similar case, the reasoning of the state supreme court of Pennsylvania in 1867 was particularly revelatory. In overturning a lower-court decision barring segregation on the railroad, the state supreme court argued, in part:

> The public also has an interest in the proper regulation of public conveyances for the preservation of the public peace. A railroad company has the right and is bound to make reasonable regulations to preserve order in their cars. . . . It is much easier to prevent difficulties among passengers by regulations for their proper separation, than it is to quell them. . . . If a negro take his seat beside a white man or his wife or daughter, the law cannot repress the anger or conquer the aversion which some will feel. However unwise it may be to indulge the feeling, human infinity is not always proof against it. It is much wiser to avert the consequences of this repulsion of race by separation, than to punish afterward the breach of the peace it may have caused.[32]

Of particular note here is the presumed natural antipathy of whites to blacks, such that it became normal to assume some whites would respond violently against blacks in close proximity. In the convoluted reasoning of the argument, however, the black person moving about freely on a public conveyance was understood to be not the victim of prejudicial violence but the cause. The conclusion that blacks must be segregated thus relied on the tacit assumption that the "public" had an interest in "proper regulation," just as the public would later have an interest in the proper regulation of the airwaves. The "public" referred to in the term "public conveyances" and the "public" whose peace must be preserved was the same "public" that could be expected to react violently to the intrusion of blacks on its space. In fact, one could argue that white violence against intrusive blacks was expected in this decision, and in the culture it reflected, as a legitimate characteristic of public space.

With the *Brown v. Board of Education of Topeka* decision, the concern over racial interaction in public space moved from public conveyances to public schools, but the logic remained the same: Since not admitting black students to school on September 4 was an attempt to protect them, when a federal court judge ordered the board of education to begin immediate integration, Faubus was forced to call out the National Guard to preserve order. The very term "National Guard" evokes exactly the power struggle at stake in Faubus's resistance to federal orders, in that the guard is actually a state militia—the well-maintained militia referred to in the Constitution's Second Amendment—trained and maintained by the federal government and available for appropriation to federal service. Otherwise, however, the governor is its commander in chief. It can function both as a *state* militia and as a *national* guard without contradiction so long as it is recognized that the state takes priority over the nation. As with the founding of Texas, so throughout the South, the notion of the American nation derives from the sovereignty of the state. For the original Texans, this "American" principle, as we have seen, even extended across national boundaries to take precedence not only over the American federal government but also over the Mexican. In both cases, the governing principle was white privilege. Although conceding the Supreme Court's claim that separate but equal schools presented emotional difficulties for black students, Faubus echoed the themes of the Texas Revolution when he argued that "there are very strong emotions on the other side, people that see a picture of the mongrelization of the race, they call it. They are very strong emotions, and we are going to whip this thing in the long run, by Americans being true to themselves and not merely by law."33

While this attempt to buy time seems to suggest gradual progress toward integration, its rejection of legal means validates extralegal Americans as the Americans who are "true to themselves." The South thus becomes the source of the "true" American. The true American, whether in 1950s Arkansas or in 1830s Mexico, was the extralegal white man who followed Davy Crockett's motto: "Make sure you're right; then go ahead." The "very strong emotions," therefore, rather than threatening the law of the land asserted its underlying principles. Those principles included the right of Americans to act on their very strong emotions and the right of the governor to mobilize the militia to protect blacks from those rightfully emotional acts.

As in the period after the Civil War, the problem in the South, from Faubus's perspective, was that the federal government had endangered public welfare by propelling blacks into white space, where they brought with them the threat of sexual assault. This concept was invoked in Faubus's telecast by the term "mongrelization," which drew on arguments connecting the black profile to public menace that had been accumulating since the Civil War. If blacks were allowed in white space, they would not only provoke natural white violence but would also "amalgamate" with whites, thus causing the deterioration of the "Anglo-Saxon race" by introducing inferior strains into the gene pool. "If there is an amalgamation of the races," Louisiana senator Allen Ellender proclaimed on the floor of the U.S. Senate as late as 1938, "decay of our civilization will surely follow; and amalgamation cannot be stopped, in my mind, if we permit colored people to keep on encroaching on the whites socially."[34]

"Pitchfork Ben" Tillman, a white supremacist active in South Carolina in the 1870s who eventually became governor of the state, declared,

> Now I have alluded to the fact of this villainy, anarchy, misrule and robbery, and I cannot, in any words I possess, paint it. There is no man on this floor living in the country who dared during that dark period [Reconstruction] to leave his fireside without dread that when he returned he would find some harm to his family; and he dared not go forth without being armed, fearful of robbery. The sky was lit almost every night by the glare of burning dwellings and ginhouses.[35]

And James Kimble Vardaman, who ran for governor of Mississippi in 1900, stated, "We would be justified . . . in slaughtering every Ethiop on the earth to preserve unsullied the honor of one Caucasian home."[36] Tillman said in 1913 that "from forty to a hundred Southern maidens were annually offered as a sacrifice to the African Minotaur, and no Theseus has arisen to rid the land of this terror."[37]

The Negro A Beast, published in 1900, typified many books that identified Negroes as subhuman. It argued that a black person was no more entitled to freedom than a dog or an ape, and it viewed the Civil War as God's wrath for the error of mixing Negroes with humankind. The consequences of that error were that "to-day our wives and our daughters are not safe from their brutal assaults beyond the range of our shot guns. They degrade our religion, debauch our youths, plunder our citizens, murder our officials, rape our women, and conduct themselves generally as the curse they are and will always be so long as they are allowed to defile our land with their presence."[38] So profound was the impact of assertions such as these that they became virtual commonplaces of American culture at the turn of the twentieth century. Thus, in 1919, South Carolina congressman James F. Byrnes could declare with confidence on the floor of Congress, "Another peculiar thing is that while the press of the North and the negro press will join the press and pulpit of the South in their condemnation of the criminality of the mob, they seldom join in the condemnation of the criminal assaults upon white women, which is generally the cause of the lynching."[39]

As in the case of integrating public conveyances, the black person described in these remarks always caused racial violence, including—or perhaps especially—white violence against blacks, and the white Southerner was always the victim. (Many in the South, even today, refer to the Civil War as "the War of Northern Aggression.") In 1929, Claude Bowers wrote, "Rape is the foul daughter of Reconstruction. . . . All over the South, white women armed themselves in self-defense. Before the Klan appeared and after the Loyal Leagues had spread their poison, no respectable white woman dared venture out in the black belt unprotected. . . . Negroes who had criminally attacked white women, tried and sent to penitentiary, were turned loose after a few days' incarceration."[40]

Although the black vilified in these widely circulated narratives of the beleaguered South was a person who frequently attacked white women and rarely received adequate punishment, the historical facts, as Gossett made clear, suggested a very different story:

> Of the 3,811 Negroes lynched between 1889 and 1941, only 641, or less
> than 17 percent, were even accused of rape, either attempted or
> committed. Negroes were lynched for such "crimes" as threatening to sue
> a white man, attempting to register to vote, enticing a white man's servant
> to leave his job, engaging in labor union activities, "being disrespectful to"
> or "disputing with" a white man, or sometimes for no discoverable reason
> at all.[41]

The bulk of the violence against Southern blacks took place in the decades immediately preceding and following the turn of the century. It was almost as if, in the absence of a slave system and in preparation for the twentieth century, a generation of blacks born into ostensible freedom had to be disciplined afresh. Characteristically, this violence was defended so as to cast the white Southerner as the victim. "The white man in lynching a Negro," wrote Winfield H. Collins in *The Truth About Lynching* (1918), "does it as an indirect act of self-defense against the Negro criminal as a race . . . in order to hold in check the Negro in the South."[42]

Faubus thus joined a long tradition of Southerners, always in a defensive position, who were merely responding to the violence perpetrated against them, to the violence of their own response, to potential violence against the purity of the races. Above all, they were defending, as they saw them, the Constitution and principles of American freedom. In this way, they were the true Americans, even in their lawlessness, preserving the law of the land, the word and spirit of the Constitution. This notion is stated explicitly in the "Southern Manifesto," a document signed in October 1957 by nineteen Southern senators and eighty-one Southern congressmen. "The unwarranted exercise of power by the Court," it declared, "contrary to the Constitution, is creating chaos and confusion in the States principally affected. It is destroying the amicable relations between the white and Negro races that have been created through 90 years of patient effort by the good people of both races. It has planted hatred and suspicion where there has been heretofore friendship and understanding."[43]

The South in the Adult Western

This theme was iterated throughout an array of television narratives that delivered the "true" West to the adult viewers of America. Sheldon Hackney, former director of the National Endowment for the Humanities, pointed out the significance of the desegregation of Little Rock Central High as *dramatizing* the ideas expressed in *Brown v. Board of Education of Topeka*:

> When the Arkansas National Guard turned back the nine teenagers, literally blocking the door that led to educational opportunity and preventing model young Americans from treading the primary avenue of self-improvement that Americans had come to recognize as a fundamental right, the public saw a *dramatization* of the evil of exclusion. . . . When put into *human drama*, it was hard for Americans to imagine why young African Americans should be denied access to the means of self-improvement. . . . The *visual drama* of the confrontation in Little Rock drove home the moral lesson throughout the country that excluding any American from this central dynamic was intolerable [emphasis added].[44]

Hackney's stressing the power of "visual drama" helped explain how media coverage affected attitudes toward civil rights and, equally, why prime-time television drama could be effective in rereading these events, turning the specific visual dramas on newscasts into aberrations in a larger historical landscape. Repeatedly episodes of top Western shows, set in artificially white societies, redeemed aggrieved Southerners by uniting them in the common cause of the wagon train, cattle drive, or Western settlement. These "good" Southerners were distinguished from the aberrant "bad" Southerners, such as Jesse James, or Quantrill, or some local enforcers. One adult Western hero, Bronco Layne, in the series *Bronco* (1958–1962), is a former Confederate Army captain who after the Civil War finds his home in Texas confiscated. As a form of knight errant, he wanders the West working many jobs, including one as a federal undercover agent who reports to his former Confederate commanding officer, now occupying a high post in a proto-FBI branch of the government.

Both Bronco and Yancy Derringer, in the show by the same name (1958–1959), are Southerners serving as secret agents of the federal government. Although these roles could suggest co-optation of Southern values—and no doubt were read that way by some non-Southern viewers—they make the Southerner the true heroes of the series, the true representatives of American values. They also position these heroes as keepers of the peace, mediating between the lawless South and the corrupt North. Sharing their secret motives with the viewers, they implicitly remind the audience that, despite appearances, the true Southerner was a loyal American.

In an episode of *Bronco* titled "The Shadow of Jesse James," for example, Bronco Layne is working as a deputy marshal for his former commander, General Joe Shelby, who is now a U.S. marshal in Kansas City. The aftermath of the Civil War permeated the struggle—of which this episode was one example—to bring law and order to the West. The episode thus opens with a montage of Civil War action, while viewers are told: "During the Civil War, two battle flags symbolized honor, courage, and devotion of the highest order for all those who served under them. But there was another flag, the black flag of the Missouri guerilla fighters, that was followed by brutal savage men, led by such famous killers as Quantrill, Bloody Bill Anderson, George Todd, and Jesse James." The post–Civil War goal, therefore, was to end a lawlessness initiated during the war but not connected to the war's antagonists or to the issues surrounding the war. The warring parties—and by implication the issues that motivated them—

were all honorable. Slavery, of course, is never mentioned, and blackness is present only in association with the outlaw flag that signifies neither North nor South (despite its Southern origins).

The job of these former Confederate officers—neither of whom have Southern accents—is to capture the renegades Cole Younger and Jesse James. The episode distinguishes the "good" Southerner, Younger (who is wounded saving Bronco), from the evil renegade, Jesse James. The conclusion connects Younger's virtue to his being a Southerner, as Bronco told Shelby: "I put Cole on my horse and gave him a chance to escape. He didn't take it." Shelby responds, "I didn't hear that, but off the record I might have done the same. Cole's still one of my boys." On the record, Shelby represents the United States of America, but off the record he still considers himself the commander of Confederate troops, recognizing Bronco as his subordinate (and confederate) in both roles. Just as Bronco is secretly a federal agent, Shelby is secretly a Confederate officer. The two of them both valorize the extralegal Younger as the representative of their values, the values of the West. When the episode concludes with the message that it took Younger's friends twenty-five years to win him a pardon, the implication is that he earned his pardon based on the loyalty he had shown to his former fellow Confederate soldiers, who now stand for the values of the nation.

The use of real names and these "historical" facts manifested television's attempt to stress the authenticity of adult Westerns, so that the fictional Bronco Layne could share historical space with real heroes and outlaws, people whose history extended beyond the parameters of the episode. While it was a historical fact that it took twenty-five years to win a pardon for Cole Younger, the episode based that factual pardon on Younger's behavior in this fictional event. Younger's pardon was deserved based on the testimonials of fictional characters. Bronco thus helped reveal Younger's *true* colors, which were not the colors of the black flag to which he had gravitated but those of the Confederate stars and bars, under which both he and Bronco had served—colors that symbolized "honor, courage, and devotion to the highest order."

In this episode and throughout the series (at some times more explicitly than others) Bronco asserts the connection between the Southerner and the nation with the unspoken message that the Southern cause in the Civil War had been honorable, as were the people who had fought for it. Younger's parole and subsequent pardon—actually the result of his good behavior in prison—here are associated with his having been a good Confederate soldier. The honor, courage, and loyalty to the Southern cause endear him to the episode's representatives of national authority, Bronco and Shelby. They seem, implicitly, to have acquired that authority as a logical transfer of the authority they had earned in the Confederacy, making this earlier relationship to the Union not so much adversarial as competitive. Their shifts, like those of corporate executives changing firms or athletes changing teams, entail no change in values.

Their former Confederate allegiance, therefore, did not alienate them from the national audience. The episode suggests, furthermore, that the same patriotic sympathies should be extended to Younger because of his military service under Shelby and Bronco, who number among the friends who fought to pardon him and who eventually succeed. Black viewers, of course, might have been less inclined to see Younger's loyalty to the Confederacy as proof that he deserved to be pardoned, as might viewers of all races who believed that profoundly different values and attitudes defined the adversaries in the Civil War, and that devotion to a state committed to the preservation of slavery did not transparently translate into devotion to American national interests. Once the issue of race is introduced, in fact, Bronco's and Shelby's deft conversion seem as dubious as does the idea that the winners of the bloodiest war in American history would immediately bring into their high ranks the officers of the opposing army.

One alternative, of course, was to diminish the role of race and of slavery in understanding the motives surrounding the Civil War. This has been a position held by some historians, but it is extremely problematic, as certain facts remain incontrovertible, the most significant being that no other causes of the war would have been sufficient if the Southern states did not practice slavery. Although the majority of Southerners did not own slaves, and the majority of slaveowners owned fewer than five slaves, the South had developed a well-entrenched economic and social caste system inextricably connected to the "peculiar institution." Whether the individual Southerner fought the war to protect that institution, or to support a state's right to maintain that institution, or simply out of a loyalty to a specific state that allowed that institution and was affiliated with other states on the basis of their commitment to that system, it is impossible to remove slavery from the equation and produce a formula for civil war. Equally irrelevant is the distinction between those who supported the abolition of slavery, those who supported its containment, and those who supported its extension, or the conflict between economic interests based on the distinction between wage slavery and chattel slavery. If slavery had not been practiced in the United States, the Civil War could not have occurred. As the economic historian Roger Ransom succinctly states, "the presence of slavery in the United States represented a contradiction that eventually could only be removed by an armed conflict between the slave South and the nonslave North."45

In constructing a unified nation, that is, in accommodating the institutionalized racism and extralegal violence that became a structural part of American culture and history after the failure of Reconstruction, it was extremely efficacious to allow race-based slavery to occupy a blind spot in American history. This was what happened when the adult Western became the idealized projection of Cold War norms, requiring the United States to be one nation united by common values; hence, the assimilation (without any apparent angst) of Shelby and Bronco asserted a televisual truth about essential Americanism that transcended regional difference. Against this model, the newscasts of Southern whites threatening schoolchildren or beating Freedom Riders or threatening reporters could be read as aberrations, in contrast to the assurance that true Southerners were in fact true Americans.

This assumption was much easier to make when one erased the issue of race, as the adult Western relentlessly did, substituting for the injury to slaves the injury to the South. Repeatedly in these Westerns the Southerners were asked to forgive the North, a historically atypical request, to say the least, when we consider that war reparations are usually paid by the vanquished, not the victor. To the victor, in other words, goes the right to determine injuries and identify injured parties. In an odd substitute mythology, the South was viewed as having been unfairly punished. Not only had its land been ravaged by war but its civilization had been dismembered by occupying troops, carpetbaggers, and (although never mentioned in these adult Westerns) blacks: free blacks, ignorant blacks, voting blacks, office-holding blacks. Furthermore, decent Southerners continued to be persecuted by Southern renegades: Quantrill's Raiders, the James gang, bands of "Regulators."

The focus on the interests of the West as the channel for Southern honor similarly informs an episode of *Cheyenne* titled "The Blind Spot" (September 21, 1959). Instead of Quantrill or James, in this episode a group of Texas "Regulators" is the source of the animus that inappropriately separates North and South. Arriving in a Texas town still haunted by the aftermath of the Civil War, Cheyenne rescues a man who is being beaten by masked riders who terrorized the town. As the episode develops, Cheyenne assists

the town in healing the rifts created by the war, a role for which he is particularly well suited: "I fought for neither North nor South," he explained.
"I was a scout against the Indians during the War."

Given that Cheyenne never indicated for *whom* he was a scout, this statement makes sense only if the West is construed not as an extension of
Northern or Southern interests but as a transcendent space, where regional
differences diminished before a common foe: the Indians of the 1860s
West (and the communists of the Cold War West). Being *against* the Indians
means, implicitly, being *for* the West, that is, for America, rather than for
any one region. Cheyenne's past in the West therefore signifies the North's
and South's destiny, just as the past of the adult Westerns represented the
future of the Western bloc.

The central figure in the episode, Mr. Clayborne, faces serious problems
both in this Texas community and in his family. Clayborne's son had fought
for the North in the war and served as a guard at Leavenworth prison, and his
wife had passed away on the day of the Appomattox surrender. The war had
left comparably deep scars on Clayborne's community. "After the war," he
explains, "the scum of both North and South passed into Texas. It's these
misfits who hide their faces and ride at night. The decent people are against
their methods." As in the *Bronco* episode, the decent Southerner stands apart
from the violent renegade. Although the renegades emanated from both
North and South, their rise to power resulted directly from Northern aggression, an example of yet one more way that the North had injured the South.

When Cheyenne asks why the decent people don't stop the Regulators,
he is told, "It's difficult. Remember the war is still fresh in everybody's
mind." This statement is ambiguous. It might imply that people exhausted
by conflict are easily oppressed, or it might mean that the occupation by
Northern troops had deprived decent Southerners of authorities whom
they could trust. In any case, it makes clear that the war had disempowered
the decent people, who are now subject to the dictates of the Regulators.
Although Mr. Clayborne has a black servant, and the despised tactics of the
Regulators resemble those of the Klan, in no way does the narrative touch
on the issue of race (unless we count Cheyenne's participation in the war
against the Indians or the fact that the character Cheyenne is part Indian).
The Regulators in this story regulate not race but rather economic relations: "This is a cotton town and the bottom has fallen out of the cotton
market. The only place to sell cotton is the North and certain business
interests are against it."

The people who pick the cotton, however, make no appearance in this episode; they serve as invisibly as did the antebellum slaves. Therefore, when the resolution between father and son pivots on Mr. Clayborne's Southern honor and the biblical call to forgive one's enemies, the Southerner can forgive the North without having to ask forgiveness from the slave. Racial issues are moot because the problem is the Civil War rather than its causes.

This episode finds the solution to its problems through the decent Southerner's return to political and, more important, moral authority. The Southerner who ran things prior to the war becomes the repository of values once he can see his way to forgiving past wrongs. "Remember," Cheyenne cautions Clayborne at the end, "from now on you and [your son] had better be a team." The interests of the West mandate that teamwork.

This episode strongly underscores the themes found in Faubus's resistance to desegregation. Articulating a theme echoed by many of the adult Westerns, Faubus located the problems of the South in the undermining of legitimate Southern authority. In an affidavit filed on September 19, 1957, Faubus asserted that federal court judge Ronald Davies, who had ordered immediate desegregation of Central High, "has shown a personal prejudice against [Faubus] and a personal bias in favor of the plaintiffs."[46] In Faubus's view the Southerner was the victim rather than the perpetrator of prejudice. And, as in "The Blind Spot," the source of both the prejudice and the potential violence was the illegitimate intervention of the North.

Faubus could not concede, he stated in a televised speech, that "the United States in this or any other court may question his discretion or judgment as chief executive of a sovereign state and the performance of his Constitutional duties under the Constitution and the laws of his state since they do not and cannot coincide that the Governor may be so questioned."[47] The usurpation of the governor's power had resulted in the forcible imposition of a minority demand on the will of the majority, a form of untenable violence: "It is my firm belief that [integration] can be successful only if it is accomplished in a peaceful manner, which means accepted by a majority of the people of any area affected."[48]

Faubus quite clearly meant the white majority or the voting majority, groups that at that time were for the most part synonymous. The black population was a burden or danger that could be imposed on the "majority" but never included in composing that majority. Faubus similarly excluded blacks from the "public" when he stated, "When a law is in harmony with public standards, its upholders, the police, will find allies in the people. When the law is not thus in harmony, the police appear as public enemies. Then peaceable enforcement becomes impossible."[49] This white public was being forced into a state of disharmony with the law, and the police were being denied their rightful allies. These conditions, which fostered violence, followed from illegitimate Northern intervention.

After President Eisenhower, on September 24, finally sent federal troops—the 101st Airborne—to Little Rock, Faubus sent a letter to the "Commander of Occupational Troops" alleging that the troops in the high school had been "invading the privacy of the girls' dressing rooms."[50] These charges combined the allegation of Northern aggression with the resulting threat to Southern women that, as we have seen, was a common motif in the aftermath of the Civil War.

Like his Southern ancestors, Faubus did not let the presence of Union forces or subjugation to Northern authority weaken his principles. After the 1957–1958 school year and the graduation of the first black student from Little Rock Central High, Faubus signed legislation closing the Little Rock public schools to prevent integration from continuing. They remained closed for a full academic year until, in June 1959, the bill closing the schools was ruled illegal. Adult Western episodes such as "The Blind Spot," associated as they were with America's "true" history, lent Faubus's charges an aura of historical veracity. The attempt to impose the will of the North on the sovereign state of Arkansas and to force people into conflict with the law was consistent with the historical abuse that the South had suffered at Northern hands. Faubus's claims indicated that, despite injunctions of the sort Cheyenne gave to Mr. Clayborne, the South had not found a way to forgive the North, and, therefore, the two regions had not managed to work as a team in the interest of the West. Instead, the South remained vulnerable to "the scum from the North and the South," the rise of lawlessness, and the resulting threat to the safety of Southern womanhood.

Wagon Train's "Willie Moran Story," as I noted, required that Moran, the former Union soldier, redeem himself to be worthy of the Southern widow. He did so by virtue of his heroics in fighting Quantrill's raid, an event in which he joined forces not only with Major Adams but also with the Southern colonel whose wagon was part of the train. The colonel, formerly a Confederate officer (who continued to wear his officer's hat) remained eternally the—albeit sometimes arrogant—Southern gentleman. He disdained Willy, in other words, both for his allegiance and for his manners. In

Black students leaving Little Rock's Central High School under trooper escort. *Library of Congress, Prints and Photographs Division* [LC-USZ62–111232].

justifying Adams's trust and winning the colonel's respect, Moran was able to focus the wagon train's (and the viewer's) attention on the true enemy: the violent renegades who had given Southerners a bad name.

In another *Wagon Train* episode, "The Colter Craven Story" (November 23, 1960) (directed by John Ford), an Eastern doctor has become an alcoholic because of the traumatic experience of losing most of his patients at the battle of Shiloh. He is with the wagon train because he hopes to lose himself in the West, but Major Adams has no sympathy for the doctor. Adams, as J. Fred MacDonald explains, was himself "the essential pioneer, full of purpose and discipline and out to create a new Eden."[51] He confronts Craven: "Who are you to sit in judgment of yourself? What makes you think you ought to be infallible? You aren't the only one who was at Shiloh. You're not the only man who wanted to push his memories back into a bottle and put the cork back in. What right have you got to make yourself personally responsible for that war?" Ultimately, inspired by Adams's story of Ulysses S. Grant's personal redemption, the doctor is able "to perform [a Caesarian delivery] and save the mother, child, and himself."[52] Once again, in other words, Major Adams's wagon train/Salvation Army does the trick. The trick in this case is not only to save the soul of Dr. Craven but also to separate the personal from the political in the interest of the West.

An episode of *Tombstone Territory*, allegedly out of the pages of the *Tombstone Epitaph*, brings the editor of the paper and the sheriff to the small, deserted town of Osage, where they encounter a small group known as Hicks's Raiders. This "rag-tag group" put together by Hicks after the Civil War has "been riding and raiding ever since." Although it is fifteen years after the end of the war, and many miles west of the Confederate states, these raiders still cling to their Southern identity, which informs and motivates their behavior. "Now, listen to me," Hicks says at one point, "is there anything left inside of any of us? We come from the South. We knew what we were fighting for. We didn't ask the women to do our dying for us either." "We're going to fight like men, like soldiers," says one of the raiders named Shelton, "or we're not going to fight at all."

In the end, their Southern honor motivated Hicks's Raiders to join the sheriff in fighting off an Indian attack. The Indians are an inverse version of Hicks's Raiders. They too are a bunch of rag-tag renegades, held together by the chief who assembled them. What differentiates them from Hicks's Raiders is that they cannot call upon Southern tradition and Southern honor, so that in the final confrontation, Hicks's Raiders, rearmed and reinvigorated, decide to "die here with a purpose." The pursuit of that purpose shifts their focus from defense of the South to conquest of the West. The Raiders lead a wagon charge into the Indians and kill the chief, effectively defeating the renegades. "The Indians won't charge again," the sheriff explains, "now that their chief is dead," to which the Epitaph editor adds, "Thanks to the last of Hicks's Raiders and the last of the fighting Confederates." This statement is less an epitaph than an indication of how the spirit and values of the South live on in the West.

Yancy Derringer, too, secretly channeled the ideals of the South into the interests of the nation. In the guise of a professional gambler, distinguished by his white suit and hat, his numerous hidden weapons, and an ever-present, ever-silent Indian companion, Pahoo, Derringer operates as a secret federal agent "outside the law" in New Orleans, shortly after the Civil War. In many ways, in other words, he is an adult Western version of the Lone Ranger. (X Brands, who played Pahoo, in fact bore some resemblance to Jay Silverheels, who played Tonto.) Like the Lone Ranger's mask, Derringer's gambler outfit ostensibly associates him with a criminal element, and Derringer's array of special weaponry signifies, as did the Lone Ranger's silver bullets, a special, almost talismanic arsenal. Derringer thus combines the qualities of the mythic Western hero—the quintessential man in a white hat—with those of Paladin, the dark knight errant of Have Gun, Will Travel. In many ways, Paladin was the Lone Ranger's alter ego, a man in black who worked for money rather than the ideal of a tamed West. Rather than roam the countryside, he made business trips from his urban and urbane San Francisco hotel residence. If the Lone Ranger occupied a timeless West and Paladin a temporally delimited West Coast hotel, Derringer combined the powers of the two champions by secretly infusing his mercenary role in historically specific New Orleans (occupied by federal troops) with the timeless national values that the Lone Ranger exemplified.

An episode of *Yancy Derringer* titled "State of Crisis" demonstrates this role by having Derringer single-handedly save the economy of the entire nation. The alleged crisis in the plot is the infusion of high-grade counterfeit money into New Orleans. Under martial law, a new set of officials have taken charge of the city who, in their search for the counterfeit money, have confiscated all the money in all the "gambling clubs," including the one Derringer patronizes. This ruthless confiscation of funds and the destruction of legitimate businesses evokes once again the abuses of the occupying armies that permeated post–Civil War Southern mythology. It echoes that moment when Confederate dollars became worthless, and the South was helplessly at the mercy of Northern abuse of power. In this episode, however, Derringer reveals the new Northern officials to be fraudulent. "You know the whole new administration of New Orleans is as bogus as that money," he explains. They are master forgers: "They forged the documents to give them power to move in and take over, and the bogus money gives them power to impound the real stuff." At stake is the ability to differentiate legitimate wealth from counterfeit, legitimate authority from bogus, the ostensible interests of the national economy from the actual. Derringer sees clearly where the South's and the nation's best interest lies, and therefore he understands why the new administration is fraudulent. Explaining the scheme, he compares the con men to barbarians:

> "They are getting away with it. They move in and in forty-eight hours
> sack New Orleans and they're gone. You know that's just like the
> ancient days."
> "You mean like the Trojan Horse?"
> "No, like when the barbarians sacked Rome, carted it away, piece by
> piece."

Derringer's analysis is, of course, correct. The con men have raided all the clubs and are about to move against the banks and the cotton market. While Derringer astutely differentiates the legitimate Northern officials from the illegitimate, his imagery blurs exactly those distinctions: the image of the barbarians sacking Rome suggests the Northern pillaging of the South in general, and Sherman's march to the sea in particular. The description thus calls into question the authority not only of these con men but also of the entire Northern occupation. Even the "good" Northerners are easily duped by phony credentials, and it takes the Southerner to save the economy.

In his confrontation with the bogus Major Allen, Derringer says directly:

> "Unfortunately you're not the government."
> "Oh? And exactly what am I?"
> "A swindler, Mr. Allen, a thief, and a highwayman. There's nothing small or mean about your talents. As a matter of fact you're a thief on such a high level that you almost command admiration, and you almost got away with it."

The legal authority to stop Allen, however, comes from an extralegal source: "You're coming along with Pahoo and me," Derringer tells Allen. "If you make one false move he'll blow your head off."

When Allen protests that that would be murder, Derringer inverts the legal relationship: "On the contrary, we'd just be shooting a prisoner trying to escape. You see, I'm making a citizen's arrest for forging, pillaging and looting, masquerading as an army officer."

In this understanding of the law, the citizen takes priority over the soldier, such that it is the citizen's prerogative not only to take prisoners but also to shoot them if they try to escape. Abduction and execution metamorphose into the legal responsibility of Southern citizens and define the appropriate response to the illegitimate tampering by Northern troops with Southern customs and economy. When Derringer points out that his commission "is signed by the President of the United States," the proof is once more unmistakable. Derringer, no matter how lawless he might appear, no matter how extreme his actions, represents true American values—a point Orville Faubus had made just a year before this episode aired.

The Rebel as Civil Rights Hero

Repeatedly, adult Westerns worked to construct an image of the historically and symbolically true West as the place where the Northerner and Southerner united to recognize their common interest in the welfare of the West. An implicit compromise—one that indeed reflected the actual compromise of the post-Reconstruction era—was that the price of this reunification was the acceptance of the notion of white supremacy. In such a context, the rejection of segregation could be viewed as a breach of contract, a reneging on the compromise that had settled the 1876 Tilden-Hayes election. In seeking desegregation, the North unfairly impinged on the rights of the South, reminiscent of the time when the South was controlled by an occupying army. Throughout the South, in the aftermath of *Brown v. Board of Education of Topeka*, such charges repeatedly surfaced, on the floor of Congress and state legislatures, in legal briefs, at public meetings and mob actions, in school doorways.

Through the second half of the 1950s, while the conflict between North and South grew in these venues, television's vision of a segregated West proliferated with concomitant tenacity. It was almost as if television were keeping the promise that had unified the nation, while the federal government and the Supreme Court were undermining it. If "the intent of segregation by law," as Goldenfield convincingly argues, "was not merely to separate the races but to denigrate one and elevate the other; to offer constant reminders of inferiority as if repetition would bring a self-realization among blacks that they were, in fact, an inferior race,"53 then it is hard to ignore the effect of prime-time television's visual segregation. Speaking simultaneously in the name of reality and in the interest of the West, 1950s television echoed the 1850s instrumentalist Supreme Court by implicitly connecting national interests to Southern property rights and making a national priority the channels of trade that allowed America to become an effective commercial network.

The most astounding example of this identification between the aggrieved Southerner and the interests of the West, I think, is the television show *The Rebel*. The show, which premiered on October 4, 1959, chronicled the adventures of Johnny Yuma, a veteran of the Confederate Army. "Johnny Yuma," the title song tells us, "was a Rebel; he roamed through the West." Yuma's identification with the Confederacy, however, was not regional. Rather, it reflected his commitment, like Crockett's at the Alamo, to a generic American sense of justice and fair play. His leaving his Western hometown to enlist in the Confederate Army thus signified his integrity. Like all true Americans, he could be drawn to the cause of freedom, wherever it took him, whatever it cost. The show's evocation of classical virtues—although not its direct association of those virtues with the Confederacy—was noted by *Los Angeles Times* television critic Cecil Smith, who felt that the series "could have been set in ancient Greece or medieval Europe . . . as well as the post–Civil War frontier." Smith also compared Johnny Yuma to a "Young David with his slingshot walking toward Goliath."[54]

But the historical specificity of Yuma's circumstances is very much the point. In one episode, he relates in flashback his plan to assassinate General Ulysses S. Grant by hiding in the attic of the Appomattox courthouse. He relents, however, because he is moved by Grant's respect for Lee and his soldiers and, particularly, by Grant's decision to allow the soldiers to keep their horses. In this odd reversal of roles, Grant and the North earn the mercy of the Rebel in a context attesting to the Rebel's integrity. The flashback is related as a form of anecdotal instruction to a boy whose father had been killed during the war by Union soldiers. The lesson for the boy, then, is that Yuma had almost made the same mistake as the boy by not realizing that the Union leaders had actually shown respect for the Confederates. Grant had even refused to take Lee's sword. The audience, however, receives a different form of cautionary lesson: Grant becomes the model Northerner who recognizes the Southerner's integrity and, therefore, understands that the Southerner should not be defanged. Compared to this ideal, many contemporary Northerners who would defame Southern honor and interfere with the Southern way of life fall short. They lack the values, in other words, that reflect the apparently legitimate ire of the honorable ex-Confederate. If Grant had not had their values, then the Rebel would have killed him.

In the premiere episode of the series, the important link of the Rebel to the West, rather than the South, is established quickly and emphasized repeatedly. Before the opening credits appear, viewers see this Rebel fending off an Indian attack, using his dead horse as a shield, shooting one Indian and killing another in hand-to-hand combat. Clearly, this is not the land of cotton but a more unsettled Indian territory. The locale, moreover, is arid, suggesting the Southwest region, a suggestion reinforced by the Rebel's having the same name as an Arizona city. Johnny Yuma's outfit also identifies him with the frontier rather than with Dixie. He wears, for no logical reason, his Rebel enlisted man's cap—though certainly something with a brim wide enough to shield him from the sun would be more sensible and look less out of place—and striped Confederate Army pants, but his shirt is fringed buckskin. Although from the perspective of forty-five years later this mix-and-match might seem more apt for the Village People than for an adult Western hero, in the context of its time it probably seems no more ludicrous than Davy's coonskin cap. Further, it echoes a fashion motif that scatters remnants of Confederate Army garb over an array of shows and characters to indicate, if nothing else, that the settling of the West represents the unification of (white) Americans in the interest of the nation. To put it simply, in the West of the adult Western, Confederate symbology is far more commonplace than black cowboys. The combination of cap and buckskin thus mark Johnny Yuma as that quintessentially American combination of idealism and pragmatism, in the mold of his buckskinned (television) ancestor, Davy Crockett.

After the titles, the premiere episode begins with Yuma, carrying his saddle, walking down a dusty road into a small town. As it turns out, this is his hometown, and although its location is not specified, it is clearly not in the South. No one in the town has a Southern accent and, more importantly, the town seems to contain no Confederate sympathizers. The thugs now running the town, having killed the former sheriff (Yuma's father), are in fact overtly hostile to Yuma, even before they know his name, based simply on his outfit. (This should, of course, be viewed not as a fashion judgment but as an act of prima facie prejudice.) When a parched and exhausted Yuma dunks his head in a water trough, Jess (Strother Martin) says to his boss (Dan Blocker), "I think I need to have me some fun with that little Rebel . . . can I have me some fun?" He then approaches the trough and the following interchange takes place:

> "Hey you, Reb, hey you, Reb—this here water's for horses; it ain't for
>   no jackasses. I come here to water my horse."
> "Then you do that."
> "Well, not with your face in it. I don't want him contaminated."
> "Don't push."
> "Why, Reb, you oughta be used to being pushed. Why, we pushed you
>   clear from Gettysburg though Georgia. You gotta admit you've been
>   pushed real good."
> "Yeah. The war's done."
> "So it is, but I'm not. I'm going to enjoy pushing you pretty good."

This interchange ends when Yuma draws a (huge) gun and threatens to blow Jess's eyes out, a perfectly appropriate threat, since Yuma's transgressions are purely in the eyes of the beholder; he is not being threatened because he has drunk from the trough but because, based on his appearance, he can be presumed to have contaminated it. The trough, Jess points out, is a segregated drinking place, reserved for horses and restricted from

The combination of cap and buckskin marked Johnny Yuma as that American combination of idealism and pragmatism. *Photofest*.

rebels. Clearly the irrational restriction is motivated not by the practical threat Yuma posed to the water supply but by the symbolic threat his appearance poses to the post–Civil War hierarchy. That hierarchy is connected to the violation of Southern soil and Southern rights, as underscored by Jess's direct reference to the Union Army as an invading force.

When Yuma says that the war is done, he is asserting the restoration of his rights as an American, rights that he has enjoyed before the war. Jess acts villainously in refusing to acknowledge those rights, insisting that the war has forever changed the Rebel's status.

But that was exactly what the Civil War did. It legally negated some privileges of the Southerner, chiefly in regard to slavery and more generally in regard to race, even if the legal sanctions were not enforced and the practices of the South allowed the reinstitution of laws that normalized racism. "In the war's immediate aftermath," Eric Foner writes, "federal policy regarding black labor was established by the army. And the army seemed to many freedmen to have only one object in view—to compel them to return to work on the plantations."[55] Thus, the goal of landownership for blacks was a Reconstruction policy as early as 1866, but by the time of the 1876 Tilden-Hayes compromise that ended Reconstruction, Southern land had largely been restored to its white owners, with the newly freed blacks composing a labor force in large part economically shackled to tenant tracts and dependent on white landowners.[56]

From 1870 on, moreover, the Ku Klux Klan used violence widely, aggressively, and potently in the interest of restoring white racial supremacy.[57] While the direct agents of this violence came from a general membership composed of ordinary farmers and laborers, Klan leadership that included "planters, merchants, lawyers, and even ministers"[58] formulated policy and chose the targets. For the most part, Southern Reconstruction governors were incapable of dealing with the Klan, and it was not controlled until the federal government intervened, in 1871, with legislation prohibiting many of the Klan's abuses and, more significantly, empowering the federal government to prosecute offenders. With Hayes's inauguration, however, the federal government returned Southern governance to Southern whites and the South replaced Reconstruction with Redemption, a policy committed to "reducing the political power of blacks, and reshaping the South's legal system in the interests of labor control and racial subordination."[59]

Our introduction to the Rebel, however, rereads this history, seeing the Rebel as the victim rather than the perpetrator of blind prejudice, extended even to the sphere of public facilities. This Western town is, it turns out, like the South an occupied place, and the men who torment Yuma simply on the basis of his appearance are also those who have killed his father and are continuing to exploit the town. For example, they are using supplies without paying for them. In the context of the tenant-farmer economy that arose in the South after the war, this detail provides another reversal of Southern conditions, for instead of the store's being the exploiter, it is the victim of exploitation. This capacity for exploiting the Rebel's hometown, moreover, is directly linked to the consequences of the Civil War. When Yuma asks the editor of the newspaper (John Carradine), "Why haven't you sent for government troops?" he is told, "We have. . . . I guess they're too busy attending to the defeated South or the undefeated Indians."

The inversion of the Southern Rebel and the Southern black are further suggested when Jess later torments Yuma with a variant of "Dixie"—"I'm glad I'm not in a land of cotton./The Rebs lost the war and their bones are rotten"—and then yells, "Hey you, cottontail, you better scat while you can." The cottontail rabbit, of course, suggests not a Rebel soldier but a character out of slave folklore. The Rebel, in this unjust world, has thus become the cottontail, the oppressed minority figure, subject to the ridicule and violence of the majority.

For Yuma, of course, the solution is simply to get new clothing, that is, to show he submits to post–Civil War authorities and values. But, as the series represents it, that would be wrong and cowardly. No matter how much the Southerner might suffer from prejudice, harassment, discrimination, and violence, the interests of the West require that he stick to his principles. After ridding the town of the bullies, therefore, he turns down the offer to stay on as sheriff, opting instead to display his Rebel hat and the principles it signifies in whatever part of the West needs him, as a kind of knight errant, going where there is nothing but a mess of trouble—Americans in trouble. His theme song tells us,

> He packed no star as he wandered far.
> He searched the land, this restless land.
> He was panther quick and leather tough,
> And he figured that he had been pushed enough.

This theme is marked by a confused sense of direction. As a wanderer, Yuma has no direction, only a random motion, but as someone who has been pushed enough, his motion is characterized by resistance to immobility. Once again, we see his thematic kinship to the defenders of the Alamo, who had wandered to Texas so that they could refuse to be pushed, thus effecting the intransigent claim of manifest destiny. In Texas, as in the Indian Territory, it was the *settlers* who had been pushed enough. In the contemporary South, it was the Southerner who had been pushed beyond reason to abandon rights and privileges. Through his identification with the South as the beleaguered victim of prejudice and violence, Yuma can bring to the West the principle of resistance—a wandering, expansionist resistance—out of which the destiny of the West would be forged.

The inversion pertains not just to civil rights but also to the political reality of American mythology, in which the Southerner, as the representative of the manifest destiny of the Anglo-Saxon race, becomes the exemplary hero of the West and by extension of the free world. The importance of whiteness in that world is underscored in the premiere of The Rebel at a moment when the reality of the adult Western is enfolded into the other realities that circumscribe the narrative, the reality of a performer directly addressing real people in their real homes, conveying the commercial truths that underwrite the medium. In this moment of truth, when the network meets its real obligation to deliver the audience to the sponsor, viewers make direct eye contact with Nick Adams, the real star of The Rebel, sitting next to a box of Cheer detergent: "Hi. I'm Nick Adams, and this is tonight's sponsor, Cheer, the folks who know how to get a white shirt really white. Just check mine. Cheer gets it so white that even I can see Cheer gets it whiter."

Since The Rebel was broadcast in black-and-white, viewers cannot tell if Nick Adams's shirt is really white. They have only the authority evoked by his direct address, as though he were really speaking to them, augmented by the residual authority he accrues from his role. No doubt his association with the Confederate cause helps them understand why he values whiteness so much, just as Cheer's sponsoring of The Rebel helps prove the detergent's commitment to the cause of whiteness. As a commercial earlier in the show proclaims, "Cheer washes so white you can tell the difference," and "Try Cheer and see the difference in whiteness for yourself!" In comparison to Cheer's pure white, the commercials imply, items washed by other products are just passing for white. But users of Cheer will be able to segregate the true white from the ersatz and make their sheets (and hoods?) as white as the true white of Nick Adams's shirt.

Nor should we forget, in stressing the important difference of Nick Adams's shirt, that the whole series depended on the crucial difference effected by sartorial decisions. Adams's shirt was no less important in the commercial than Yuma's hat was in the series, for without the sign of the Rebel, Yuma could not evoke the acts of prejudice around which the dramatic action revolved. The messages of Yuma's hat and Adams's shirt were more than parallel; they were synonymous, both attesting to the wearer's commitment to the supremacy of whiteness. It was fitting that Adams and Yuma should share this common distinction because, as the opening credits informed us, Adams was the cocreator of the series.

West of the South

These episodes only scratch the surface. They identify some of the ways that prime-time programming, at the moment when national newscasts began televising the civil rights struggle, represented the South and the Southerner as victims. To some extent, adult Westerns portrayed the South as the conscience of the nation. Perhaps these portrayals help explain why, late in 1958, despite the fact that he had shut down the Little Rock public schools (or possibly because he had), Governor Faubus was, according to a Gallup poll, among the ten most admired men in America.[60] In any case, one reiterated suggestion of adult Westerns was that the nation's capacity to fulfill its true destiny depended upon the South's putting its grievances behind it. In the interest of the West, the South had to forgive the North and, like Willie Moran in the premiere *Wagon Train* episode, the North had to redeem itself in the eyes of the South.

To make these stories work, adult Westerns regularly divorced "true Southern values" from Southern violence. Notably, in black-and-white prime time, that violence was never motivated by race. The television West of the 1950s and early 1960s—virtually free of black faces—often attributed violent impulses to renegades, raiders, and regulators, aberrant personalities who might have shared and/or preyed upon the South's rightful sense of indignation. At the same time, television seemed to erase not only black characters but black presence itself from Southern and Western history, from the streets of Yancy Derringer's New Orleans, from the antebellum paddleboat in the series *Riverboat*, and from the towns along the Mississippi River where the boat docked.

It is not surprising that Dodge City should have been the place that introduced Americans to the adult Western and attested to its veracity, for in many ways the city united themes and images central to the Western. The legends of the West, its "facts and fantasies were brilliantly blended by [*Gunsmoke* creator] John Meston in [his] portrayal of Dodge City, Kansas, in the 1870s. Meston's cow town was a microcosm of the American West."[61]

Fort Dodge was founded in 1865, chiefly as an outpost for troops fighting Indians, and Dodge City, five miles west of the fort, was founded in

1872. In the same year the Atchison, Topeka, and Santa Fe tracks were laid through the town. From its inception, therefore, Dodge City was connected with the Indian frontier and with the railroad. (One of the responsibilities of the soldiers stationed at Fort Dodge was to protect the men laying rails against Indian attack.) Dodge City was also the center for buffalo hunting—no doubt at least one of the reasons the Indians were attacking—and it was the place where two cattle trails, the Western Trail and the Western branch of the Chisholm Trail, connected with the rails that would carry the cattle to Eastern slaughterhouses. Dodge City quickly became a major cattle town, so that by 1875, just three years into the city's existence, longhorns from Texas had replaced buffalo as the focus of its economy. The city was full of cowboys—the majority of them Texans who had driven their herds north through east-central Texas—and it was replete with everything that would entertain those Texas drovers. Two of Dodge City's saloons, in fact, were named Alamo and Lone Star. At a third saloon, the Long Branch, Luke Short ran gambling enterprises in the 1870s, although the records are unclear regarding whether the owner of the Long Branch at the time was Matt Dillon's "friend," Miss Kitty, or whether she acquired the property later.

Dodge City is important, moreover, not only as the place where the West connected with the East but also as the place where the strong abolitionism of the Kansas frontier intersected with Texas culture. Texas, particularly east Texas, bore distinctly Southern traits, as Texas was a Mexican territory settled overwhelmingly by American Southerners, a sovereign state dominated by Southerners, and a slave-holding state that joined the Confederacy. Dodge City, therefore, was the place where the North met the South at the beginning of the West; it was the place where Texas entered the nation as a Western rather than a Southern state. And Texas, perhaps even more than Kansas, figures prominently in Western image and mythology. Much of Western legend, as we have seen, locates itself in Texas, from the Lone (Texas) Ranger and the Alamo to the cattle drives that epitomized cowboy culture and the Indian campaigns that opened up the Southwest.

The history of Texas, however, has been strongly infused by a black presence.[62] Black cowboys participated in the cattle drives along the famous trails that took herds to Kansas, and they were present in the cattle towns, such as Dodge City and Wichita, where those drives culminated. While there is some debate over the actual percentage of black cowboys, what seems certain is that there were many, including several known for great accomplishments. It also seems clear that, as Odie Faulk writes about cowboys in his history of Dodge City, "because of the shared hard work and the common danger, there was rough equality among these men, even the blacks. . . . In the early days of the open-range cattle era, there was little discrimination against these blacks in town or on the ranch."[63]

In addition to the cowboys, the general population of Kansas in 1870 was over 5 percent black, and that of Texas over 30 percent. West Texas was patrolled primarily by black soldiers from the all-black Ninth and Tenth Cavalries. Black cavalrymen helped protect the workmen who laid the rails through Dodge City, and black cavalry units secured some of the territory through which the cattle trails ran.[64] From the end of the Civil War until the end of the nineteenth century, black soldiers protected Kansas, west Texas, New Mexico, and Arizona (along with other parts of the western territories) from Indians. Blacks also participated in the cattle drives that, perhaps, contributed even more to Western mythology than to Western economy. While there were some all-white cattle drives, many crews had black cowboys, some even a majority of blacks. On the integrated crews, the number of black cooks was disproportionately high. In a typical crew of eleven men—a trail boss, a cook, a wrangler, and eight herders—the cook, who tended to be an older, more experienced former cowboy, was usually second in charge. The cook carried the guns, traveled ahead of the drive to select the campsites, and took charge if the trail boss was incapacitated.[65]

Adult Westerns altered both the race and the authority of cooks, turning them into white men characterized by comic ineffectuality. In *Rawhide*, for example, Wishbone was several decades older and a foot shorter than the trail boss, Gil Favor, ramrod Rowdy Yates (Clint Eastwood), and most of the other cowhands. Like all the cowboys—other than the Mexican wrangler—on that crew or any other drovers they came across, he was white. So were all the people in the episodes that the cattle drive met in the Texas towns along the way, even though the population of Texas at that time was almost one-third black.[66]

Even though in several ways these black cowboys and soldiers were not treated with equality, the conditions of the West necessarily required more interdependence than discrimination. Taylor explained,

> The workplace racism that permeated plantations in east Texas or in the Old South did not exist on the plains. Nor were racial sentiments openly expressed in the most famous end-of-the-trail town, Dodge City, Kansas. Kansas's reputation for racial tolerance and the promise of hundreds of black cowboys spending wages in saloons, restaurants, hotels, brothels,

and other businesses along the notorious Front Street encouraged social mixing in this raw new town, founded in 1875. White and black drovers shared hotel rooms, card games, café tables, and on occasion jail cells. One attempt to exclude blacks from a hotel was recalled years later precisely because of its failure.[67]

This was the Dodge City that Wyatt Earp was hired to protect, initially in 1876, then leaving briefly, and returning to the post of deputy marshal from 1877 to 1879: "A black man, an innocent observer of a gambler's quarrel, was the first person killed in Dodge City. His death and subsequent murders prompted town merchants to form a vigilance committee and to hire a series of marshals, of whom Wyatt Earp and Bat Masterson were the most famous."[68]

But the Kansas of 1875 Dodge City was not the Kansas of 1954 Topeka. By World War II, Kansas had lost touch with its abolitionist history, and the landmark 1954 Supreme Court decision in *Brown v. Board of Education of Topeka* made the Kansas state capital forever a national symbol of segregated schools. The presence of segregated schools, of course, indicated a significant black population. In 1950, Kansas had the third-highest percentage of blacks among the Western states (not including California), behind only Texas and Oklahoma, both of which were segregated. Arizona, which also had segregated schools, had the fourth-highest percentage of blacks. Its schools were desegregated in part by state law in 1951 and in part by the state judiciary in 1952.

These facts provide a significant context for the adult Westerns. While many adult Westerns were set in the generic West (e.g., *Cheyenne, Maverick, Have Gun Will Travel, Wanted Dead or Alive, Restless Gun, Tales of Wells Fargo, Wagon Train, Trackdown, Colt .45, Man from Blackhawk, Zane Grey Theater*), those that were set in specific places showed an overwhelming preference for Kansas (*Wyatt Earp, Gunsmoke, Wichita Town, Bat Masterson*), Texas (*Bronco, Jim Bowie, The Texan, Texas John Slaughter*), and Arizona (*Broken Arrow, The Deputy, Johnny Ringo, Tombstone Territory, Texas John Slaughter, Wyatt Earp*).

The Kansas of 1955 television Dodge City thus bore no resemblance to either 1950s or 1870s Kansas. In the same way that *The Rebel* reread Southern segregation, Dodge City Westerns revisited *Brown v. Board of Education of Topeka*, assuring the American public that Kansas was not really a state with a black population or a history of integration; it was *really* the West, the real West that epitomized American frontier values, historically, nationally, and globally. In order to do so, the television Wyatt Earp (like his successor, Matt Dillon) avoided Dodge's real black citizens and real black drovers, even though, as the opening episode of the series assured us, Earp was "a real Western hero." That is to say, he was a real hero, reinvented according to that magic black-and-white screen of Cold War reality. That reality required a commercially acceptable, homogeneous, normative vision of the West that reconfigured manifest destiny as domestic security on the one hand, and as a strategy of communist containment on the other.

The Ninth and Tenth Cavalry to the Rescue

The real Texas John Slaughter, a cattle baron whose exploits Disney heralded, was known to have at least two black cowhands. "One was a near giant named Jim. . . . He came with Slaughter's herds from Maverick, Texas, through New Mexico to Slaughter's San Bernardino ranch. . . . Another was known as Bat, and it was Bat who accompanied Slaughter and his foreman into Mexico on a dangerous cattle-buying expedition."[69] In chronicling Slaughter's exploits, however, Disney kept these cowboys out of the story. At the same time, he attributed to Slaughter a role in capturing Geronimo. "In this atomic age with all the talk about guided missiles, H-bombs, and so on," Disney started his introduction to that episode,

> one might not be too impressed with such primitive weapons as these [tomahawk and spear or arrow]. But lest we forget, one of the most violent campaigns in this country's history was waged with just such weapons. It started in May 1885 when Geronimo led a renegade band of Chiracahuas on the last and most vicious series of raids in all of their blood-soaked history. 5000 American troops poured into this area with but a single objective—capture Geronimo. And yet for some 15 months the campaign of terror continued. General Miles, sent to replace the frustrated General Crook, finally called upon his old friend John Slaughter and requested his help in tracking down this renegade Apache, Geronimo. The program you are about to see titled "The End of the Trail" is based upon this true historical incident in the life of that most remarkable man, Texas John Slaughter.

By explicitly comparing Indian weapons to H-bombs and guided missiles, Disney made the Indian wars the precursors of the Cold War, implying that the "redskins" were to the Old West what the Reds were to the Western bloc. Disney also subordinated the power of five thousand troops to that of one man, an interesting shift, given that some of those five thousand and, in general, a large number of the troops that fought the Indians, especially in west Texas and the greater Southwest, were black.

The Ninth and Tenth Cavalry, regiments formed immediately after the Civil War, were rapidly deployed in the West to avoid conflict with Southerners who were already hostile enough to white occupying troops. (A similar strategy would be used ninety years later in Little Rock. When the 101st Airborne surrounded Central High, only white troops were dispatched to the site; the black troops in the division, a significant number, were left behind at the armory so as not to arouse the ire of the white citizens of Little Rock.) By 1869, the federal troops assigned to occupy Texas, therefore, assumed a racial geography. East of the 100th meridian, which divides the state roughly in half, were forty-six white infantry companies and one black company, nineteen white cavalry divisions, and two black divisions. No white infantry or cavalry, however, patrolled the area west of the meridian; that task was assumed exclusively by nine black infantry companies and eleven black cavalry troops. The safety of west Texas thus depended far more on the black soldier than on the Texas Ranger.

The Ninth and Tenth Cavalry shortly became known as the most effective, feared, and respected of the Indian fighters. (Many speculate, for obvious reasons, that George C. Custer might have been better off had he not refused a lieutenant colonelcy with the Ninth Cavalry prior to acquiring the same position with the Seventh.) The "buffalo soldiers," as the black troops were called by Indians, by all accounts had much more to do with the pursuit of Geronimo than did John Slaughter. Their accomplishments were all the more impressive given that they were, especially at first, allocated substandard horses, clothing, and equipment. Depending on where they were stationed, moreover, they were not always treated fairly by the residents of local communities. Nevertheless, they were fundamental to frontier security. One incident, summarized by Quintard Taylor, is illustrative of the important role played by the black soldiers:

In May of 1880 . . . when warned of an impending attack by [the Apache band led by] Victorio on the tiny settlement of Tularosa, New Mexico, Sergeant George Jordan led twenty-four soldiers of the Ninth Cavalry on an all-night ride to the settlement. Upon arriving, the soldiers turned a corral and an old fort into a defensive stockade and gathered the frightened settlers into it. Soldiers and citizens fought off repeated attacks by the Apache, who then tried to capture the town's horses and cattle. Anticipating their plan, Jordan sent troopers to assist two soldiers and a herder who had been earlier assigned to protect the livestock. Jordan's decisive leadership and bravery earned him the Congressional Medal of Honor.[70]

As this incident made clear, any realistic representation of the frontier after the Civil War—especially the Texas, Kansas, New Mexico, and Arizona frontiers—would have to include the importance of black troops.

Although one episode of *Zane Grey Theater* (aired in November 1959) does acknowledge the existence of black cavalry troops, it does so in such a way as to inversely interpret their role, in the same way that *The Rebel* reinterprets the role of the Southerner in contemporary civil rights conflicts. An episode called "The Mission" starts with a voice-over narrator telling us,

> The West was growing. The last frontier was rapidly becoming the newest civilization. But violence and death were still the rule, not the exception; there was still the hunter and the hunted. Scattered throughout the frontier and pitifully few were the forts of the United States Army, the bastions of law and order. The men of the United States Cavalry were more than soldiers; they were guides, guardians, giants, a handful to cover 100,000 square miles. But [at this point shots of black cavalry appeared on the screen] these were not gods. They were men, all kinds of men.

This brief opening passage makes a sharp distinction between the general description of the U.S. Cavalry—"guides, guardians, giants"—and the description when the black cavalry appear: "These were not gods. They were men, all kinds of men." This introduction is making clear that (unlike most Western heroes) the buffalo soldiers are not "larger than life." The host, Dick Powell, in his role as the series historian/curator, then appears to explain that "of all the men who brought justice to the frontier, none did a bigger job than the United States Cavalry." Powell's introduction thus conflates military presence with law enforcement—the bringing of *justice* to the frontier, thus lauding the cavalry for assuming a judicial role prohibited in American democracy. Since "justice" is the provenance of courts and laws, only under martial law can the military be involved in administering it. Soldiers, therefore, may be tried in civilian courts whereas, under normal circumstances, civilians may not be tried by the military. In rendering justice as the product of military action, Powell's introduction supplies not a domestic narrative but rather one connected to the American military's interna-

A black corporal (Buffalo Soldier) in the Ninth Cavalry, 1891. *Library of Congress, Prints and Photographs Division* [LC-USZ62–132221].

tional role in containing communism and spreading democracy. Such was the mandate for action in Korea and Vietnam, for supporting a coup in Guatemala or in Iran. Such was the general understanding of the international function of the U.S. military in the Cold War.

"One of the most respected units was the Tenth Cavalry," Powell goes on, "a group composed of Negro soldiers. They even had their own standard to ride under." Despite the earlier qualifications, Powell indicates that this unit of "men, all kinds of men" is separate but equal to its white "guide, guardian, and giant" counterparts. "The Tenth Cavalry," Powell points out, "played a big part in the capture of the very famous Apache Chief, Geronimo." (The episode of *Texas John Slaughter* that might have set Powell straight, we should remember, had not yet been produced.) Eliding the distinction between the actors and the actual soldiers, Powell concludes his introduction by saying, "Tonight we'll show some members of the famous Tenth in a true story. Our star will be that very famous entertainer, Sammy Davis, Jr."

Clearly, this was a "famous" episode. Geronimo was *famous*; Sammy Davis, Jr., was *famous*; and the Tenth Cavalry was *famous* (although no one who had previously produced the thousands of films or television episodes set in the regions it protected seemed to have heard of it). How did all this fame—of their foes, of their exploits, of the people who portrayed them—befall ordinary men ("all *kinds* of men")? The episode had to reconcile the fame ascribed to the black cavalry with the ordinary stature of its soldiers. It did so not by making them prototypes of contemporary civil rights heroes or by rendering them Western heroes of exceptional prowess, along the lines of Davy Crockett, Wyatt Earp, or Texas John Slaughter (who a few television years later would single-handedly succeed where whole black companies had apparently failed). Rather, their fame accrued to the role they played in the Cold War context hinted at in the introduction.

The episode starts with a small company of buffalo soldiers on horseback, complaining about their insignificant assignments. These interchanges imposed on the story a World War II logic that, for the most part, relegated black divisions to secondary roles, away from action. The implication of that policy, as of this episode, was that black soldiers were not suitable as combatants. This was equally true in the Civil War, where black troops had to seize opportunities for dangerous attacks and incur huge casualties in order to prove their value. This may have been the case, in fact, at any time when black soldiers were called upon to fight white enemies. But on the frontier, prejudice functioned in exactly the other way: To the extent that they were considered expendable, black soldiers were given the most hazardous patrols.

In this episode of *Zane Grey Theater*, however, they believe that they have been given yet one more trivial task, that of transporting horses. "Don't worry," one of the soldiers says. "The Army ain't never lost a horse yet." Another says, ironically, "That's the trouble with you guys—you just don't realize how important we are."

When the discussion turns to Indians, one of the black soldiers says, "I'd give two years of my life to kill a Comanche." Obviously, these soldiers have not been allowed to fight Indians, despite their strong desire to do so. Deprived of their combat roles, they seem more like domestic servants, emasculated and in no way associated with violent activity. In the lexicon of the 1950s—North and South—they are "good Negroes," not the kind engaged in urban violence or civil rights protests. They just want a chance to demonstrate that they are loyal Americans. They express part of that loyalty by showing that they share the same prejudices as white men.

"There's but one way to bring in a Comanche," Sammy Davis, Jr., as Corporal Harper, states, "and it ain't on a horse, it's across it." Like the premiere episode of *The Rebel*, this discussion refocuses the issue of prejudice. The blacks are the perpetrators of prejudice—saying in effect that there was no good Injun but a dead Injun—rather than its victims.

Their mission, however, turns out to be very important. It is assigned to them in the hope that, as generally insignificant soldiers, they would be more innocuous when they secretly bring a Comanche chief back to the fort where he has promised to sign an important treaty. The evil Apaches want to prevent this signing at all costs because they fear that if this chief signs, then others will follow, causing the war against the white man to collapse. The Comanche chief wants the killing to stop, and the Apaches want it to continue.

This, of course, is the Cold War narrative suggested in the show's introduction. The Comanche chief represents a fissure in the Red(skin) alliance, one that could mark the beginning of the end of the Red(skin) bloc. The buffalo soldiers are being given an opportunity to serve the West by carrying out this secret mission. Unfortunately they fail even at this noncombat role, for they are ambushed and trapped by the evil Apaches. As the wounded sergeant says, "I messed it—first real job we get and I messed it." The episode, despite its praise for the "famous Tenth Cavalry," thus provides a cautionary note about giving blacks tasks that exceed their capacity for good judgment. In this case, a misjudgment threatens the security of the West. The treaty could end the killing, could make the West safe, but now the killing might continue because they "messed it."

The Apache leader further complicates the problem by asking the black soldiers to surrender the chief: "You are fools to die for a land that does not want you. You are our brothers. We do not wish to kill you. You have until tomorrow, sundown. Send us the Comanche, and you can ride away without fear." The Apache, who seems extremely knowledgeable about U.S. race relations, is equally articulate in using that knowledge to undermine

U.S. solidarity. Illustrating conventional American Cold War wisdom, he provides one more example of how the nation's racial divisions can be advantageous to the nation's Red enemies. The Apache's speech effectively evokes black antipathy, not toward "the land that does not want" them but toward the Comanche chief: "Yeah, you fought all right, slaughtering women and children, burning and killing everything you came across." The chief, however, retains the equanimity of a true statesman, insisting, "Treaty important. You and your people, me and my people."

This chief's speech, which has the characteristic grammar and accent of traditional movie Indians, attested, in the terms of this adult Western drama, that he was authentic, in contrast to the Apache, whose accent is as pristine as his grammar and usage. The Apache's articulation, his education, and his rhetorical skill thus became suspect. One can never know, after all, how these reds get their information, and therefore one can never trust their motives. In any case, the authentic chief—that is, the one who has never seen a preposition, not to mention an infinitive, he didn't hate— effectively refutes his red adversary's subversive speech in several ways. By referring to "you and your people," meaning all American citizens, he identifies the black soldiers along national, rather than racial, lines. While the suspect Apache says that the nation does not want them, the authentic Comanche sees them as an integral part of that nation, risking their lives not for some other people but for their own people.

The Comanche chief also reminds them that the cause of peace requires personal sacrifice: "My life not important. Treaty can stop killing." In a late-night conversation with Harper, now in charge of the mission, he returns to the question of racial allegiance evoked by that articulate Red menace, the Apache. "We much a same," the Comanche chief tells Harper, "you and I" (rising to a new eloquence by using "I" to demonstrate that he knows it is properly not the *object* but the *subject* of the verb "a"). Harper, however, who has yet to overcome the prejudice toward Comanches that he expressed at the outset, will not accept the idea that he has anything in common with this redskin: "Now, don't start with that 'brother' stuff."

This gives the Comanche chief the opportunity to redefine "brotherhood." Whereas the Apache had defined it on racial grounds, such that he and the buffalo soldiers are brothers because they are both nonwhite, the Comanche chief defines brotherhood in Christian terms, stating: "Men not brothers for what they are here [touching his face] but what they are here [touching his heart]." The Comanche chief thus supplies Harper with the terms under which he can fit in, be a brother to both Indians and whites. To do so, he has to overcome his racism, his sense that skin color matters. By overcoming his racist attitudes toward the Comanches, he may find redemption.

The final lesson the chief imparts is that one must look at the big picture rather than at the petty battles. When asked if the treaty wouldn't mean defeat for his people, the chief replies, "I wish my people to live with dignity. Treaty can do that. What matter if battle lost if peace won?"

This interchange with the chief makes clear that Harper needs to redeem himself—for his racism, for his incompetence, for his shortsightedness, and for his selfishness. And in the end, he does exactly that. He allows the chief to escape by switching outfits with him. Only after the chief and the other soldiers are safely away does the Apache get close enough to see that the man in the Indian headdress is actually Harper. Thus, the black soldiers' first important mission succeeds not because they are superior fighters or, in fact, show any form of prowess but rather because one of them is willing to sacrifice himself for the good of the nation.

Apparently, according to this "true" story, the buffalo soldiers became famous in this manner, in spite of their noticeable liabilities, the most noteworthy of which was their racism. Since no historical record documents this event, and history has proven the Comanche chief to have been wrong in that no known treaty with the Indians has allowed them to live with dignity, it must be assumed that the inherent "truth" was allegorical rather than factual. As an allegory, it suggests that blacks caused the nation's race problems, and hence those problems will disappear only when blacks are willing to make sacrifices for the greater good.

This position might not have been consistent with the nightly news about civil rights and Southern injustice, but it was consistent with the norms created by black-and-white prime-time television and epitomized in that apotheosis of Western living, Disneyland. If *The Rebel*, like all the adult Westerns, owed a debt to *Disneyland*, that debt, by 1959, had in part been repaid by turning a significant chunk of prime time into "Frontierland," while it advertised the West as the place where one could tell the difference in whiteness.

At the same time, because the status of American civil rights was important to both East and West Cold War propaganda, television became a cogent interpreter of America's historical and racial realities, representing those realities in one way on news shows and in another in the Western. This juxtaposition allowed the image of the West reflected by the adult Westerns to contextualize the image of a racially torn nation reflected by the evening news. The adult Westerns conflated America's history and destiny into a mythic "truth" against which the conflicts over racial discrimination could be read as inaccurate or as partial—both in the sense of being incomplete, like the story of the Alamo, and being biased, like the treatment of Johnny Yuma as he implicitly remembered the Alamo in the process of representing the values of the South in the name of the West. The adult Western thus practiced the same segregation that the courts had outlawed in schools and Congress was in the process of outlawing in public facilities. In the face of legal decision and social protest, prime-time television remained, throughout the 1950s, the West's real separate but equal public space.

6 The New Frontier

Into the center of that separate but equal Western space on a summer night in 1960 rode a new presumptive hero of the West. Accepting the presidential nomination of the Democratic Party, John Kennedy can be viewed as merging the two aspects of American imperialism that I have been discussing: the narratives of the American West and the political mandate to lead the Cold War West. On July 15, 1960, occupying the time slot that normally followed *Rawhide* and that would be filled, in the following season, by *Route 66*, speaking in Los Angeles, John F. Kennedy introduced the theme of the "New Frontier" with an astonishing number of temporal and spatial dislocations:

> I stand here tonight facing west on what was once the last frontier. From the lands that stretch 3000 miles behind us, the pioneers gave up their safety, their comfort and sometimes their lives to build our new West.
>
> They were not the captives of their own doubts nor the prisoners of their own price tags. They were determined to make the new world strong and free—an example to the world to overcome its hazards and its hardships, to conquer the enemies that threatened from within and without.[1]

In this construction, the "last frontier"—which California was, but no longer is—was actually the penultimate frontier, situated temporally, not geographically, in the timeline of the imagination as the place we used to think of as the frontier. But that place itself was the site of directional disorientation. This "new world" as he called it, albeit unsettled, somehow needed also to be made "free," "strong and free," not as a place to live in but as an inspiration to those who live everyplace else: "an example to the world to overcome its hazards and its hardships." The last frontier was thus paradigmatic America, the New World that would stand as an emblem of freedom to the Old World, and the pioneers who "gave up their safety, their comfort and sometimes their lives," were surrogates for America's founding fathers, who, in the Declaration of Independence, pledged their lives, liberty, and common fortune to the cause of independence.

Facing west from Los Angeles, as he was, Kennedy was actually looking away from the West just as, in this scheme, the West looked away from the America whose interests and privileged narratives it was reinventing as it was reiterating them. It was reiterating those narratives, moreover, at least as Kennedy described it, in the context of a universal paranoia, a determination to conquer in advance "enemies that threatened from within and without." Since the West was both a moveable space and a vacancy filled by the praised pioneers, it was impossible to specify *what* the enemies were "within." The hostile world simply surrounded all of the surfaces—interior and exterior—of America, which was, in perpetual reiteration, the West. That was why Kennedy could go on to announce one more relocation:

> Some would say that those struggles are all over—that all the horizons have been explored—that all the battles have been won—that there is no longer an American frontier.
>
> But I trust that no one in this assemblage would agree with that sentiment.[2]

The reason Kennedy's trust was well founded was that the West had never been America's reiteration so much as its simulation, a point supported by even a cursory examination of the sights and experiences most common to all Americans that summer, supported by the narratives they most frequently and extensively shared and the public spaces they most universally occupied—supported, that is, by television. By 1960 television had come, unquestionably, to comprise the most significant public sphere of American life, and the television programming of 1960, as we have seen, revealed emphatically that the frontier was the ubiquitous reference point for the simulation of American civilization. Among the thirty prime-time Western series in the 1959–1960 season were a majority of the most popular shows on television, including *Gunsmoke*, *Wagon Train*, *Have Gun Will Travel*, *The Rifleman*, *Wanted Dead or Alive*, *Maverick*, *Cheyenne*, and *Bonanza*. The New Frontier—that mobile place where the narrative of the West became the simulacrum of America—was no longer geographical. It was a televisual space that by 1960 had become so vast that it indeed circumscribed in every temporal direction the podium from which Kennedy spoke.

In a sense, then, it was quite apt that Kennedy identified himself as the hero of the New Frontier in that he was, as is generally conceded, the first genuinely televisual president. More even than in the Nixon debates, in his press conferences Kennedy milked the medium's potential, turning the political forum into an entertainment event by exploiting the sense of intimacy and spontaneity from which television drew its authority. Not only in providing the margin of victory (three million of the four million voters making up their minds on the basis of the debates voted for Kennedy) but in governing, Kennedy believed, according to Ted Sorensen, that "his greatest weapon . . . was television."[3] The same month that Eisenhower selected Nixon as his running mate, Kennedy, while taking a CBS course on how to use television, was informed that "three hundred Capitol Hill news correspondents voted him the 'handsomest' member of the House."[4] Christopher Matthews, comparing Nixon's political ability with Kennedy's gift for media, notes about the concurrence of these two events in 1952, "Salieri had learned the powers of craft; Mozart had begun to discover his talent."[5]

Although he was not a trained performer, he was, as David Farber points out, "the first President to use live televised press conferences, speeches, and special appearances . . . as a basic aspect of his presidency. As Kennedy said to an aide, while watching a film of one of his press conferences, 'We couldn't survive without television.' No President since Kennedy has enjoyed such control over his TV image."[6]

As in Kennedy's New Frontier speech, the West was the frontier of science and the destiny of the nuclear age, and if America won the Cold War, the West would be what lay before us: "We stand today on the edge of a new frontier—the frontier of the Nineteen Sixties—the frontier of unknown opportunities and perils—the frontier of unfulfilled hopes and threats." In a sense, the frontier to Kennedy was the common denominator for everything: space, technology, geopolitics. "The New Frontier is here," Kennedy announced, "whether we seek it or not. Beyond that frontier are uncharted areas of science and space, unsolved problems of peace and war, unconquered pockets of ignorance and prejudice, unanswered questions of poverty and surplus."[7]

Every aspect of American life, every detail of its past, every potential for its future was thus reconfigured in terms of the frontier. The West was not a border at the edge of civilization but a circumstance—the circumstance—of American life at the precipice of the new decade. Just as the interstate made distance temporal rather than geographical, so the New Frontier converted the West from a geographical to a temporal configuration. That temporal configuration was eternity. In every direction, the West designated, for as far as the eye and the mind's eye could see, America's essence and destiny.

No president since Kennedy has enjoyed such control over his TV image. *Library of Congress, Prints and Photographs Division* [LC-USZ62-133061].

In creating this multifarious timeframe, Kennedy was echoing the multitudinous West of prime-time television, and even more the frontier of mass communication that was rapidly becoming a quintessential American characteristic. Television was the frontier of a new communication medium, and, as President Kennedy would announce almost exactly a year later in regard to Germany—in a speech encouraging Americans to build bomb shelters—"today the endangered frontier of freedom runs through Berlin."[8]

The bomb shelter thus became a way of building on the shared space of a nation united, virtually knitted together, by TV antennae, freeway spurs, and prime-time narratives of Western domination and Anglo-Saxon privilege. Mobilizing the frontier spirit of the American citizenry, Kennedy was urging suburbia to reimagine itself in the image of the nineteenth-century settlers, as he had in the New Frontier speech when he said, "I believe the times require imagination and courage and perseverance. I am asking each of you to be pioneers toward that New Frontier."[9] In this context, Kennedy was creating outposts at the edge of the nuclear frontier, in an age when intercontinental ballistic missiles (ICBMs) had reconfigured the global boundaries. Like television, and the interstate highway system, and the initial New

Frontier speech, ICBMs measured distance temporally, so the same suburb could now lie, equally, thirty-five minutes away from an urban center and forty minutes from nuclear annihilation. On this ubiquitous frontier, the bomb shelter represented, at least symbolically, the task of settling the New Frontier in the same way that America's symbolic ancestors had settled the old frontier.

Kennedy made this connection explicit: "As Americans know from our history on our old frontier, gun battles are caused by outlaws and not officers of the peace."[10] Certainly no Americans—including Kennedy—were more actually the sons and daughters of these frontiersmen and pioneers than were those who had actually ridden to Grandmother's house by horse-drawn sleigh. Thus, Americans, in this Texas-style showdown with the Russians, were being given a second chance to avow their frontier heritage, in the same way that they claimed their Pilgrim ancestors by singing along with the songs they learned in school or heard on television.

At the same time, the bomb shelter was a litmus test for the kind of family suited for survival on this New Frontier. It is hard to imagine the family—only parents and siblings—that could be isolated for six weeks or more in a space one-third the size of the average subway car, with about one-eighth the ventilation, eating only Spam, powdered milk, and canned beans, without bathing and with nothing on television, listening over and over on the battery-driven phonograph to the original cast album of *Carousel*, along with 45-rpm recordings of "How Much Is that Doggie in the Window?" "Hound Dog," and Ferrante and Teicher playing "The Theme from *Exodus*."

The only families conceivably capable of surviving this ordeal would have been those found on 1950s television sitcoms—and Westerns such as *Wagon Train* and *The Rifleman*—that could amicably resolve every internal problem, settle every domestic disagreement, and permanently overcome every hurt and slight in twenty to forty-five minutes. The bomb shelter provided the opportunity, in other words, for Americans to prove they were worthy of survival because they had lived up to the norms prescribed by over a decade of national Cold War television. To put it another way, if the New Frontier ran through Berlin, then the bomb shelter was the little house on the prairie.

The brief period we can call the Kennedy era—1960 to 1963—thus represented the culmination of the 1950s adult Western in the sense that, as Kennedy brought the Western to life in and around Berlin and Cuba and Southeast Asia, the genre all but disappeared from the television screens.

Each year after Kennedy's election, the number of television Westerns declined, as did their general popularity. While *Gunsmoke* remained extremely popular into the 1970s, most of the other hit adult Westerns of the 1950s were off the air by 1964. Of the Westerns on television, only *Gunsmoke* and *Bonanza*, the 1960s' most popular television show of any genre, appeared regularly in the top ten or twenty programs.

Bonanza, which premiered in September 1959 and lasted into the 1970s, was in many ways the quintessential Kennedy Western, a consolidation of the 1950s adult Westerns around the themes of the New Frontier. Significantly, it was one of the first of what has been called "property Westerns," that is, Westerns focused on maintaining a spread and defending it against encroaching enemies. The heroes of *Bonanza* were not going anywhere; they were simply preserving what they had. Unlike the principal figures of the 1950s adult Westerns, they were not law officers, nor did they travel from town to town in search of work or wealth or adventure. Nor were they marginal small ranchers, like the Rifleman. They were established, and they were the establishment. They set the tone for the small number of TV Westerns that would have any success through the 1960s: *The Virginian, High Chaparral, The Big Valley*.

The "Ponderosa," the estate on which *Bonanza* was set, was a one-thousand-square-mile timberland ranch in Nevada, owned by the Cartwrights. Ben Cartwright, three times a widower, ran the ranch with his three sons, one from each marriage. Although technically "new wealth," in that Ben had founded and developed the Ponderosa himself in the world of rapidly spreading prosperity, the Cartwrights in less than a generation had become the landed gentry of their region. As such, the series made clear, they were the unofficial upholders of the community's laws and values, responsible not only for their business practices but also for a form of public service. To this task they brought not only wisdom but also superior skills with fists and weapons. They represented Western heroes, in other words, not as settlers of the frontier but as protectors of the settled West.

It is hard to miss some similarities between the Cartwrights and the Kennedys, especially in terms of the Kennedys' image in the 1950s and 1960s. A patriarch of relatively new wealth, Joseph Kennedy was an odd blend of immigrant and aristocrat. To solidify his tenuous claims on his aristocratic position, he dedicated his three sons to public service.[11] *Bonanza* similarly unequivocally linked morality to prosperity, wisdom to wealth, such that the series was a consolidation of the postwar economic accomplishments that vouchsafed the rewards of Western industriousness as a form of Western industry. As in the opening *Maverick* episode, the common good in *Bonanza* was the product of individual, not communal, enterprise, and the patriarchal order solidified the gains by investing secular power with religious authority.

The opening episode established these issues well, marking the Ponderosa as the secular and sanctified apotheosis of the American estate. The episode began with patriarch Ben "Pa" Cartwright and his eldest son, Adam, on horseback atop a wooded bluff that overlooked the expanse of their estate:

> "Look at it, Adam. Feast thine eyes on a sight that approacheth Heaven itself."
>
> "You been to a lot of places and you seen a lotta things, Pa, but you never seen or been to Heaven."
>
> "Maybe I never been to Heaven. Maybe I'm never going to get the chance, but Heaven is going to have to go some to beat the thousand square mile of the Ponderosa."

As the biblical connotations evoked by Ben's archaic usages suggests, his son is indeed the American "Adam," heir to the Puritans who colonized New England with a millennial purpose. Adam's mother (Ben Cartwright's first wife), in fact, had come from sturdy New England stock, making him the literal as well as the figurative heir to Yankee America. In this role, Adam is responsible for overseeing the legacy of the East and maintaining its authority in the expanded and settled American domain. His response to Ben articulates this responsibility:

> "As long as it's ours . . . as long as we can keep it in Cartwright hands."
>
> "Know anyone who could take it from us, son?"
>
> "I know those who would try—the Virginia City bunch if we gave them half a chance."

Like JFK in his "New Frontier" speech, Adam is expressing concern about "the enemies that threatened from within and without." And like the Kennedys, the Cartwrights represent not the pure New England stock but a more hybrid, emigrant tradition. The Kennedys were descendents of Irish immigrants who arrived in Boston in the early 1850s, almost exactly the time that the fictional Ben Cartwright arrived in Nevada to found the Ponderosa. Along the way, Ben acquired two sons: Adam, born in Boston to a (non-Irish) New Englander (who died shortly thereafter), and Hoss, born in Missouri to a Swedish immigrant (subsequently killed by Indians). After he was settled in Nevada, Ben made a trip to New Orleans, married a New Orleans maiden, and returned to the Ponderosa with her. Their son, Joe, was born in Nevada. (Shortly thereafter the third Mrs. Cartwright died when her horse stepped in a chuckhole and threw her.)

Aside from the obvious lesson that one ought not to sell life insurance to a Ben Cartwright bride—or for that matter, any woman attracted to any of the Cartwrights, before or during the show's thirteen-year run—Ben's family history consolidates an (Anglo-Saxon) American history. This genetic demography of the West in *Bonanza* takes on a political dimension in that Joe and Adam, at least, seemed to have inherited from their mothers not only physical but also political genes so that this family Western, set during the Civil War (but outside its purview) evoked familial fights that expressed the sons' respective Northern and Southern alliances. "Imagine my Pa being married to a Yankee," Little Joe scoffed. "What's so wrong about a Yankee?" Adam asks, and Little Joe retorts, "If you don't already know, guess there's no use in my telling you."

Much of Adam's and Joe's feuding in this initial episode pertains to Adam's perception that Joe is lazy: "You're a Cartwright—do you know what that means? . . . It means you're supposed to be a man now, fit to do a man's work," by which Adam means taking care of the Ponderosa. The stereotypical laziness of the Southern black is thus first displaced onto the white youngest son, who then in the interest of the Ponderosa has the chance to disprove the stereotype. In so doing, he provides the "Yankee granite-head," as he calls his brother, the opportunity to admit that he has misjudged his brother, the "poor boy outta New Orleans."

As the episode's opening interchange indicated, the Ponderosa belonged to the Cartwrights not just because they have earned it but also because they have a heavenly mandate, like the Christian knights of old. "The Ponderosa," the series producer, David Dortort explained, "is not just a dusty, down-at-the-heels ranch. There's power, wealth and permanence there, and as such it is the most important single home on television. The great house is like the castles of old, its occupants, kings, princes, knights. . . . We are against the phoney West. Our men swear allegiance not to the silver but to the land."[12] The Cartwright family represented the apotheosis of the masculine, Anglo-Saxon West, the composite of regional interests and Anglo-Saxon origins that yielded a fragile realm, not unlike the Camelot of the 1962 Broadway musical, the title song of which JFK embraced and that retrospectively became his unofficial theme.

In the half decade since the advent of the adult Western, the real West, in other words, had transformed itself from a land of settlers and cowboys to a land of wealth and power. The Cartwrights, therefore, did not enact the emigrant or pioneer experience but rather validated it with the evidence of heaven on earth. To call the Ponderosa ranch house the most important single home on television implicitly linked it, moreover, with the White House. What other house, after all, could justify that claim? At the same time, the term "single house" evoked connotations of the single-family house in which each year a growing number of the show's viewers lived. As the site of wealth and power, like the heraldic fortress, the Ponderosa represented the best imaginary version of the suburban man's house that, as the adage goes, was his castle.

"The Cartwright attitude toward the Ponderosa," as Gary Yoggy succinctly states, "is almost paranoid."13 As more than a decade of Cold War paranoia had reiterated, in other words, America's imagined heaven on earth teetered precariously between nuclear annihilation and internal subversion. The precariousness of Western values, and practices, and prosperity was very much a theme of the New Frontier speech as it was, subsequently, of Kennedy's inaugural address:

> We dare not forget today that we are the heirs of that first revolution. Let the word go forth from this time and place, to friend and foe alike, that the torch has been passed to a new generation of Americans—born in this century, tempered by war, disciplined by a hard and bitter peace, proud of our ancient heritage—and unwilling to witness or permit the slow undoing of those human rights to which this Nation has always been committed, and to which we are committed today at home and around the world.
>
> Let every nation know, whether it wishes us well or ill, that we shall pay any price, bear any burden, meet any hardship, support any friend, oppose any foe, in order to assure the survival and the success of liberty.14

The Cartwright boys, then, like the Kennedy clan, were entrusted with the relentless task of defending the West as its own best version of itself, as Camelot, the New Frontier, the American Dream.

Crucial on the Ponderosa, therefore, was the capacity for hard work, man's work. The moral authority earned through hard work also had to be maintained that way so that the West in this series would become the place where the Protestant ethic could be tested and proved. An episode titled

"The Mill" (October 1, 1960) deals with Tom Edwards, a neighbor bitter because of a paralyzing hunting accident, who has fallen into the power of his malevolent ranch hand and servant, Ezekiel (Claude Aikens). Each evening Ezekiel stays up drinking and gambling with Edwards until Edwards's losses leave him hopelessly indebted to Ezekiel. When sober, Edwards resents Ezekiel and wishes to be rid of him but cannot fire him because of the gambling debts; when drunk he prefers Ezekiel's company to his wife's and seems to absorb Ezekiel's suspicions and jealousies.

Ezekiel is thus the figure of sin and temptation, leading Tom to prefer vice to work, feeding his suspicion and jealousy, tricking him into selling his soul to this deceiving servant (referred to at one point as "you snake"). In the episode, Ben Cartwright becomes Ezekiel's overt rival for Tom's soul. Whereas Ezekiel wishes to draw Tom ever more deeply into his debt, Ben wishes to save Tom's soul by making him once more financially independent, able to pay off his debt to Ezekiel and thereby extricate himself permanently by firing the hand. To this end, Ben makes an investment in the Edwards ranch by fronting the costs to construct a mill on Edwards's stream so that Edwards might earn a living by meeting a market demand (there is no mill nearby). It is agreed that Adam, using his engineering skill, will design the mill and supervise his brothers in building it, and Ben will receive a return of his initial investment and 12.5 percent profit before turning the mill over to Edwards. Work and redemption are thus inextricably connected in this allegorical drama, as are capital investment and good works, market forces and salvation. Thus, at the moment that the mill goes into operation, it is virtually impossible to tell if work, engineering, and capital enterprise are being worshipped with religious zeal or whether religion is being manifested in the intricacies of the free-market system.

Just before the final steps are completed, Little Joe asks Adam why they have to go on, protesting that they have done enough work for ten men that day. Adam galvanizes them to one last effort at setting the water wheel in place through an encomium to work and to seeing that work turns into profit: "Because I want to see it work. I want to see this mill grind wheat. I want to eat bread from this mill that we built." When the mill starts working Hoss offers this prayer, "Oh millstone, oh grind our wheat, and oh wheat, make our bread, and oh bread, make us as bright as our brother Adam. Amen." This Walt Whitman/Carl Sandburg version of "give us our daily bread" recapitulates the drama's theme of using engineering and in-

dustry to turn the millstone—representing Tom Edwards's handicap, physical and spiritual—into a source of production and thus of redemption. In
this way, the Cartwrights not only represent Western (Cold War) values but
also exemplify how those values redeemed the West, that source of raw material so lauded in the Kaiser industry commercials of the *Maverick* show.
Not only Tom Edwards but the West itself is being redeemed. Thus, the
paraplegic, decadent, self-pitying Edwards and the unexploited Western
terrain come to share a common lack of productivity that put them both in
contrast with the productivity of the Cartwrights, who, as workers, inves-
tors, and engineers, can find a way for the West to bring us our daily bread,
a way that is, like the resolution of the silver mine dispute in *Maverick*, beneficial to all parties.

But that resolution is always defined within the context of a Protestant
ethic that vindicated the notion of manifest destiny (of the Anglo-Saxon
race). This vindication, moreover, comes with divine endorsement. The
quasi-biblical pronouncement made by Ben at the outset of the series became a motif running through it. Even more blatantly than "The Mill,"
"Springtime" (October 1, 1961) is a series of thinly disguised Christian parables. In order to deal with his sons' spring fever, manifested as fighting
and general rowdiness, Ben sends them out to accomplish three discrete
tasks. Each task has a beneficial result in ways that suggest a controlling
hand, a divine scheme at work. The tasks involve Christian images (fishes,
loaves, wine) and values (charity, redemption), so each section of the episode functions as a separate lesson not only for the Cartwright progeny but
also for the audience. In the case of the audience, the lesson was double.
They are instructed not only in Christian virtue but also in fact that these
parables can be attributed to the sagacity of Ben, who—in choosing these
missions for his sons—clearly seems to know something about their purpose that is more than merely pragmatic. He knows how to create the conditions for what looks like divine intervention, and what better credential
could one have to preside over the American Dream?

The Cartwrights were entrusted with the estate of the New Frontier, furthermore, because they could overcome their regional differences, even before the outcome of the Civil War was certain, and make things work. One
testament to this technological supremacy was the show's format. As the
first Western broadcast in color, *Bonanza* not only demonstrated its ability
to master the technology of television but also established itself as a pioneer at the frontier of television's future. It established that supremacy,

moreover, in one of the whitest of the West's territories. In 1860, the entire Nevada territory had fewer than fifty blacks. Over the next decade that number did not increase to even four hundred, despite the general westward migration after the Civil War and, specifically, the migration of many freed slaves to areas in the West.[15] Even as late as 1920, it still had under five hundred black residents.

In the 1964–1965 season, as the writers looked for a way to write Adam (and actor Pernell Roberts) out of the series by marrying him off, Roberts suggested in a memo that "the network cast the role of my bride as an Indian girl, and get a Negro to play the part." He wanted to ameliorate recent "events in the South [that] have done tremendous damage to our national prestige and have clearly indicated the grievous wrong that has been perpetrated upon American Negroes." It was unclear why Roberts suggested that a Negro actress play an Indian character rather than a black character. Perhaps he believed that advocating black/white miscegenation would be going too far, or perhaps he thought that introducing a Negro character into the West would strain the credibility of the series. Nor was it clear how this "would be one of the most progressive statements in television drama, as both the Negro and the American Indian have consistently been exploited 'second class citizens.'"[16] Especially puzzling was the idea that the American Indian would improve her "second-class citizen" status if played by a Negro.

The premises of Roberts's suggestion (not followed), in other words, were as confused as the genetic politics that defined the WASP tensions kept in balance on the Ponderosa. They were as confused, as well, as the temporal frame that delimited history as shown in the series. Although Ben referred to events on the Ponderosa that had occurred fifteen to twenty years earlier—a period necessary to account for Joe's birth and his mother's death in the West—the region where the Ponderosa was located did not come under settlement until the 1850s, that is, less than a dozen years earlier. Similarly, Virginia City, in the series deemed to be as old as the Ponderosa, was not settled until 1859, at which time it had few inhabitants and even fewer permanent buildings.

If the prehistory of the Ponderosa was not consistent with historical events, it nevertheless seems clear that the first seasons were set shortly before and during the Civil War. Although the show encouraged a sense of historical specificity through its array of historical characters and allusions, in order to correlate *Bonanza* with any historical context one must assume that the episodes were not televised in the order in which events occurred in the life of the Cartwrights. The first episode, involving Lotta Crabtree's visit to the Comstock, referred to an event in 1863. The fourth episode dealt with the Paiute Indian War, which took place in 1860, and the fifth episode with Mark Twain's employment as a Virginia City journalist in 1862. The eighth episode showed Adam interacting with engineer Philip Diedesheimer to help make the silver mine shafts safe; Diedesheimer did this in 1860. The tenth episode dealt with the performer Adah Menken's 1864 visit to Virginia City. In any case, regardless of the episode order, *Bonanza* seemed clearly to concentrate on the period almost exactly one century before the show's 1959 premiere. Thus, "House Divided" (January 9, 1960) dealt with the 1858 Lincoln-Douglas debates, and an episode in the fourth season, "The War Comes to Warshoe" (November 4, 1962), dealt with Nevada's joining the Union, an event that revived the North/South antipathy in the Cartwright household when Adam objected to Joe's plans to marry the daughter of a Confederate sympathizer.

The point is not to identify the show's errors in chronology or historical detail. If these historical errors (along with many others) may suggest some sloppiness or indifference, they were nevertheless purposeful in that they represented the intentions of their producers. Those producers chose the time and place they thought best to present the Western estate as an ideal exemplifying the best possible result of the frontier spirit. For the producers, the Ponderosa, in its time and place, identified the kind of estate God intended America to inherit. In that regard, they consciously chose a place far in the West, bordering on but not part of California, a state that may have been farther west but lacked adequate association with cowboys. (Paladin, after all, always left San Francisco before he donned his Western outfit.) California, with its Spanish and Asian populations, also had a marked multiethnic heritage. In this regard, Virginia City and the Ponderosa became the Western outpost of the WASP frontier, located so that it could have commerce with the world of the cosmopolitan West Coast even before that world was fully formed.

Setting the initial seasons *during* the Civil War, especially when so many of the historical problems might have been avoided if the series were set a decade later, gave *Bonanza* a temporal position analogous to its unique geographical position. Its action took place at a time prior to the events portrayed in almost all the other adult Westerns. Wyatt Earp was marshal of Dodge City from 1876 to 1879, and Matt Dillon of *Gunsmoke* was the town's marshal for roughly twenty years starting around 1870. *Wagon Train* was set in the 1870s and *Rawhide* in the late 1860s. The events portrayed in *The Rebel*, of course, began shortly after the Civil War, as did those of *Bronco*, whose hero was a contemporary of Cheyenne, despite the fact that Cheyenne in the same time frame witnessed the massacre at Little Big Horn, which took place in 1876. The more general point is that the West of the adult Western was a place anchored by an array of sites and events and traversed by a finite number of figures who moved between them. The overwhelming bulk of these sites were established after the Civil War, as were the events that distinguished them, either in the history of the West or in the fictional world of the adult Westerns. As a group, these events, true or apocryphal, plausible or incredible, acquired composite significance by virtue of the way that they illustrated the methods and values that settled the West, in the way they manifested, in other words, the pioneer spirit that Kennedy's speech sought to renew.

In this light, *Bonanza* as the culmination of westward settlement should have been set, perhaps, like *The Rifleman*—or like *Bonanza*'s property Western successors—in the 1880s. Positioned as it was, prior to the great wagon trains and cattle drives, prior to the expanse of lawmen and cavalrymen, prior to many decades of Indian wars, *Bonanza* was claiming a prophetic position in the history of the West. It was proclaiming itself, in advance, as the place all the other settlers would be seeking, the end that justified their means. To put it another way, *Adam* Cartwright's estate proved the existence of the New Eden that Major *Adams* would lead his pilgrims toward a decade later.

That this prophetic goal of the West should necessarily be established before the nation had settled the question of slavery seems particularly stunning. At best, one could say that in the world envisioned by *Bonanza* the issue of slavery was irrelevant to any conception of an American heaven on earth. Certainly this would be true if we consider that the series portrayed the dispute between North and South as having to do with a difference in the genes that determined the disposition of two white half brothers rather than as a result of the values attributed to the genes that determine skin color.

Bonanza, in addition, strongly advocated property rights and the relative sovereignty of estates. "There is never any doubt that the Cartwrights will fight together to the death to protect their land," Gary Yoggy notes. "In the third episode . . . Ben declares to a group of miners . . . that 'nobody's going to destroy the Ponderosa,' adding that he will kill any man who tries, 'if he has to.' . . . The battle between the Cartwrights and those who would take from them what is rightfully theirs continued season after season."17

On the Ponderosa, the Cartwrights more or less enforced the law. While Nevada was a territory, not a state, and hence not able to claim state's rights, the Ponderosa exercised a limited version of those rights through the semiautonomy of its estate. In the period directly before the Civil War, *property* rights—representing slaveholding interests—were in direct legal conflict with *human* rights. The status of the black person as human or as property thus focused much of the legal conflict leading up to the Civil War, and, to the extent that the "property Westerns" were implicit advocates for property rights, Westerns such as *Bonanza* could be read as inflecting the argument toward the South. If this inflection toward property rights might have been too subtle to be significant, the autonomy of law enforcement, the relative sovereignty of the Ponderosa, certainly was not, as it strongly resonated with the arguments made by Orval Faubus and articulated in the "Southern Manifesto" signed by every Southern member of the House and Senate. In the view of that manifesto, the Southern states, not the federal government or any other outside authority, had the right to determine the laws of the South.

As circumstances pushed the Kennedy administration to be more actively involved with the issue of civil rights, once again the adult Western that best mirrored the Kennedy clan and their New Frontiers reread the mid-twentieth-century house divided as an Anglo-Saxon heaven, one in which white people preserved their earned privilege by demonstrating that they were all brothers under the skin. To put it another way, while Martin Luther King, among others, was making a call for universal brotherhood, *Bonanza* was promoting a much more xenophobic definition of the concept, one more consistent with the white utopia of Disneyland, especially in the park's first decade. In the world of *Bonanza*, the estate that exemplified the American Dream, materially, politically, and theologically, came to be in a territory virtually devoid of blacks that was aligned with neither slavery nor abolition.

In addition to being fundamentally WASP, this ideal American estate was profoundly patriarchal and exclusively male, a utopia with no lasting female presence. Women, in fact, always constituted a problematic disruption. Either they perpetrated corruption and deceit (which from the opening episode threatened not only patriarchal authority but also the very future of the Ponderosa) or—as with Ben's three wives—they were the source of longing, loss, and sorrow. Dortort explicitly affirmed the

show's intentional masculine preeminence. Yoggy accurately summarizes
Dortort's objectives:

> Dortort wanted to reinstate [the American father] as the head of the
> American household in his depiction of the patriarch of the Cartwright
> family. Ben Cartwright was not only a father his sons could respect, but a
> stern, though gentle, role model for fathers across the land. By
> strengthening the image of the father figure, *Bonanza* became a sort of
> virile, Westernized version of *Father Knows Best*. Even more than this,
> however, Dortort took pride in the fact that there were no moms in the
> show—nor for that matter any continuing woman characters whatsoever.[18]

Father Knows Best, however, had an assertive (albeit supportive), instrumental (albeit housebound) wife and two female siblings (nicknamed
"Princess" and "Kitten"). The sitcom that *Bonanza* more closely resembled,
My Three Sons, premiered a year later as an all-male version of *Father Knows
Best*. In the Douglas household of *My Three Sons*, as on the Ponderosa, a man
performed all the cooking and housework (at first the maternal-side grand-
father, "Bub," and subsequently the maternal-side uncle, Charlie). An explicit connection between this male version of the suburban American
Dream and *Bonanza*'s 1860s Western version appeared in the liner notes of a
hit album of songs and stories that Lorne Greene (the actor who played Ben
Cartwright) recorded in 1964. These notes took the form of a letter, dated
1860, from Ben Cartwright to:

> My Three Sons:
>   I trust, now that you are men, that these songs will be passed on by you
> to your children with the same fondness, pride and love as I now feel. For
> these are the songs and stories that tote up to the sum of riches, the
> greatest wealth possible—the remembrance of human experience. This
> memory is the champagne of the history of the American West, and all
> those years were vintage ones.
>   Long after we are all gone—maybe a hundred years from now—if we
> could return just once to re-hear these songs and stories, I am hopeful that
> they would be told in this form. And quite possibly some feller named
> LORNE GREENE, who looks like me, could re-tell and re-sing these things to
> three fellers who look like you.[19]

Once again the American estate established its citizenship by sharing
songs and stories that affirmed the common Western history claimed by

Bonanza's Ben Cartwright and his three sons. *Photofest.*

John Kennedy in facing down the Russians in Berlin. It was the ersatz heritage that his father, Joseph Kennedy, no doubt claimed for his three sons, just as it was the Western heritage passed on by "some feller named LORNE GREENE" to his twentieth-century contemporary, the fictional Steve Douglas, a man who lived with his three sons in the suburban male-dominated community for which the Ponderosa was the prophetic pioneer. As Kennedy made clear, the New Frontier rendered every American home an outpost, turned every American citizen into a pioneer, converted the entire nation into a vast Ponderosa, that is, an estate authorized by the history of expansion and the taming of the savage and the outlaw. Everywhere America, or at least white America, was part of Frontierland. In this way Disneyland anticipated what the interstate highway system, television, and JFK (and arguably Vietnam) confirmed.

If *My Three Sons* represented the twentieth-century sitcom cousin of *Bonanza*, another aspect of the New Frontier sensibility could be seen in an updating of the pre-property Westerns. Because these "lawman/restless gun" Westerns presented the American frontier before it was consolidated into a patriarchal estate, the entire West became the tableau for the countless acts of individual heroism that constituted the cumulative settling of the region. The updated adult Westerns, emphasizing the "new" of the New Frontier, transferred to the contemporary scene these narratives of the cowboy as knight errant. In a small number of Kennedy-era series, latter-day Paladins, Johnny Yumas, Bronco Laynes, and Cheyennes replaced in the public imagination the bulk of 1950s Westerns. While *Gunsmoke* and *Bonanza* remained extremely popular through the entire decade, the 1960s produced few successful new Westerns and no successful lawman/restless gun Westerns. A few contemporary series, however, reenacted on the American highways the adventures of the restless Western heroes. The first—and one of the most enduring in the American imagination—was *Route 66*.

The 1960 season introduced a prime-time show that represented the new decade—*Route 66* spoke to the restlessness of a younger generation. Searching for purpose as much as for adventure, the two lead characters crisscrossed the country in a Corvette convertible. The location shooting of *Route 66* resulted in an expansive production style with an emphasis on motion. The tone of the show was aptly labeled by one critic "purely new-American."[20]

The series, which ran from 1960 to 1964, featured two men, Buzz Murdock (George Maharis), who had grown up in the St. Francis Home for Foundlings in New York City, and Tod Stiles (Martin Milner), the son of an affluent father. When Todd's father died, he discovered that his entire inheritance consisted of a new (1960) Corvette. With nothing to lose, he and Buzz decided to ride around the country, working when and as necessary. In the first episode, Buzz explains how he knows Todd—"I had a job with

Todd's dad on a barger in the East River"—and what motivates the two of
them: "Now, Todd, he's looking too. He had it made—Yale, prep school,
and just like that his Dad drops dead. So I say, who needs New York. Only
the buildings got roots there, and they don't go too deep. Sure, we're looking. Todd says if we keep moving we'll find a place to plant roots and stick.
With me it's fine just moving."

Like the vast audience of mid- and late adolescents who had grown up
watching adult Westerns, they were struck with the frontier spirit, or that version of it that could turn itinerants on horseback into modern knights. They
were doing, perhaps, what Little Joe Cartwright would do if Ben suddenly
died, having left Joe nothing but a palomino. At the same time, Buzz and
Todd lacked the direction, both literally and figuratively, of those who rode
the Old West. In the nineteenth century, the direction was clear: "Go West,
young man." Wherever in the West they went, in other words, those settlers,
pioneers, cowboys, rangers, soldiers, and lawmen were forging the frontier,
doing what had to be done to settle the unruly margins of civilization.

For the restless young men of the New Frontier, however, the psychological impulse was no clearer than the geographical direction. Although they
had a strong kinship with the gunmen and their sidekicks, and they had,
like the nineteenth-century pioneers, a strong belief that America contained whatever they were looking for, they knew neither what it was nor
where. With the New Frontier speech as their implicit credo, and their
sponsor's jingle ("See the USA in your Chevrolet, America is asking you to
call") as their unofficial theme song,[21] Todd and Buzz seemed to recognize
that by the 1960–1961 television season, all of America—where one could
roam in any direction on the open highway—had become the West.

The disparity between the show's title and its actual locales underscored the universality of their frontier. Route 66—at the time one of the
longest noninterstate routes in America—ran south from Chicago, then
turned west and ended in southern California. The episodes of the show,
however, took place in areas such as Pittsburgh or Seattle or Philadelphia.
Uniquely for television, each episode of the show was shot on location.
Thus the cast, like its characters, was on the road most of the year. In the
first year of the series alone, they visited over thirty cities. Like Kennedy's
New Frontier, in other words, "Route 66" was a state of mind, one that
merged the ethos of the adult Western with the geography of America and
the destiny of the West. It was, in other words, the spirit of the Cold War,

that is, of black-and-white television and the interstate highway system, those two powerful instruments of homogeneity that reinvented national space so as to create a coherent yet timeless American frontier.

Lest we fail to see that *Route 66* was a New Frontier Western, the opening episode provides several broad hints. In that episode, "Black November" (October 7, 1960), Todd and Buzz have made a wrong turn off Route 66, somewhere in the Deep South. Following side roads, they find the town of Garth, which has fallen outside of time. It has absolutely no contact with the outside world—no signs of even one antenna at time when over 90 percent of all American households have televisions—and it resembles architecturally a small town in a TV Western, complete with a general store and a mechanic/blacksmith. The empty, unpaved streets, the old wooden buildings, and the rustic surroundings give it the atmosphere of a Western ghost town. When people do appear, they range from suspicious to overtly hostile, even threatening Todd and Buzz with guns.

The town, Todd and Buzz learn from the one friendly person—the daughter of the owner of the general store—doesn't have a sheriff. The tyrannical Mr. Garth, whom everyone seems both to obey and to fear and who runs the town, discourages strangers, and the mechanic warns Todd and Buzz to "go away while [you're] still ahead." Unfortunately, because the axle of their Corvette has been damaged, they cannot get out of town before sundown. They have to stay there, in fact, until the blacksmith can make—that's right, *make*—a new part for their car.

If it weren't already evident that the town is hiding a dark secret, the arrival of Garth's somewhat crazed son makes this clear. At the edge of town, near the stockade that detained German prisoners of war during World War II, Todd sees Garth's son putting flowers on two graves while talking to the ground and crying: "I know it's cold down there. I know because the sun can't reach you." "Then he looked up at the tree and cursed it," Todd explains. "'How can the sun reach you,' he said, 'with that standing over you.' I never heard anything like it; it gave me the shivers."

The secret that Garth is trying to hide by isolating the town, the secret that is destroying his son with guilt and shame, is that during World War II, when Garth learned that his oldest son had been killed in Europe, he led a mob that murdered one of the German prisoners and, as well, the town minister who tried to defend him. This plot twist is simultaneously clichéd and peculiar. The lynching of a prisoner whose clan had killed the son of a town patriarch was the basis for numerous Westerns, as was the preventing or uncovering or revenging of a lynch party. In typical fashion, our saddle-tramp heroes wandered into a secretive one-horse town where the citizens acted peculiar. The heroes were warned to get out of town, but they couldn't until their horses could rest or the town smithy could re-shoe them, or repair the bridle, or whatever. In the course of their unin-tentionally prolonged stay, they befriended, even romanced, the sweet girl at the general store, stood up to the town roughs, and helped the downtrodden, spineless son develop enough backbone to expose his cor-rupt father, thereby freeing the town of its oppression.

Clearly "Black November" was a thinly veiled Western. It was very close, in fact, to the excellent 1954 contemporary Western film, *Bad Day in Black Rock*, starring Spencer Tracy, in which a World War II veteran uncovered in a small Western town the wartime murder of a Japanese American. Even the episode's title echoed the film's title by tying the word "black" to a calendar unit. But the episode of *Route 66* is not set, as one might expect, in the West. Instead, it takes place in the Deep South, where a lynching motif has signif-icantly different associations. If a Southern town were hiding a secret con-nected with lynching, the odds would be much stronger that an Aryan would be the perpetrator than the victim. Once again, however (à la Johnny Yuma), this New Frontier Western announces its connection with the adult Westerns by erasing from Western history the presence of blacks, and eras-ing from American history the injury done to them. The "black" of "Black November" thus stands not for a black person but for the injury done to a white person. In this Southern town, seen in the context of a New Frontier Western, the German is the victim of the lynching.

An even more sustained substitution of white for black can be found in the most successful of the New Frontier Westerns, *The Fugitive*. In the se-ries, Richard Kimble (David Janssen), wrongly convicted of murdering his wife and sentenced to death, fortuitously escapes because of a train derail-ment on his way to death row. Changing his identity constantly, he roams the country, hiding from the law and also searching for the one-armed man who might have actually committed the crime. The conditions that frame the series seem strikingly to replicate for the fugitive Richard Kimble the conditions endemic to being a fugitive slave. Living outside due process, as the uncontestable property of the state, his humanity, his very right to life, was by definition tenuous and situational. He lived, not only in the eyes of the law but also in the eyes of the citizenry, under the presumption of guilt. Because, like the fugitive slave, Kimble had no legal recourse and had to be voiceless in his own defense, as the episodes developed, he constantly effected conflict between local action and federal enforcement, between individual citizens and the arm of the law. Unlike the fugitive slave, however, he could, in the tradition of the "good outlaw" or the decent gunman, enlist assistance through his good deeds. He was able to employ his prowess—as a doctor and as a tough man—to gain local support and evoke gratitude.

In the opening episode, for example, he aids a woman who is being abused by her estranged husband. Kimble, here known as Jim Lincoln, is working as a bartender in Tucson, Arizona, at a saloon called the Branding Iron. (As with the premiere episode of *Route 66*, the setting strongly alludes to the Western.) When Kimble found a man physically abusing Monica, the saloon's piano player, Kimble knocked him down with one punch. The contemporary equivalent of a cattle baron, the man, Ed Welles, owns 250,000 acres of land (an estate about one-third as large as the Ponderosa) and is a powerful and influential member of the community. When Kimble goes home, Ed threatens him, showing Kimble his custom-made six-gun and warning him, "Get out of my sight!" Kimble and Monica, nevertheless, begin seeing one another, so Ed contacts local detectives to run Kimble out of town. When they tell the fugitive to "leave Tucson tonight," Monica decides to run away with him, and they head for the bus station. Before the bus (or stagecoach?) can leave, Ed catches up with them and attempts to gun Kimble down. Fortunately, the hero is saved when a bus-station lawman shoots Ed first. Kimble, of course, has to flee the scene of this shoot-out before he is apprehended by the law.

Like many heroes of adult Westerns, Kimble was a good Samaritan in disguise, an outlaw with not only skills but also values superior to those of the general population. In order to help tame an unruly society, however, he had to operate on the margins of the law. This motif, of course, was central to the Western, for the Western hero needed to supplement the law. He had to be able to triumph in those places where the law was not yet fully established. This was equally true for Paladin, the hired gun of *Have Gun, Will Travel*; bounty hunter Josh Randall of *Wanted Dead or Alive*; and Matt Dillon, the marshal of Dodge City (who was not afraid to draw first or to shoot a man in the back, if necessary).

In this regard, Kimble's marginal status, his constant wandering, and his need to act outside the law to achieve justice all identified him as heir to the heroes of many adult Westerns. This association was underscored, especially in many of the early episodes. Consider how much this description

Richard Kimble in one of the many episodes of the *Fugitive* that evoke aspects of an adult western. *Photofest*.

of the initial events in episode 3, by *The Fugitive* chronicler Bill Deane, makes it almost indistinguishable from a Western:

> Kimble is dropped off in a West Virginia hamlet, which has become something of a ghost town since the coal mines stopped producing. He stops for a beer and soon finds himself surrounded by locals who have no

use for strangers in their town. They harass and rough up Kimble, touching off a playful barroom brawl. Deputy Marlin enters, seeking to restore order and vowing to lock up whoever started the melee; the locals indicate that Kimble started it. Kimble tries to escape, winding up in a fistfight with the deputy. Kimble gets the better of the lawman and is about to leave when he is clubbed from behind by Sheriff Bradley. The unconscious stranger's effects are checked turning up no identification. While the sheriff contemplates this over a beer, Kimble regains consciousness and slips away.[22]

In episode 16, Kimble is a ranch hand who saves the owner's life when she is almost thrown by a bucking bronco. Subsequently, he is enlisted by her husband to teach her to ride a horse and shoot a gun "like the ranch-girl she was brought up to be."[23] And in a two-part episode (episodes 22 and 23), Kimble, fleeing the law, helps a nun get through Nevada's desert mountains to Sacramento. Not only the setting but the events echo a Western, especially the point at which Kimble gets into a fight over a poker hand, which includes the Western clichés of the overturned poker table, the fistfight, and the drawn gun.

Like the Western hero, moreover, Kimble must always live up to or live down his reputation. In numerous episodes Kimble, identified as the outlaw, implicitly proved his innocence by performing some good deed or heroic act, such as rescuing children from a burning bus, performing an emergency caesarian delivery, saving an injured dog, and even, once, saving the life of his relentless antagonist, Lieutenant Gerard.

It was necessary for Kimble to prove himself through his deeds because, circumscribed by the plot mechanism, for Kimble, like the fugitive slave under the court rulings of the 1840s and 1850s, personal-liberty laws did not apply. Kimble's chief distinction in this regard, however, was that he was white and hence able to disappear in the public space, while remaining, nevertheless, prominent within our privileged televisual gaze, exploiting the celebrity that came with being framed. He lacked both the public visibility and the social invisibility of the black. He became, in other words, the inverse of the black American in that he was able to travel unobtrusively through the public (i.e., televisual) space while still being central to its narrative. The *motions* of this inverse fugitive slave, moreover, replaced images of a civil rights *movement* and the *march* on Washington with the fictional movements of a man manifesting the migratory status of a fugitive slave, expunged of its racial threat. For the Richard Kimble of that show, public spaces provided safety, not danger, escape, not entrapment. His local experience reiterated the theme that America was a place of opportunity, not a community under siege and in need of police protection.

The America of the open road available to the middle-class white men infected with Kennedy adventurism was the America represented by *Route 66* and *The Fugitive*. Replacing all but a handful of the more than forty Western series that dominated prime time from 1956 to 1961 with this story of a latter-day outlaw roaming the countryside, Richard Kimble became the Lone Ranger of the New Frontier. There were of course many differences between the two characters, the most significant of which was that the Lone Ranger chose his outsider status. Nevertheless, like Richard Kimble's wanted poster, the Lone Ranger's mask—the sign of the outlaw—marked him with the presumption of guilt, which, like Kimble, he repeatedly had to dispel through his deeds. As in the tradition of numerous Westerns, Kimble thus became the knight errant in the guise of the dark stranger. (Both the benevolent outlaw Western and its latter-day incarnation as the open-road picture would, of course, shortly after the TV fugitive's vindication, collide irrevocably with their own suppressed violence in the films *The Wild Bunch* and *Easy Rider*.)

Conversion from black-and-white to color marked *The Fugitive*'s final season. The final episode was not broadcast until August 1967, after the rerun season had concluded. It became at the time the single most watched show in the history of television, garnering nearly three-quarters of the nation's television viewers. During that summer, *The Fugitive* reruns shared television space with rampant reportage of urban riots, of tanks in the streets of Detroit and National Guardsmen policing Newark, New Jersey. Invoking another historical way to frame Richard Kimble, we could say that the series spanned the time between Martin Luther King's culmination of the nonviolent phase of the civil rights movement and the rise to national prominence of the Black Panther Party. In this regard, the narratives of the black-and-white television series, of course, were possible exactly because they never tried to account for black America or the possibility that a black Richard Kimble would find the roads to escape somewhat less congenial to hitchhikers.

Conclusion

When we take into account the fact that the average baby boomer, by age sixteen, had watched between twelve thousand and fifteen thousand hours of television,[1] it is hard to overestimate the medium's influence on the second half of the twentieth century. This is especially the case when we realize that they were watching a relatively small selection of images, most of which adhered to a strict broadcast code that precluded a vast array of attitudes and issues. This official code was augmented by several other equally strict, albeit unofficial, practices that included banning blacks and blacklisting as well as myriad forms of collusion with the federal government and many concessions to Southern governance so as to create the impression of a normally white nation engaged in a Cold War where the issues were black-and-white.

Cold War television gave us a nation, in other words, with the same ethos as Disneyland, a place marred on its first day of construction by a color problem: In the Anaheim orange grove that was to become the park, the trees were marked by red and green ribbons to indicate which should be cleared and which should be saved, but on groundbreaking day the color-blind bulldozer operator mowed them all down. In a small way, this detail ironically echoes the general invisibility of color in television's representation of America, and in Disney's. In his indiscriminate leveling, the color-blind construction worker was also ironically emulating the action of the interstate highway system that would bulldoze its way through the communities where people of color resided.

Today, thanks to that color-blind bulldozing, the actual Route 66, like its television series namesake, no longer exists. Its role has been usurped by interstate highways and other forms of controlled-access roads. Television, the medium that made it famous, has also disappeared—television, that is, as a free, broadcast medium, television as an American pastime, television as the community of common images that provided the nation with visual coherence, television as the focus of national attention. Like Route 66, these manifestations have disappeared, leaving only their traces in myth and memory.

While the broadcast media are heavily concentrated, the number of viewing options is not. Instead of a nation monopolized by a small number of television signals, we have a nation individuated by a plethora of monitors. At any given time, on some of those monitors a (relatively small) percentage of viewers watch a hit network show. (In the weeks of 1956, when *The Nat King Cole Show* attracted 10 percent to 12 percent of the potential viewing audience, it was never among the top one hundred shows;[2] the same ratings today would keep it safely in the top ten shows in the country.) At the same time, groups of other viewers—each an extremely small portion of the total population—watch cable shows about animals or deserts, home improvement or history, food or sports, to name just a few of the options. Other viewers, simultaneously, are using their monitors to watch a film or sports event on a premium channel, while yet other groups use them to look at DVDs or play computer games or edit their own digital images. Some viewers are using those monitors to send e-mail or surf the Web.

Instead of a national audience, we have a nation of fragments. Those fragments, moreover, are segmented not only by their tastes and desires but by their affluence, by the kinds of monitors they can purchase and the services they can afford to access on them. While it would be folly to underestimate the effect of the multifarious media on the future of a fragmented nation, it seems doubtless that it will not play the same kind of powerful, formative, and unifying role that television played in defining public space and setting national norms from the late 1940s through the mid-1960s, and to some degree in disrupting them through the 1970s.

It would take another, very different book to examine how and why television programming changed in the color era, why in the 1975–1976 season there was not a single Western on prime-time network television, why by the mid-1970s dramas of any sort had virtually disappeared from the top twenty television shows. Certainly in the color era, black faces started showing up with some frequency and prominence. And certainly today, if you are among the relatively small number of people watching a show on one of the major networks, you cannot help but notice how much black Americans have achieved: They have become lawyers, judges, police lieutenants . . . on television.

At the same time, over 50 percent of America's prison inmates are black. And, as has now become a well-documented fact, blacks moving through the public space by driving on interstate highways are subjected to inordinate persecution. U.S. customs officials have been nine times more likely to frisk or x-ray black women travelers than white women travelers, despite the fact that black women were found with contraband *half* as frequently as white women.[3]

Katheryn Russell succinctly explains, "Policies which allow enforcement officers to use Blackness as an indicator of criminality (in the absence of empirical support), have the effect of *creating* Black criminality. This is particularly problematic at the pre-arrest stage. When racialized practices occur at the pre-arrest stage, they significantly increase the probability that Blacks will enter the criminal justice system."[4] The disproportionately high number of blacks who enter the system thus seems to confirm the idea that black populations are more heavily criminal despite evidence to the contrary. This makes the practices of law officers patrolling the roadways all the more problematic. Much evidence has confirmed that "driving while black" on an interstate highway makes one a target for the police.

While it would be absurd to blame this kind of behavior on Cold War television, it seems clear that it was a powerful instrument in perpetuating the racialization of space that has scarred American society for nearly four centuries. As Sandra Bass argues,

> For a better part of our history, race has been a central determinant in
> how public spaces were constructed and in the regulation of behavior in
> public spaces. Federal, state, and local governments as well as private
> actors engaged in a range of discriminatory practices in order to create
> and then preserve racial discrimination and segregation. . . . Segregation
> was a central tool for keeping African-Americans in their "place"
> whether that be defined as a specific part of the city or a lower status in
> society at large.
>
> Race and space have been important factors in social and public policy
> and thus they have also had a significant impact on the development of
> policing in America. Race as a means of defining space and regulating
> behavior in public spaces and thus, as an organizing element in police
> work, reaches back to the earliest days of policing.[5]

We have seen the significant ways in which Cold War television, especially in the black-and-white era, not only helped legitimize racial segregation but also helped motivate the force invoked to maintain it. Although a white America does not exist and never did, some imaginary America, associated with highways and suburbia, with public space and domestic security, with the idea of the West, remains cogent for a significant portion of the American population.

NOTES

Chapter One. Black Bodies, White Space, and a Televisual Nation

1. Cornel West, *Race Matters* (Boston: Beacon Press, 1993), p. x.

2. The best work on the case is James Goodman, *The Stories of Scottsboro* (New York: Vintage, 1994).

3. Gilbert Osofsky, *The Burden of Race: A Documentary History of Negro-White Relations in America* (New York: Harper and Row, 1967), p. 310.

4. Paul Finkleman, *An Imperfect Union: Slavery, Federalism, and Comity* (Chapel Hill: University of North Carolina Press, 1981), p. 146 (footnote).

5. Richard Bardolph, *The Civil Rights Record: Black Americans and the Law, 1849–1970* (New York: Thomas Y. Crowell, 1970), p. 6.

6. E. Franklin Frazier, *The Negro in the United States* (New York: Macmillan, 1957), p. 160.

7. Toni Morrison, *Playing in the Dark: Whiteness and the Literary Imagination* (Cambridge, Mass.: Harvard University Press, 1992), p. 52.

8. Richard Dyer, *White* (London: Routledge, 1997). See also Theodore Allen, *The Invention of the White Race* (London: Verso, 1994); Ruth Frankenberg, *White Women, Race Matters: The Social Construction of Whiteness* (Minneapolis: University of Minnesota Press, 1993); Thomas Gossett, *Race: The History of an Idea in America* (New York: Schocken, 1995).

9. Cheryl Harris, "Whiteness as Property," *Harvard Law Review* 106, no. 8 (June 1993), p. 1724.

10. Dyer, *White*, p. 57.

11. Roland Barthes, *Mythologies*, Annette Lavers, trans. (London: Hill and Wang, 1972), p. 11.

12. See Catherine Lutz and Jane Collins, *Reading National Geographic* (Chicago: University of Chicago Press, 1993).

13. Henry Louis Gates, *Colored People: A Memoir* (New York: Knopf, 1994), p. 20.

14. Ibid., p. 20.

15. Donald Bogle, *Primetime Blues: African Americans on Network Television* (New York: Farrar, Straus and Giroux, 2001), p. 58.

16. Quoted in J. Fred MacDonald, *Blacks and White TV: Afro-Americans in Television since 1948* (Chicago: Nelson-Hall, 1983), p. 78.

17. Winthrop D. Jordan, *White over Black: American Attitudes toward the Negro, 1550–1812* (Chapel Hill: University of North Carolina Press, 1968), p. 97.

18. Ibid., p. 123.

19. John Hope Franklin and Alfred A. Moss, Jr., *From Slavery to Freedom: A History of African Americans*, 7th ed. (New York: Alfred A. Knopf, 1994), p. 154.

20. See Robert Cruden, *The Negro in Reconstruction* (Englewood Cliffs, N.J.: Prentice Hall, 1969). Consider, for example, the *Laws of Mississippi* (1865), which required every freedman to have written evidence of "lawful home or employment" and a written contract for all labor over one month performed by freedmen, free Negroes, or mulattos. It further held that "if the laborer shall quit the service of the employer, before

expiration of his term, without good cause, he shall forfeit his wages for that year, up to the time of quitting." In addition, civil officers were instructed to "arrest and carry back to his or her legal employer" a freedman who quit before the expiration of his term of service (Bardolph, *The Civil Rights Record*, p. 38).

21. Alan Nadel, *Invisible Criticism: Ralph Ellison and the American Canon* (Iowa City: University of Iowa Press, 1988).

22. Douglas S. Massey and Nancy Denton, *American Apartheid: Segregation and the Making of the Underclass* (Cambridge, Mass.: Harvard University Press, 1993), p. 9.

23. Ibid., p. 19.

24. Ibid., p. 35.

25. Ibid., p. 51.

26. Tom Lewis, *Divided Highways: Building the Interstate Highways, Transforming American Life* (New York: Penguin, 1999), p. 79.

27. Franklin and Moss, *From Slavery to Freedom*, p. 453.

Chapter Two. Television, Reality, and Cold War Citizenship

1. Eric Barnouw, *The Golden Web: A History of Broadcasting in the United States, Volume II—1933–1953* (New York: Oxford University Press, 1968), p. 126.

2. Winthrop Jordan, *White over Black: American Attitudes toward the Negro, 1550–1812* (Chapel Hill: University of North Carolina Press, 1968), has documented extensively how replete with that notion all the inventions of America, from colonization onward, have been. See also George Fredrickson, *The Black Image in the White Mind* (New York: Harper and Row, 1971).

3. Nina Leibman, *Living Room Lectures: The Fifties Family in Film and Television* (Austin: University of Texas Press, 1995).

4. Lynn Spigel, "Television in the Family Circle: The Popular Reception of a New Medium," in Patricia Mellencamp, ed., *Logics of Television: Essays in Cultural Criticism* (Bloomington: Indiana University Press, 1990), p. 76.

5. Lynn Spigel, *Make Room for Television: Television and the Family Ideal in Postwar America* (Chicago: University of Chicago Press, 1992), p. 37.

6. Quoted in Paul Carter, *Another Part of the Fifties* (New York: Columbia University Press, 1983), p. 115.

7. Quoted in Douglas T. Miller and Marion Nowak, *The Fifties: The Way We Really Were* (New York: Doubleday, 1977), p. 91.

8. Thomas Doherty, *Cold War, Cool Medium: Television, McCarthyism, and American Culture* (New York: Columbia University Press, 2003), p. 158.

9. William Boddy, *Fifties Television: The Industry and Its Critics* (Urbana: University of Illinois Press, 1990), p. 17.

10. Bruce Owen, Jack Beebe, and Willard Manning, *Television Economics* (Lexington, Mass: D. C. Heath, 1974), p. 12.

11. William F. Baker and George Dessart, *Down the Tube: An Inside Account of the Failure of American Television* (New York: Basic Books, 1998), p. 69.

12. Quoted in J. Fred MacDonald, *One Nation under Television: The Rise and Decline of Network TV* (New York: Pantheon, 1990), p. 51.

13. Nancy Bernhard, *U.S. Television News and Cold War Propaganda, 1947–1960* (Cambridge: Cambridge University Press, 1999), p. 13.

14. Ibid., p. 47.

15. Ibid., p. 48.

16. Ibid., p. 136.

17. Ibid.

18. Harry Castleman and Walter Podrazik, *Watching TV: Four Decades of American Television* (New York: McGraw-Hill, 1982), p. 53.

19. H. G. Christensen, "Long Shots and Close-Ups," *Television: The Magazine of Video Fact* 3, no. 2 (February 1946), p. 29.

20. Ibid.

21. Maurice Gorham, *Television: Medium of the Future* (London: Percival Marshall, 1949), p. 130.

22. Orin E. Dunlap, Jr., *The Future of Television* (New York: Harper and Bros., 1942), p. 165.

23. Gilbert Seldes, "The Future of Television," *Atlantic* 3 (1949), p. 36.

24. *Time*, May 24, 1948, p. 72.

25. Ibid., p. 73.

26. James Caddigan, "Station Operations: Setting Up a Special Events Department," *Television: The Magazine of Video Fact* 2, no. 10 (December 1945), p. 12.

27. Castleman and Podrazik, *Watching TV*, p. 19.

28. Ibid., p. 33.

29. See Alan Nadel, *Containment Culture: American Narratives, Postmodernism, and the Atomic Age* (Durham, N.C.: Duke University Press, 1995); Tom Englehardt, *The End of Victory Culture: Cold War America and the Disillusioning of a Generation* (New York: Basic Books, 1995); Elaine Tyler May, *Homeward Bound: American Families in the Cold War Era* (New York: Basic Books, 1988); Lary May, ed., *Recasting America: Culture and Politics in the Age of Cold War* (Chicago: University of Chicago Press, 1989); Ellen Schrecker, *Many Are the Crimes: McCarthyism in America* (Boston:

Little, Brown, 1998); Stephen J. Whitfield, *The Culture of the Cold War* (Baltimore: Johns Hopkins University Press, 1991).

30. See Ellen Schrecker, *No Ivory Tower: McCarthyism and the Universities* (New York: Oxford University Press, 1986).

31. Jeanne Allen, "The Social Matrix of Television: Invention in the United States," in E. Ann Kaplan, ed., *Regarding Television: Critical Approaches—An Anthology* (Los Angeles: American Film Institute, 1983), p. 112.

32. Caddigan, "Station Operations," p. 13.

33. Ibid.

34. J. Fred MacDonald, *Television and the Red Menace: The Video Road to Vietnam* (New York: Praeger, 1985).

35. Ibid., p. 126.

36. Ibid., p. 124.

37. Ibid., p. 122.

38. Only in the mid-1950s were these shows on network television.

39. MacDonald, *Television and the Red Menace*, p. 117.

40. David Marc, *Demographic Vistas: Television in American Culture* (Philadelphia: University of Pennsylvania Press, 1984), p. 5.

41. J. Fred MacDonald, *Blacks and White TV: Afro-Americans in Television since 1948* (Chicago: Nelson-Hall, 1983), p. 59.

42. "The Television Code of the National Association of Radio and Television Broadcasters," in William Y. Elliott, ed., *Television's Impact on American Culture* (East Lansing: Michigan State University Press, 1956), p. 328.

43. Ibid.

44. Ibid., p. 329.

45. Dunlap, *The Future of Television*, p. 15.

46. Ibid., p. 16.

47. "The Television Code," p. 329.

48. Ibid., pp. 330–331.

49. Ibid., p. 334.

50. George Kennan, "The Sources of Soviet Conduct," *Foreign Affairs* 25 (1947), pp. 566–582.

51. Quoted in Spigel, "Television in the Family Circle," p. 81.

52. Castleman and Podrazik, *Watching TV*, p. 53.

53. Doherty, *Cold War, Cool Medium*, p. 31.

54. Castleman and Podrazik, *Watching TV*, p. 53.

55. Doherty, *Cold War, Cool Medium*, p. 25.

56. Ellen Schrecker, *The Age of McCarthyism: A Brief History with Documents* (Boston: Bedford Books, 1994), p. 224.

57. Ibid., p. 154.

58. Quoted in Eric Barnouw, *A Tube of Plenty: The Evolution of American Television*, 2d rev. ed. (New York: Oxford University Press, 1990), p. 207.

59. MacDonald, *Blacks and White TV*, p. 64.

60. See Boddy, *Fifties Television*, p. 201; Erik Barnouw, *The Television Writer* (New York: Hill and Wang, 1962), p. 28.

61. Harold A. Carlborg, "Billion Dollar Whipping Boy," *Television Age*, November 4, 1957, p. 90.

62. Castleman and Podrazik, *Watching TV*, p. 78.

63. Henry Clay Gipson, "Educational Films and Television," *Television: The Magazine of Video Fact* 2, no. 4 (May 1945), pp. 13–14.

64. David Marc, "Beginning to Begin Again," in Horace Newcomb, ed., *Television: The Critical View*, 4th ed. (New York: Oxford University Press, 1987), p. 329.

65. James Monaco, "The TV Plexus," in Carl Lowe, ed., *Television and American Culture* (New York: H. W. Wilson, 1981), p. 24.

66. Mary Gannon, "*Mademoiselle* Tries Out Television," *Television: The Magazine of Video Fact* 2, no. 8 (October 1945), p. 11.

67. Leibman, *Living Room Lectures*, p. 111.

68. Boddy, *Fifties Television*, p. 196.

69. Lee De Forest, *Television Today and Tomorrow* (New York: Dial Press, 1942), p. 349–350.

70. Quoted in MacDonald, *One Nation under Television*, p. 54. It is worth noting the ways in which Weaver anticipated claims about the World Wide Web.

Chapter Three. Disneyland, the Interstate, and National Space

1. William Boddy, *Fifties Television: The Industry and Its Critics* (Urbana: University of Illinois Press, 1990): "The demise of the DuMont television network was due principally to the allocation and assignment policies of the FCC in its *Sixth Report and Order*, which simply did not permit national competition of four major networks. . . . As [broadcast economist Stuart] Long argued, 'This decision in effect sacrificed the DuMont network in order that at least ABC might survive and prosper to offset the obvious dominance which NBC and CBS had gained in the industry during the freeze years'" (p. 56).

2. Ibid., p. 146.

3. "Disney in TVland," *TV Guide*, January 23, 1954, p. 5.

4. Ibid.

5. "Love That Television," *TV Guide*, August 13, 1955, pp. 4–5.

6. Leo Bogart, *The Age of Television: A Study of Viewing Habits and the Impact of*

Television on American Life (New York: Frederick Ungar, 1956), p. 15.

7. Steven Watts, *The Magic Kingdom: Walt Disney and the American Way of Life* (Boston: Houghton Mifflin, 1997), pp. 366–367.

8. Karal Ann Marling, *As Seen on TV: The Visual Culture of Everyday Life in the 1950s* (Cambridge, Mass.: Harvard University Press, 1994), pp. 80–81.

9. Quoted in Robert De Roos, "The Magic Worlds of Walt Disney," in Eric Smoodin, ed., *Disney Discourse: Producing the Magic Kingdom* (New York: Routledge, 1994), p. 56.

10. Ibid.

11. Ibid., p. 54.

12. Walter Lowe, "Hollywood Follows Disney into TV," *New York Herald Tribune*, June 5, 1955, p. 25.

13. Karal Ann Marling, "Imagineering the Disney Theme Parks," in Karal Ann Marling, ed., *Designing Disney's Theme Parks: The Architecture of Reassurance* (Montreal: Canadian Centre for Architecture; Paris and New York: Flammarion, 1997), p. 35.

14. Mark H. Rose, *Interstate: Express Highway Politics, 1941–1956* (Lawrence: Regents Press of Kansas, 1979), p. 1.

15. Marling, "Imagineering the Disney Theme Parks," p. 35.

16. Judith Adams, *The American Amusement Park Industry: A History of Technology and Thrills* (Boston: Twayne, 1991), p. 10.

17. Ibid., p. 55.

18. Neil Harris, "Expository Expositions: Preparing for the Theme Parks," in Marling, ed., *Designing Disney's Theme Parks*, p. 27.

19. A. Q. Mowbray, *The Road to Ruin* (New York: J. B. Lippincott, 1969), p. 18.

20. Adams, *The American Amusement Park Industry*, p. 94.

21. Watts, *The Magic Kingdom*, p. 394.

22. Marling, "Imagineering the Disney Theme Parks," p. 31.

23. John M. Findlay, *Magic Lands: Western Cityscapes and American Culture after 1940* (Berkeley: University of California Press, 1992), p. 71.

24. George Lipsitz, "The Making of Disneyland," in William Graebner, ed., *True Stories of the American Past* (New York: McGraw-Hill, 1993), p. 190.

25. Watts, *The Magic Kingdom*, p. 358. See pp. 363–371 for a concise chronicle of Disney's entrance into television.

26. Ibid., p. 327.

27. Quoted in ibid., p. 367.

28. Richard V. Francaviglia, "Main Street USA: A Comparison/Contrast of Streetscapes in Disneyland and Disney World," *Journal of Popular Culture* 15, no. 1 (Summer 1981), pp. 148–149.

29. Findlay, *Magic Lands*, p. 68.

30. Ibid.

31. Francaviglia, "Main Street USA," p. 147.

32. Marling, *As Seen on TV*, pp. 92–93.

33. Ibid., p. 93.

34. Ibid.

35. Lipsitz, "The Making of Disneyland," p. 189.

36. Findlay, *Magic Lands*, p. 69.

37. Marling, "Imagineering the Disney Theme Parks," pp. 74, 75.

38. Findlay, *Magic Lands*, p. 69.

39. Arthur Gordon, "Walt Disney," *Look*, July 26, 1955, p. 29.

40. Findlay, *Magic Lands*, p. 67.

41. Ibid., p. 320.

42. Adams, *The American Amusement Park Industry*, p. 96.

43. Findlay, *Magic Lands*, p. 78.

44. Watts, *The Magic Kingdom*, p. 396.

45. Quoted in Adams, *The American Amusement Park Industry*, p. 97.

46. Findlay, *Magic Lands*, p. 318.

47. Marling, *As Seen on TV*, p. 286.

48. Quoted in ibid., p. 125.

49. Quoted in Richard Schickel, *The Disney Version: The Life, Times, Commerce, and Art of Walt Disney* (New York: Simon and Schuster, 1968), p. 263.

50. Paul Goldberger, "Mickey Mouse Teaches the Architects," *New York Times Magazine*, October 22, 1972, p. 20.

51. Findlay, *Magic Lands*, p. 69.

52. Quoted in ibid., p. 70.

53. Watts, *The Magic Kingdom*: "[Disney] offered the [FBI] 'complete access to the facilities of Disneyland for use in connection with official matters and for recreational purposes.' For its own part, the FBI approved Disney as a 'SAC contact,' a largely honorary designation given to friendly community members who were willing to talk with the agency's special agent in charge for their region" (p. 349). "We also know," Eric Smoodin pointed out, "the FBI remained at least somewhat suspicious of Disney until his death." See Smoodin, *Animating Culture: Hollywood Cartoons from the Sound Era* (New Brunswick, N.J.: Rutgers University Press, 1993), p. 5.

54. Watts, *The Magic Kingdom*, p. 284.

55. Schickel, *The Disney Version*, p. 14.

56. Findlay, *Magic Lands*, p. 77.

57. Francaviglia, "Main Street USA," p. 148.

58. Adams, *The American Amusement Park Industry*, p. 97.

59. Findlay, *Magic Lands*, p. 70.

60. Watts, *The Magic Kingdom*, p. xvi.

61. Findlay, *Magic Lands*, p. 10.

62. Marling, *As Seen on TV*, p. 123.

63. Goldberger, "Mickey Mouse Teaches the Architects," p. 19.

64. Lipsitz, "The Making of Disneyland," p. 189.

65. Findlay, *Magic Lands*, pp. 54–55.

66. Lipsitz, "The Making of Disneyland," p. 316.

67. Findlay, *Magic Lands*, p. 20.

68. Ibid., p. 51.

69. Watts, *The Magic Kingdom*, p. 288.

70. William Graebner, ed., *True Stories of the American Past* (New York: McGraw-Hill, 1993), p. 180.

71. George Kennan, "The Sources of Soviet Conduct," *Foreign Affairs* 25 (1947), pp. 566–582.

72. Many people have written about the role and influence of Kennan's essay; *Strategies of Containment* by John Gaddis remains one of the most useful guides to the myriad forms the policy of containment has assumed, and it has an extensive bibliography. In my book *Containment Culture: American Narratives, Postmodernism, and the Atomic Age* (Durham, N.C.: Duke University Press, 1995), I engage at length the cultural implications of the policy; Stephen J. Whitfield, *The Culture of the Cold War* (Baltimore: Johns Hopkins University Press, 1991), provides a quick review of some of the cultural forms that containment took. See also Elaine Tyler May, *Homeward Bound: American Families in the Cold War Era* (New York: Basic Books, 1988); Tom Englehardt, *The End of Victory Culture: Cold War America and the Disillusioning of a Generation* (New York: Basic Books, 1995); Lary May, ed., *Recasting America: Culture and Politics in the Age of Cold War* (Chicago: University of Chicago Press, 1989).

73. Findlay, *Magic Lands*, p. 55.

74. Watts, *The Magic Kingdom*, p. 305.

75. Ibid., p. 307.

76. Ibid., p. 305.

77. Findlay, *Magic Lands*, p. 21.

78. Ibid., p. 27.

79. Ibid., pp. 53–54.

80. Mowbray, *The Road to Ruin*, pp. 177–183.

81. Thomas J. Sugrue, *The Origins of the Urban Crisis: Race and Inequality in Postwar Detroit* (Princeton, N.J.: Princeton University Press, 1996), p. 47.

82. Ibid.

83. Stephen B. Goddard, *Getting There: The Epic Struggle between Road and Rail in the American Century* (Chicago: University of Chicago Press, 1994), p. 194.

84. Ibid., p. 200.

85. Douglas S. Massey and Nancy Denton, *American Apartheid: Segregation and the Making of the Underclass* (Cambridge, Mass.: Harvard University Press, 1993), pp. 53–54.

86. Lipsitz, "The Making of Disneyland," p. 191.

87. Findlay, *Magic Lands*, p. 74.

88. Schickel, *The Disney Version*, pp. 318–319.

89. Lynn Spigel, *Make Room for Television: Television and the Family Ideal in Postwar America* (Chicago: University of Chicago Press, 1992), p. 110.

90. Ibid., pp. 111, 112.

91. Ibid., p. 38. Cecilia Tichi, *Electronic Hearth: Creating an American Television Culture* (New York: Oxford University Press, 1991), discusses at length the ways in which the early television was imagined as a hearth.

92. Lipsitz, "The Making of Disneyland," p. 190.

93. Ibid., p. 189.

94. Watts, *The Magic Kingdom*, pp. 316–317.

95. Marling, *As Seen on TV*, p. 124.

96. "Fess Parker: King of the Wild Frontier," *TV Guide*, April 30, 1955, p. 6.

97. "Love That Television," pp. 4–5.

98. Watts, *The Magic Kingdom*, p. 315.

99. Ibid., p. 314; see also Paul F. Anderson, *The Davy Crockett Craze: A Look at the 1950s* (Hillside, Ill.: R and G Productions, 1996).

100. Raymond Williams, *Television: Technology and Cultural Form* (Hanover, N.H.: Wesleyan University Press, 1992), pp. 72–112.

101. See Jack Zipes, "Breaking the Disney Spell," in Elizabeth Bell, Lynda Haas, and Laura Sells, eds., *From Mouse to Mermaid: The Politics of Film, Gender, and Culture* (Bloomington: Indiana University Press, 1995), pp. 21–42.

102. Watts, *The Magic Kingdom*, p. 317.

103. "Old Horse Operas Never Die: They Just Go On Making Hay," *TV Guide*, January 15, 1954, pp. 20–21.

104. Rogers and Autry built on their exceptional movie popularity from the preceding decade, while Boyd was turned into a major children's star by virtue of his seizing the moment of early television.

105. Dan Jenkins, "Children Made Roy King of the Cowboys," *TV Guide*, January 17, 1954, p. 5.

106. James Atkins Shackford, *David Crockett: The Man and the Legend* (Chapel Hill: University of North Carolina Press, 1956), calls Col. *Crockett's Exploits and Adventures in Texas, Written by Himself* "the source of so many errors, fabrications, and misrepresentations that . . . it deserves . . . its final refutation" (p. 273). See pp. 273–281.

107. Houston's primary strategy in the early part of the revolt was continuous retreat.

108. Mark Deer, *The Frontiersman: The Real Life and the Many Legends of Davy*

Crockett (New York: William Morrow, 1993), p. 230.

109. T. R. Fehrenbach, *Lone Star: A History of Texas* (New York: Macmillan, 1968), p. 196.

110. Deer, *The Frontiersman*, p. 231.

111. Ibid., p. 234.

112. See Lawrence D. Rice, *The Negro in Texas, 1874–1900* (Baton Rouge: Louisiana State University Press, 1971), pp. 3–4.

113. Fehrenbach, *Lone Star*, p. 305.

114. Jeff Long, *Duel of Eagles: The Mexican and U.S. Fight for the Alamo* (New York: William Morrow, 1990), p. 100.

115. Deer, *The Frontiersman*, p. 232.

116. Long, *Duel of Eagles*, p. 51.

117. Reginald Horsman, *Race and Manifest Destiny: The Origins of American Racial Anglo-Saxonism* (Cambridge, Mass.: Harvard University Press, 1981), p. 213.

118. Ibid., p. 231.

119. Paul Andrew Hutton, "David Crockett: An Exposition on Hero Worship," in Michael A. Lofaro and Joe Cummings, eds., *Crockett at Two Hundred: New Perspectives on the Man and the Myth* (Knoxville: University of Tennessee Press, 1989), p. 23.

120. Margaret J. King, "Disneyland and Walt Disney World: Traditional Values in Futuristic Form," *Journal of Popular Culture* 15, no. 1 (Summer 1981), p. 117.

121. Findlay, *Magic Lands*, p. 9.

122. Watts, *The Magic Kingdom*, p. 370.

Chapter Four. The Adult Western and the Western Bloc

1. J. Fred MacDonald, *Who Shot the Sheriff? The Rise and Fall of the Television Western* (New York: Praeger, 1987), p. 41.

2. "Hold Her Cowboy," *TV Guide*, March 31, 1956, p. 4.

3. "Wyatt Earp—Review," *TV Guide*, October 8, 1955, p. 18.

4. Hugh O'Brien, "Marshal Earp," *TV Guide*, January 21, 1956, p. 8.

5. Welcome Ann Earp, "My Cousin Wyatt," *TV Guide*, January 21, 1956, p. 9.

6. Advertisement, *TV Guide*, October 4, 1958, p. A39.

7. Robert Stahl, "The Facts Are Enough," *TV Guide*, February 21, 1959, pp. 12–14.

8. "Riding High in Dodge City," *TV Guide*, December 6, 1958, p. 10.

9. Quoted in MacDonald, *Who Shot the Sheriff?* p. 75.

10. Quoted in Gary A. Yoggy, *Riding the Video Range: The Rise and Fall of the Western on Television* (Jefferson, N.C.: McFarland, 1995), p. 85.

11. In Gunsmoke's first four television seasons, 138 of the 155 scripts were adaptations of earlier radio broadcasts.

12. Alex McNeil, *Total Television: A Comprehensive Guide to Programming from 1948 to 1980* (New York: Penguin Books, 1980), p. 788.

13. Quoted in Yoggy, *Riding the Video Range*, p. 85.

14. Walter Blair, "Introduction," in Michael A. Lofaro and Joe Cummings, eds., *Crockett at Two Hundred: New Perspectives on the Man and the Myth* (Knoxville: University of Tennessee Press, 1989), p. 5. In regard to Crockett's death, see Dan Kilgore, *How Did Davy Die?* (College Station: Texas A&M Press, 1978).

15. The policy of "containment" was official foreign policy from 1948 until at least the end of the Vietnam era, when, it could be argued, it was replaced by "détente," although one could view

détente as a manifestation of containment. Throughout the quarter century or more, numerous strategies were employed in the name of containment. For the best analysis of the policy, its vicissitudes and manifestations, see John Lewis Gaddis, *Strategies of Containment: A Critical Appraisal of Postwar American National Security Policy* (New York: Oxford University Press, 1982); two good collections of essays are Charles Gati, *Caging the Bear: Containment and the Cold War* (New York: Bobbs-Merrill, 1974); and Thomas G. Paterson, *The Origins of the Cold War* (Lexington, Mass.: D. C. Heath, 1970).

16. See Alan Nadel, *Containment Culture: American Narratives, Postmodernism, and the Atomic Age* (Durham, N.C.: Duke University Press, 1995), especially chapters 1 and 10.

17. Raymond Williams, *Television: Technology and Cultural Form* (Hanover, N.H.: Wesleyan University Press, 1992), pp. 53–54.

18. This point was not lost on Ronald Reagan, who derived much rhetorical power from the use of the anecdote and the small-town setting. See Lou Cannon, *President Reagan: The Role of a Lifetime* (New York: Simon and Schuster, 1991), pp. 121, 122; and Gary Wills, *Reagan's America: Innocents at Home* (New York: Doubleday, 1987), p. 94.

19. Religion had an extensive tacit presence in American culture of the 1950s, as typified by President Eisenhower's oft-quoted statement: "Our government makes no sense unless it is founded in a deeply felt religious faith— and I don't care what it is" and the enormous success of biblical epic films.

Some works that discuss this phenomenon, its range and implications, include Paul Blanshard, *God and Man in Washington* (Boston: Beacon, 1960); Martin E. Marty, *The New Shape of American Religion* (New York: Harper and Row, 1959); Paul Carter, *Another Part of the Fifties* (New York: Columbia University Press, 1983), pp. 114–140; James Gilbert, *Another Chance: Postwar America, 1945–1968* (Philadelphia, Pa.: Temple University Press, 1981), pp. 233–241; Nadel, *Containment Culture*, pp. 90–116.

20. The two most successful films of the 1950s—at the time in the history of American cinema ranking only behind *Gone with the Wind*—were *Ben Hur* and *The Ten Commandments*. In 1950, 1951, 1953, 1956, and 1959, the top-grossing films at the box office were all biblical epics. Cobbett Steinberg, *Film Facts* (New York: Facts on File, 1980).

21. "The Willie Moran Story" (premiere) episode of *Wagon Train*, first broadcast on September 18, 1957.

22. "The Orly French Story" episode of *Wagon Train*, first broadcast on December 12, 1962.

23. "Incident of the Golden Calf" episode of *Rawhide*, first broadcast on March 13, 1959.

24. Quoted in Steven Watts, *The Magic Kingdom: Walt Disney and the American Way of Life* (Boston: Houghton Mifflin, 1997), p. 292.

25. "The War of the Silver Kings," premiere episode of *Maverick*, first broadcast on September 22, 1957.

26. Richard Slotkin, *Gunfighter Nation: The Myth of the Frontier in Twentieth-Century America* (New York: Atheneum, 1992), p. 351.

Chapter Five. Rebel Integrity, Southern Injustice, and Civil Rights

1. "Hold Her Cowboy," *TV Guide*, March 31, 1956, pp. 4–5.

2. Henry Giroux, "Memory and Pedagogy in the 'Wonderful World of Disney': Beyond the Politics of Innocence," in Elizabeth Bell, Lynda Haas, and Laura Sells, eds., *From Mouse to Mermaid: The Politics of Film Gender and Culture* (Bloomington: Indiana University Press, 1995), pp. 45, 47.

3. In 1896, in the case of *Plessy v. Ferguson* dealing with the practice of segregating railroad passengers, the Supreme Court held by an 8–1 decision that separate but equal distinctions based on race were constitutional. This decision set a precedent that held for over fifty years and was frequently used to defend segregated schools.

4. "Historic Decision," *Newsweek*, May 24, 1954, pp. 25–26.

5. "Voice Speaks in 34 Languages to Flash Court Ruling to the World," *New York Times*, May 18, 1954, p. 1.

6. Mary L. Dudziak, "Desegregation as a Cold War Imperative," *Stanford Law Review* 1 (November 1988), p. 65.

7. Ibid., p. 111.

8. Ibid., p. 88.

9. Ibid., p. 89.

10. Ibid., p. 93.

11. Quoted in Mary Dudziak, *Cold War, Civil Rights: Race and the Image of American Democracy* (Princeton, N.J.: Princeton University Press, 2000), p. 95.

12. William O. Douglas, *Strange Land and Friendly People* (New York: Harper, 1951), p. 296.

13. James Reston, "A Sociological Decision," *New York Times*, May 18, 1954, p. 1.

14. "Text of the Supreme Court Decision Outlawing Segregation in the Public Schools," *New York Times*, May 18, 1954, p. 15.

15. Ibid.

16. Ibid.

17. Ibid.

18. Ibid.

19. See Philip Durham and Everett L. Jones, *The Negro Cowboys* (New York: Dodd, Mead, 1965); Kenneth Wiggins Porter, *The Negro on the American Frontier* (New York: Arno and the New York Times, 1971); William Loren Katz, *The Black West: A Documentary and Pictorial History* (Garden City, N.Y.: Doubleday, 1971); Quintard Taylor, *In Search of the Racial Frontier: African Americans in the American West, 1528–1990* (New York: W. W. Norton, 1998); and Gina DeAngelis, *The Black Cowboys* (Philadelphia: Chelsea House, 1988).

20. Durham and Jones, *The Negro Cowboys*, p. 159.

21. Taylor, *In Search of the Racial Frontier*, p. 162.

22. Ibid., p. 163.

23. Manning Marable, *Race, Reform and Rebellion: The Second Reconstruction in Black America, 1945–1982* (Jackson: University Press of Mississippi, 1984), p. 44.

24. Sean Dennis Cashman, *African-Americans and the Quest for Civil Rights, 1900–1990* (New York: New York University Press, 1991), p. 92.

25. Ibid.

26. Mary Ann Watson, *The Expanding Vista: Television in the Kennedy Years* (Durham, N.C.: Duke University Press, 1994), p. 111.

27. It is not only that the Western was the most popular and most prolific of the

prime-time genres but also that many of the other popular genres, for example, the situation comedy and the variety show, were less likely sites for serious investigations of race relations.

28. Quoted in Robert Somerlott, *The Little Rock School Desegregation Crisis in American History* (Berkeley Heights, N.J.: Enslow Publishers, 2001), p. 53.

29. David R. Goldenfield, "Segregation and Racism: Taking up the Dream Again," in Elizabeth Jacoway and C. Fred Williams, eds., *Understanding the Little Rock Crisis: An Exercise in Remembrance and Reconciliation* (Fayetteville: University of Arkansas Press, 1999), p. 35.

30. Quoted in Anthony Lewis, "Washington Studies Little Rock Dispute," *New York Times*, September 4, 1957, p. 37.

31. Richard Bardolph, *The Civil Rights Record: Black Americans and the Law, 1849-1970* (New York: Thomas Y. Crowell, 1970), pp. 56-72.

32. Quoted in ibid., pp. 88-89 (*West Chester and Philadelphia Railroad Co. v. Miles* [1867]).

33. Lewis, "Washington Studies Little Rock Dispute," p. 37.

34. *United States Congressional Record*, vol. 83, part 1, 75th Congress, 3d session (Washington, D.C.: Government Printing Office, January 14-20, 1938), quoted in I. A. Newby, ed., *The Development of Segregationist Thought* (Homewood, Ill.: Dorsey Press, 1968).

35. Quoted in Gilbert Osofsky, *The Burden of Race: A Documentary History of Negro-White Relations in America* (New York: Harper and Row, 1967), p. 166.

36. Quoted in Thomas Gossett, *Race: The History of an Idea in America* (New York: Schocken, 1995), p. 271.

37. Quoted in ibid.

38. Quoted in Osofsky, *The Burden of Race*, p. 187; see George Fredrickson, *The Black Image in the White Mind* (New York: Harper and Row, 1971), "Negro as Beast—Negrophobia at the Turn of the Century," pp. 256-282.

39. *United States Congressional Record*, vol. 58, part 5, 66th Congress, 1st session (Washington, D.C.: Government Printing Office, August 25, 1919), pp. 4303-4305, quoted in Newby, *The Development of Segregationist Thought*, pp. 120-121.

40. Claude Bowers, *The Tragic Era* (New York: Houghton Mifflin, 1929), quoted in Newby, *The Development of Segregationist Thought*, pp. 88-89.

41. Gossett, *Race*, p. 270.

42. Cashman, *African-Americans and the Quest for Civil Rights*, p. 34.

43. "The Southern Manifesto," www.dixienet.org/dn-gazette/two-documents.htm.

44. Sheldon Hackney, "Little Rock and the Promise of America," in Jacoway and Williams, eds., *Understanding the Little Rock Crisis*, p. 25.

45. Roger Ransom, *Conflict and Compromise: The Political Economy of Slavery, Emancipation, and the American Civil War* (Cambridge: Cambridge University Press, 1989), p. 15.

46. "Text of Affidavit Filed by Gov. Faubus," *New York Times*, September 20, 1957, p. 16.

47. "Text of Faubus Speech on Actions in School Dispute," *New York Times*, September 21, 1957, p. 11.

48. Ibid.

49. Ibid.

50. Homer Bigart, "Faubus Condemns Troops' Conduct; Is Called Vulgar," *New York Times*, October 8, 1957, p. 16.

51. J. Fred MacDonald, *Who Shot the Sheriff? The Rise and Fall of the Television Western* (New York: Praeger, 1987), p. 79.

52. Ibid.

53. Goldenfield, "Segregation and Racism," p. 33.

54. Quoted in Gary A. Yoggy, *Riding the Video Range: The Rise and Fall of the Western on Television* (Jefferson, N.C.: McFarland, 1995), p. 216.

55. Eric Foner, *A Short History of Reconstruction* (New York: Harper and Row, 1990), p. 69.

56. See ibid.; Roger Ransom and Richard Sutch, *One Kind of Freedom: The Economic Consequences of Emancipation* (Cambridge: Cambridge University Press, 1977).

57. See Allen W. Trelease, *White Terror: The Ku Klux Klan Conspiracy and Southern Reconstruction* (Baton Rouge: Louisiana State University Press, 1995); George C. Rable (Athens: University of Georgia Press, 1984); and Foner, *A Short History of Reconstruction*.

58. Foner, *A Short History of Reconstruction*, p. 187.

59. Ibid., p. 248.

60. Laurie O'Neill, *Little Rock: The Desegregation of Central High* (Brookfield, Conn.: Millbrook Press, 1994), p. 55.

61. Yoggy, *Riding the Video Range*, p. 87.

62. See Lawrence D. Rice, *The Negro in Texas, 1874–1900* (Baton Rouge: Louisiana State University Press, 1971). There was as well, of course, a Hispanic presence. The role of the treatment of Hispanics in Westerns would be the subject of another interesting—and valuable—study. Although undoubtedly this treatment involved issues of racism, they are quite distinct from the concerns focused on by this study. From the earliest days of television, there were valorized Hispanic Western heroes, the most prominent being Zorro and the Cisco Kid. In addition, numerous Hispanic characters appeared in an array of Westerns, often in positions of wealth and power.

63. Odie B. Faulk, *Dodge City: The Most Western Town of All* (New York: Oxford University Press, 1977), p. 66.

64. William H. Leckie, *The Buffalo Soldiers: A Narrative of the Negro Cavalry in the West* (Norman: University of Oklahoma Press, 1967). Leckie described in elaborate detail the troop movements and actions of the Ninth and Tenth Cavalry units in the West; he made specific references to black cavalry companies stationed at or operating in the area of Fort Dodge, pp. 32–33, 40, 44, 117, 124.

65. See Durham and Jones, *The Negro Cowboys*, pp. 45–56.

66. Taylor, *In Search of the Racial Frontier*, p. 104.

67. Ibid., p. 160.

68. Ibid., p. 161; see also Stanley Vestal, *Dodge City: Queen of the Cowtowns* (Lincoln: University of Nebraska Press, 1952), p. 31; and Faulk, *Dodge City*, p. 152. See also Casey Tefertiller, *Wyatt Earp: The Life behind the Legend* (New York: John Wiley, 1997), p. 10.

69. Durham and Jones, *The Negro Cowboys*, pp. 111, 113.

70. Taylor, *In Search of the Racial Frontier*, p. 171.

Chapter Six. The New Frontier

1. John F. Kennedy, "Presidential Nomination Acceptance Speech," *New York Times*, July 16, 1960, p. 8.

2. Ibid.

3. Theodore Sorenson, *Kennedy* (New York: Harper and Row, 1965), p. 328.

4. Christopher Matthews, *Kennedy and Nixon: The Rivalry That Shaped Postwar America* (New York: Simon and Schuster, 1996), p. 79.

5. Ibid., p. 80.

6. David Farber, *The Age of Great Dreams: America in the 1960s* (New York: Hill and Wang, 1994), p. 31.

7. Kennedy, "Presidential Nomination Acceptance Speech," p. 8.

8. John F. Kennedy, "Text of Kennedy Appeal for Increases in Spending and Armed Forces," *New York Times*, July 26, 1961, p. 10.

9. Kennedy, "Presidential Nomination Acceptance Speech," p. 8.

10. Kennedy, "Text of Kennedy Appeal," p.10.

11. *Bonanza* started in 1959; interestingly, the following season saw the premiere of the hit comedy series *My Three Sons.*

12. Quoted in Gary A. Yoggy, *Riding the Video Range: The Rise and Fall of the Western on Television* (Jefferson, N.C.: McFarland, 1995), p. 295.

13. Ibid.

14. John F. Kennedy, "Text of Kennedy's Inaugural Outlining Policies on World Peace and Freedom," *New York Times*, January 21, 1961, p. 3.

15. Quintard Taylor, *In Search of the Racial Frontier: African Americans in the American West, 1528–1990* (New York: W. W. Norton, 1998), p. 104.

16. Quoted in Yoggy, *Riding the Video Range*, p. 305.

17. Ibid., p. 295.

18. Ibid., p. 297.

19. Quoted in Yoggy, *Riding the Video Range*, p. 301.

20. Mary Ann Watson, *The Expanding Vista: Television in the Kennedy Years.* (Durham, N.C.: Duke University Press, 1994), p. 36.

21. The show also had an official theme song, a Nelson Riddle tune that achieved some lasting popularity both with and without lyrics.

22. Bill Deane, *Following the Fugitive: An Episode Guide and Handbook to the 1960s Television Series* (Jefferson, N.C., and London: McFarland, 1996), p. 11.

23. Ibid., p. 32.

Conclusion

1. Paul C. Light, *Baby Boomers* (New York: W. W. Norton, 1988), p. 123.

2. J. Fred MacDonald, *Blacks and White TV: Afro-Americans in Television since 1948* (Chicago: Nelson Hall, 1983), p. 59.

3. Katheryn Russell, "Toward Developing a Theoretical Paradigm and Typology for Petit Apartheid," in Dragan Milovanovic and Katheryn Russell, eds., *Petit Apartheid in the U.S. Criminal Justice System* (Durham, N.C.: Carolina Academic Press, 2001), p. 11.

4. Ibid.

5. Sandra Bass, "Out of Place: Petit Apartheid and the Police," in Milovanovic and Russell, eds., *Petit Apartheid in the U.S. Criminal Justice System*, pp. 43–53.

SELECTED BIBLIOGRAPHY

Books and Articles

Adams, Judith A. *The American Amusement Park Industry: A History of Technology and Thrills.* Boston: Twayne, 1991.

Advertisement. *TV Guide*, October 4, 1958, p. A39.

Allen, Jeanne. "The Social Matrix of Television: Invention in the United States." In E. Ann Kaplan, ed., *Regarding Television: Critical Approaches—An Anthology*. Los Angeles: American Film Institute, 1983, pp. 109–119.

Allen, Theodore. *The Invention of the White Race.* London: Verso, 1994.

Anderson, Paul F. *The Davy Crockett Craze: A Look at the 1950s.* Hillside, Ill.: R & G Productions, 1996.

Baker, William F., and George Dessart. *Down the Tube: An Inside Account of the Failure of American Television.* New York: Basic Books, 1998.

Barabas, SuzAnne, and Gabor Barabas. *Gunsmoke: A Complete History and Analysis of the Legendary Broadcast Series.* Jefferson, N.C.: McFarland, 1990.

Bardolph, Richard. *The Civil Rights Record: Black Americans and the Law, 1849–1970.* New York: Thomas Y. Crowell, 1970.

Barnouw, Erik. *The Golden Web: A History of Broadcasting in the United States, Volume II—1933–1953.* New York: Oxford University Press, 1968.

———. *The Television Writer.* New York: Hill and Wang, 1962.

———. *A Tube of Plenty: The Evolution of American Television*, 2d rev. ed. New York: Oxford University Press, 1990.

Barthes, Roland. *Mythologies.* Trans. by Annette Lavers. London: Hill and Wang, 1972.

Bass, Sandra. "Out of Place: Petit Apartheid and the Police." In Dragan Milovanovic and Katheryn Russell, eds., *Petit Apartheid in the U.S. Criminal Justice System*. Durham, N.C.: Carolina Academic Press, 2001, pp. 43–53.

Bell, Elizabeth, Lynda Haas, and Laura Sells, eds. *From Mouse to Mermaid: The Politics of Film, Gender, and Culture.* Bloomington: Indiana University Press, 1995.

Bernhard, Nancy. *U.S. Television News and Cold War Propaganda, 1947–1960.* Cambridge: Cambridge University Press, 1999.

Bigart, Homer. "Faubus Condemns Troops' Conduct; Is Called Vulgar." *New York Times*, October 8, 1957, pp. 1, 16.

Blair, Walter. "Introduction." In Michael A. Lofaro and Joe Cummings, eds., *Crockett at Two Hundred: New Perspectives on the Man and the Myth*. Knoxville: University of Tennessee Press, 1989.

Blanshard, Paul. *God and Man in Washington.* Boston: Beacon, 1960.

Boddy, William. *Fifties Television: The Industry and Its Critics.* Urbana: University of Illinois Press, 1990.

Bogart, Leo. *The Age of Television: A Study of Viewing Habits and the Impact of Television on American Life*. New York: Frederick Ungar, 1956.

Burns, James Macgregor. *John Kennedy: A Political Profile*. New York: Harcourt Brace, 1960.

Caddigan, James. "Station Operations: Setting Up a Special Events Department." *Television: The Magazine of Video Fact*, 2, no. 10 (December 1945), pp. 11–14.

Cannon, Lou. *President Reagan: The Role of a Lifetime*. New York: Simon and Schuster, 1991.

Carborg, Harold A. "Billion Dollar Whipping Boy." *Television Age*, November 4, 1957.

Carter, Paul. *Another Part of the Fifties*. New York: Columbia University Press, 1983.

Cashman, Sean Dennis. *African-Americans and the Quest for Civil Rights, 1900–1990*. New York: New York University Press, 1991.

Castleman, Harry, and Walter Podrazik. *Watching TV: Four Decades of American Television*. New York: McGraw Hill, 1982.

Christensen, H. G. "Long Shots and Close-ups." *Television: The Magazine of Video Fact*, 3, no. 2 (February 1946), pp. 28–29.

Col. *Crockett's Exploits and Adventures in Texas, Written by Himself*. Philadelphia: T. K. and P. G. Collins, 1836.

Deane, Bill. *Following the Fugitive: An Episode Guide and Handbook to the 1960s Television Series*. Jefferson, N.C., and London: McFarland, 1996.

DeAngelis, Gina. *The Black Cowboys*. Philadelphia: Chelsea House, 1988.

"Decision Broadcast in Thirty-Four Languages." *New York Times*, May 18, 1954, p. 1.

Deer, Mark. *The Frontiersman: The Real Life and the Many Legends of Davy Crockett*. New York: William Morrow, 1993.

De Forest, Lee. *Television Today and Tomorrow*. New York: Dial Press, 1942.

De Roos, Robert. "The Magic Worlds of Walt Disney." In Eric Smoodin, ed., *Disney Discourse: Producing the Magic Kingdom*. New York: Routledge, 1994.

"Disney in TVland." *TV Guide*, January 23, 1954, pp. 4–6.

Doherty, Thomas. *Cold War, Cool Medium: Television, McCarthyism, and American Culture*. New York: Columbia University Press, 2003.

Douglas, William O. *Strange Lands and Friendly People*. New York: Harper, 1951.

Dudziak, Mary L. "Desegregation as a Cold War Imperative." *Stanford Law Review* 1 (November 1988), pp. 61–120.

———. *Cold War & Civil Rights: Race and the Image of American Democracy*. Princeton, N.J.: Princeton University Press, 2000.

Dunlap, Orin E., Jr. *The Future of Television*. New York: Harper and Bros, 1942.

Durham, Philip, and Everett L. Jones. *The Negro Cowboys*. New York: Dodd, Mead, 1965.

Dyer, Richard. *White*. New York and London: Routledge, 1997.

Earp, Welcome Ann. "My Cousin Wyatt." *TV Guide*, January 21, 1956, p. 9.

Englehardt, Tom. *The End of Victory Culture: Cold War America and the Disillusioning of a Generation*. New York: Basic Books, 1995.

Farber, David. *The Age of Great Dreams: America in the 1960s*. New York: Hill and Wang, 1994.

Faulk, Odie B. *Dodge City: The Most Western Town of All*. New York: Oxford University Press, 1977.

Fehrenbach, T. R. *Lone Star: A History of Texas.* New York: Macmillan, 1968.

"Fess Parker: King of the Wild Frontier." *TV Guide,* April 30, 1955, pp. 5–7.

Findlay, John M. *Magic Lands: Western Cityscapes and American Culture after 1940.* Berkeley: University of California Press, 1992.

Finkleman, Paul. *An Imperfect Union: Slavery, Federalism, and Comity.* Chapel Hill: University of North Carolina Press, 1981.

Fisher, Paul L., and Ralph Lowenstein. *Race and the News Media.* New York: Praeger, 1967.

Foner, Eric. *A Short History of Reconstruction.* New York: Harper and Row, 1990.

Francaviglia, Richard V. "Main Street USA: A Comparison/Contrast of Streetscapes in Disneyland and Disney World." *Journal of Popular Culture,* 15, no. 1 (Summer 1981), pp. 141–156.

Frankenberg, Ruth. *White Women, Race Matters: The Social Construction of Whiteness.* Minneapolis: University of Minnesota Press, 1993.

Franklin, John Hope, and Alfred A. Moss, Jr. *From Slavery to Freedom: A History of African Americans,* 7th ed. New York: Alfred A. Knopf, 1994.

Frazier, E. Franklin. *The Negro in the United States.* New York: Macmillan, 1957.

Fredrickson, George. *The Black Image in the White Mind.* New York: Harper and Row, 1971.

Gaddis, John Lewis. *Strategies of Containment: A Critical Appraisal of Postwar American National Security Policy.* New York: Oxford University Press, 1982.

Gannon, Mary. "Mademoiselle Tries Out Television." *Television: The Magazine of Video Fact,* 2, no. 8 (October 1945), pp. 11–14.

Gates, Henry Louis. *Colored People.* New York: Alfred A. Knopf, 1994.

Gati, Charles. *Caging the Bear: Containment and the Cold War.* New York: Bobbs-Merrill, 1974.

Gilbert, James. *Another Chance: Postwar America, 1945–1968.* Philadelphia: Temple University Press, 1981.

Gipson, Henry Clay. "Educational Films and Television." *Television: The Magazine of Video Fact,* 2, no. 4 (May 1945), pp. 13–14.

Giroux, Henry. "Memory and Pedagogy in the 'Wonderful World of Disney': Beyond the Politics of Innocence." In Elizabeth Bell, Lynda Haas, and Laura Sells, eds., *From Mouse to Mermaid: The Politics of Film, Gender, and Culture.* Bloomington: Indiana University Press, 1995, pp. 43–61.

Goldberger, Paul. "Mickey Mouse Teaches the Architects." *New York Times Magazine,* October 22, 1972, pp. 18–24.

Goldenfield, David R. "Segregation and Racism: Taking Up the Dream Again." In Elizabeth Jacoway and C. Fred Williams, eds., *Understanding the Little Rock Crisis: An Exercise in Remembrance and Reconciliation.* Fayetteville: University of Arkansas Press, 1999, pp. 29–43.

Goodman, James. *Stories of Scottsboro.* New York: Vintage, 1994.

Gordon, Arthur. "Walt Disney." *Look,* July 26, 1955, pp. 28–30.

Gorham, Maurice. *Television: Medium of the Future.* London: Percival Marshall, 1949.

Gossett, Thomas. *Race: The History of an Idea in America.* New York: Schocken, 1995.

Graebner, William. Preface to Lipsitz, George. "The Making of Disneyland." In
    William Graebner, ed., *True Stories of the American Past*. New York: McGraw Hill,
    1993, p. 180.

Hackney, Sheldon. "Little Rock and the Promise of America." In Elizabeth Jacoway and
    C. Fred Williams, eds., *Understanding the Little Rock Crisis: An Exercise in Remembrance
    and Reconciliation*. Fayetteville: University of Arkansas Press, 1999, pp. 23–28.

Harris, Cheryl. "Whiteness as Property." *Harvard Law Review* 106, no. 8 (June 1993), pp.
    1707–1791.

Harris, Neil. "Expository Expositions: Preparing for the Theme Parks." In Karal Ann
    Marling, ed., *Designing Disney's Theme Parks: The Architecture of Reassurance*. Montreal:
    Canadian Centre for Architecture; Paris and New York: Flammarion, 1997.

Herbert, Steve. *Policing Space: Territoriality and the Los Angeles Police Department*.
    Minneapolis: University of Minnesota Press, 1997.

"Historic Decision." *Newsweek*, May 24, 1954, pp. 25–26.

"Hold Her Cowboy." *TV Guide*, March 31, 1956, pp. 4–5.

Horsman, Reginald. *Race and Manifest Destiny: The Origins of American Racial Anglo-
    Saxonism*. Cambridge, Mass.: Harvard University Press, 1981.

Hutton, Paul Andrew. "David Crockett: An Exposition on Hero Worship." In Michael
    A. Lofaro and Joe Cummings, eds., *Crockett at Two Hundred: New Perspectives on the
    Man and the Myth*. Knoxville: University of Tennessee Press, 1989, pp. 20–41.

"Infant Grown Up, The" *Time*, May 24, 1948, p. 72.

Jenkins, Dan. "Children Made Roy King of the Cowboys." *TV Guide*, January 17, 1954,
    pp. 5–7.

Jordon, Winthrop D. *White over Black: American Attitudes toward the Negro, 1550–1812*.
    New York: W. W. Norton, 1977.

Kaplan, E. Ann. *Regarding Television: Critical Approaches—An Anthology*. Los Angeles:
    American Film Institute, 1983.

Katz, William Loren. *The Black West: A Documentary and Pictorial History*. Garden City,
    N.Y.: Doubleday, 1971.

Kennan, George. "The Sources of Soviet Conduct." *Foreign Affairs* 25 (1947), pp. 566–582.

Kennedy, John F. "Presidential Nomination Acceptance Speech." *New York Times*, July
    16, 1960, p. 8.

Kilgore, Dan. *How Did Davy Die?* College Station: Texas A & M Press, 1978.

King, Margaret J. "Disneyland and Walt Disney World: Traditional Values in Futuristic
    Form." *Journal of Popular Culture* 15, no. 1 (Summer 1981), pp. 116–140.

Koon, Sgt. Stacey, L.A.P.D. *Presumed Guilty: The Tragedy of the Rodney King Affair*.
    Washington, D.C.: Regnery Gateway, 1992.

Leavitt, Helen. *Superhighway—Superhoax*. Garden City, N.Y.: Doubleday, 1970.

Leckie, William H. *The Buffalo Soldiers: A Narrative of the Negro Cavalry in the West*.
    Norman: University of Oklahoma Press, 1967.

Leibman, Nina. *Living Room Lectures: The Fifties Family in Film and Television*. Austin:
    University of Texas Press, 1995.

Lentz, Harris M., III. *Television Westerns Episode Guide, 1949–1996*. Jefferson, N.C.:
    McFarland, 1997.

Lewis, Anthony. "Washington Studies Little Rock Dispute." *New York Times*, September 4, 1957, pp. 1, 37.

Light, Paul C. *Baby Boomers*. New York: W. W. Norton, 1988.

Lipsitz, George. "The Making of Disneyland." In William Graebner, ed., *True Stories of the American Past*. New York: McGraw-Hill, 1993.

———. *Time Passages: Collective Memory and American Popular Culture*. Minneapolis: University of Minnesota Press, 1990.

Lofaro, Michael A., and Joe Cummings, eds. *Crockett at Two Hundred: New Perspectives on the Man and the Myth*. Knoxville: University of Tennessee Press, 1989.

Long, Jeff. *Duel of Eagles: The Mexican and U.S. Fight for the Alamo*. New York: William Morrow, 1990.

"Love that Television." *TV Guide*, August 13, 1955, pp. 4–5.

Lowe, Walter. "Hollywood Follows Disney into TV." *New York Herald Tribune*, June 5, 1955, p. 25.

Lutz, Catherine, and Jane Collins. *Reading National Geographic*. Chicago: University of Chicago Press, 1993.

MacDonald, J. Fred. *Blacks and White TV: African Americans in Television since 1948*. Chicago: Nelson Hall, 1992.

———. *One Nation under Television: The Rise and Decline of Network TV*. New York: Pantheon, 1990.

———. *Television and the Red Menace: The Video Road to Vietnam*. New York: Praeger, 1985.

Marable, Manning. *Race, Reform and Rebellion: The Second Reconstruction in Black America, 1945–1982*. Jackson: University Press of Mississippi, 1984.

Marc, David. "Beginning to Begin Again." In Horace Newcomb, ed., *Television: The Critical View*, 4th ed. New York: Oxford University Press, 1987, pp. 323–360.

———. *Demographic Vistas: Television in American Culture*. Philadelphia: University of Pennsylvania Press, 1984.

Marling, Karal Ann. *As Seen on TV: The Visual Culture of Everyday Life in the 1950s*. Cambridge, Mass.: Harvard University Press, 1994.

———. "Imagineering the Disney Theme Parks." In Karal Ann Marling, ed., *Designing Disney's Theme Parks: The Architecture of Reassurance*. Montreal: Canadian Centre for Architecture; Paris and New York: Flammarion, 1997.

Marty, Martin E. *The New Shape of American Religion*. New York: Harper and Row, 1959.

Massey, Douglas S., and Nancy Denton. *American Apartheid: Segregation and the Making of the Underclass*. Cambridge, Mass.: Harvard University Press, 1993.

Matthews, Christopher. *Kennedy and Nixon: The Rivalry that Shaped Postwar America*. New York: Simon and Schuster, 1996.

May, Elaine Tyler. *Homeward Bound: American Families in the Cold War Era*. New York: Basic Books, 1988.

May, Lary, ed. *Recasting America: Culture and Politics in the Age of Cold War*. Chicago: University of Chicago Press, 1989.

McNeil, Alex. *Total Television: A Comprehensive Guide to Programming from 1948 to 1980*. New York: Penguin Books, 1980.

Miller, Douglas T., and Marion Nowak. *The Fifties: The Way We Really Were.* New York: Doubleday, 1977.

Monaco, James. "The TV Plexus." In Carl Lowe, ed., *Television and American Culture.* New York: H. W. Wilson, 1981, pp. 12–24.

Monroe, William B., Jr. "Television: The Chosen Instrument of the Revolution." In Paul Fisher and Ralph Lowenstein, eds., *Race and the News Media.* New York: Praeger, 1967, pp. 83–97.

Morrison, Toni. *Playing in the Dark: Whiteness and the Literary Imagination.* Cambridge, Mass.: Harvard University Press, 1992.

Mowbray, A. Q. *The Road to Ruin.* New York: J. B. Lippincott, 1969.

Nadel, Alan. *Containment Culture: American Narratives, Postmodernism, and the Atomic Age.* Durham, N.C.: Duke University Press, 1995.

———. *Invisible Criticism: Ralph Ellison and the American Canon.* Iowa City: University of Iowa Press, 1988.

Newby, I. A., ed. *The Development of Segregationist Thought.* Homewood, Ill.: Dorsey Press, 1968.

O'Brien, Hugh. "Marshal Earp." *TV Guide,* January 21, 1956, p. 8.

"Old Horse Operas Never Die. They Just Go On Making Hay." *TV Guide,* January 15, 1954, pp. 20–21.

O'Neill, Laurie. *Little Rock: The Desegregation of Central High.* Brookfield, Conn.: Millbrook Press, 1994.

Osofsky, Gilbert. *The Burden of Race: A Documentary History of Negro-White Relations in America.* New York: Harper and Row, 1967.

Owen, Bruce, Jack Beebe, and Willard Manning. *Television Economics.* Lexington, Mass.: D. C. Heath, 1974.

Paterson, Thomas G. *The Origins of the Cold War.* Lexington, Mass.: D. C. Heath, 1970.

Porter, Kenneth Wiggins. *The Negro on the American Frontier.* New York: Arno and the New York Times, 1971.

Ransom, Roger. *Conflict and Compromise: The Political Economy of Slavery, Emancipation, and the American Civil War.* Cambridge: Cambridge University Press, 1989.

Ransom, R., and R. Sutch. *One Kind of Freedom: The Economic Consequences of Emancipation.* Cambridge: Cambridge University Press, 1977.

"The Real Wyatt Earp." *TV Guide,* May 2, 1959, pp. 8–12.

Reston, James. "A Sociological Decision." *New York Times,* May 18, 1954, p. 1.

Rice, Lawrence D. *The Negro in Texas, 1874–1900.* Baton Rouge: Louisiana State University Press, 1971.

Rose, Kenneth D. *One Nation Underground: The Fallout Shelter in American Culture.* New York: New York University Press, 2001.

Rose, Mark H. *Interstate: Express Highway Politics, 1941–1956.* Lawrence: Regents Press of Kansas, 1979.

Russell, Katheryn. "Toward Developing a Theoretical Paradigm and Typology for Petit Apartheid." In Dragan Milovanovic and Katheryn Russell, eds., *Petit Apartheid in the U.S. Criminal Justice System.* Durham, N.C.: Carolina Academic Press, 2001, pp. 3–13.

Schickel, Richard. *The Disney Version: The Life, Times, Commerce, and Art of Walt Disney.* New York: Simon and Schuster, 1968.

Schrecker, Ellen. *The Age of McCarthyism: A Brief History with Documents.* Boston: Bedford Books, 1994.

———. *Many Are the Crimes: McCarthyism in America.* Boston: Little, Brown, 1998.

———. *No Ivory Tower: McCarthyism and the Universities.* New York: Oxford University Press, 1986.

Seldes, Gilbert. "The Future of Television." *Atlantic*, 3 (1949), pp. 35–39.

———. *Writing for Television.* New York: Doubleday, 1952.

Shackford, James Atkins. *David Crockett: The Man and the Legend.* Chapel Hill: University of North Carolina Press, 1956.

Slotkin, Richard. *Gunfighter Nation: The Myth of the Frontier in Twentieth-Century America.* New York: Atheneum, 1992.

Smoodin, Eric. *Animating Culture: Hollywood Cartoons from the Sound Era.* New Brunswick, N.J.: Rutgers University Press, 1993.

———, ed. *Disney Discourse: Producing the Magic Kingdom.* New York: Routledge, 1994.

Somerlott, Robert. *The Little Rock School Desegregation Crisis in American History.* Berkeley Heights, N.J.: Enslow Publishers, 2001.

Sorenson, Theodore. *Kennedy.* New York: Harper and Row, 1965.

Spigel, Lynn. *Make Room for Television.* Chicago: University of Chicago Press, 1992.

———. "Television in the Family Circle: The Popular Reception of a New Medium." In Patricia Mellencamp, ed., *Logics of Television: Essays in Cultural Criticism.* Bloomington: Indiana University Press, 1990, pp. 73–97.

Spigel, Lynn, and Michael Curtin. *The Revolution Wasn't Televised: Sixties Television and Social Conflict.* New York: Routledge, 1997.

Stahl, Robert. "The Facts Are Enough." *TV Guide*, February 21, 1959, pp. 12–14.

Steinberg, Cobbett. *Film Facts.* New York: Facts on File, 1980.

Taylor, Quintard. *In Search of the Racial Frontier: African Americans in the American West, 1528–1990.* New York: W. W. Norton, 1998.

Tefertiller, Casey. *Wyatt Earp: The Life behind the Legend.* New York: John Wiley, 1997.

"Television Code of the National Association of Radio and Television Broadcasters, The." In William Y. Elliott, ed., *Television's Impact on American Culture.* East Lansing: Michigan State University Press, 1956, pp. 328–339.

Terrace, Vincent. *The Complete Encyclopedia of Television Programs, 1947–1979.* New York: A. S. Barnes, 1980.

"Text of Affidavit Filed by Gov. Faubus." *New York Times*, September 20, 1957, p. 16.

"Text of Faubus Speech on Actions in School Dispute." *New York Times*, September 21, 1957, p. 11.

"Text of the Supreme Court Decision Outlawing Segregation in the Public Schools." *New York Times*, May 18, 1954, p. 15.

Thompson, William Irwin. *At the Edge of History.* New York: HarperCollins, 1971.

Tichi, Celia. *Electronic Hearth: Creating an American Television Culture.* New York: Oxford University Press, 1991.

Vestal, Stanley. *Dodge City: Queen of the Cowtowns*. Lincoln: University of Nebraska Press, 1952.

Watson, Mary Ann. *The Expanding Vista: Television in the Kennedy Years*. Durham, N.C.: Duke University Press, 1994.

Watts, Steven. *The Magic Kingdom: Walt Disney and the American Way of Life*. Boston: Houghton Mifflin, 1997.

West, Cornel. *Race Matters*. Boston: Beacon Press, 1993.

Whitfield, Stephen J. *The Culture of the Cold War*. Baltimore: Johns Hopkins University Press, 1991.

Williams, Raymond. *Television: Technology and Cultural Form*. Hanover, N.H.: Wesleyan University Press, 1992.

Williamson, Joel. *The Crucible of Race: Black-White Relations in the American South since Emancipation*. New York: Oxford University Press, 1984.

Wills, Gary. *Reagan's America: Innocents at Home*. New York: Doubleday, 1987.

"Wyatt Earp—Review." *TV Guide*, October 8, 1955, p. 18.

Yoggy, Gary A. *Riding the Video Range: The Rise and Fall of the Western on Television*. Jefferson, N.C.: McFarland, 1995.

Zipes, Jack. "Breaking the Disney Spell." In Elizabeth Bell, Lynda Haas, and Laura Sells, eds., *From Mouse to Mermaid: The Politics of Film, Gender, and Culture*. Bloomington: Indiana University Press, 1995, pp. 21–42.

Selected Television Shows

The Adventures of Ozzie and Harriet. 30 minutes. ABC, October 3, 1952–September 3, 1966.

The Amos 'n' Andy Show. 30 minutes. CBS, June 28, 1951–June 11, 1953.

Bonanza. 60 minutes. NBC, September 12, 1959–January 16, 1973.

Bronco. 60 minutes. ABC, October 20, 1959–September 20, 1960.

Cheyenne. 60 minutes. ABC, September 20, 1956– August 30, 1963.

Colt .45. 30 minutes. ABC, October 18, 1957–October 10, 1962.

Dick Powell's Zane Grey Theater. 30 minutes. CBS, October 10, 1956, September 19, 1962.

Disneyland. 60 minutes. ABC, October 27, 1954–September 3, 1958 [subsequently *Walt Disney Presents*, September 12, 1958–June 17, 1959].

Father Knows Best. 30 minutes. CBS, October 3, 1954–March 27, 1955; NBC, August 31, 1955–September 17, 1958; CBS, September 22, 1958–September 17, 1962.

The Fugitive. ABC, September 17, 1963–August 29, 1967.

Gunsmoke. 30 and 60 minutes. CBS, September 10, 1955–September 1, 1975.

I Love Lucy. 30 minutes. CBS, October 15, 1951–September 15, 1956.

The Life and Legend of Wyatt Earp. 30 minutes. ABC, September 6, 1955–September 26, 1961.

Maverick. 60 minutes. ABC, September 22, 1957–July 8, 1962.

My Three Sons. 30 minutes. ABC, September 29, 1960–September 16, 1965; CBS, September 16, 1965–August 24, 1972.

The Nat King Cole Show. 30 minutes. NBC, November 5, 1956–December 17, 1957.

Rawhide. 60 minutes. CBS, January 1, 1959–January 4, 1966.

The Rebel. 30 minutes. ABC, October 4, 1959–September 24, 1961.

Route 66. 60 minutes. CBS, October 7, 1960–September 18, 1964.

Texaco Star Theater. 60 minutes. NBC, September 21, 1948–June 9, 1953.

The Today Show. 120 minutes. NBC, premiered January 14, 1952.

Tombstone Territory. 30 minutes. ABC, October 16, 1957–October 9, 1959.

Wagon Train. 60 minutes, NBC, September 18, 1957–September 12, 1962; 60 and 90 minutes, ABC, September 19, 1962–September 15, 1965.

Yancy Derringer. 30 minutes. October 2, 1958–September 24, 1959.

INDEX

ABC (American Broadcasting Company), 43, 44, 45, 75, 190n1. *See also Disneyland* (television show)

Abolitionism, 9, 145

Acheson, Dean, 113

Action-adventure series, 31

Adams, Edie, 27

Adams, Judith, 52, 58, 60–61

Adams, Nick, 143–144

Adult Westerns
  absence of blacks, 116, 130, 144, 146, 147–148
  anthology shows, 89–90
  authenticity, 116, 156
  black soldiers, 150–155
  Bronco, 126–128, 170
  characteristics, 86–87
  Cheyenne, 129–131, 132, 170
  Colt .45, 94–96, 97, 100
  confined spaces, 100
  cook characters, 146
  Death Valley Days, 90, 91(photo)
  declining popularity, 161–162
  differences from children's Westerns, 86
  Have Gun, Will Travel, 134–135, 178
  historical characters, 87, 127–128
  images of West, 136–137
  The Life and Legend of Wyatt Earp, 86, 87, 89, 94, 147–148
  locations, 147
  Maverick, 108–111
  Native American characters, 152–155
  in 1960s, 161–162, 174
  popularity, 86, 158
  Rawhide, 90, 99, 103–106, 146, 170
  realism, 86–87, 89–90
  The Rebel, 137–144, 140(photo)
  reflection of contemporary society, 87–88, 99–100, 155–156
  religious themes, 100–106
  representation of South, 119, 144
  rhetorical strategies, 88, 89–90
  The Rifleman, 94, 95(photo), 99
  Southern characters, 126–128, 129–131, 132–135, 137–144
  sponsors, 110–111
  Texas John Slaughter series, 91–94
  timeframes, 169–170
  Tombstone Territory, 90, 133–134
  values, 119
  violence in, 144
  Wagon Train, 99, 101–103, 132–133, 144, 170
  weapons, 93–94
  Yancy Derringer, 126, 134–136
  The Zane Grey Theater, 89–90, 150–155
  See also Bonanza; Gunsmoke

The Adventures of Davy Crockett, 47, 74–83, 84–85, 86, 91, 112

The Adventures of Ozzie and Harriet, 27–28

Advertising, product placement, 39–41. *See also* Commercials; Sponsors

Africa, independent states, 113

African Americans. *See* Blacks

Alabama, *Code of Alabama*, 1

Alamo, 47, 76, 77–82, 91, 92, 142

The Aldrich Family, 36

Allen, Gracie, 28

Allen, Jeanne, 30

American Broadcasting Company. *See* ABC

American Communist Party, 36

American Dairy Association, 46

American Motors, 46

Amos 'n' Andy, 7, 15, 16(photo), 37

Amusement parks
  differences from Disneyland, 59
  history, 52
  See also Disneyland

Anaheim (California), Disneyland site, 53–54, 182

Animals, anthropomorphized, 47, 65, 66
Apache Indians, 148, 149–150, 153–154
An Appeal to the World, 114
Arizona
    black population, 147
    school desegregation, 147
    Tombstone, 90
    Westerns set in, 90, 133–134, 147
Arnaz, Desi, 28, 29(photo)
Arness, James, 88, 89. *See also Gunsmoke*
Arthur, Robert Alan, 41
Automobile travel
    Autotopia (Disneyland), 54–55
    promotion of, 50–51, 53
    Route 66, 174–177
    suburban development and, 66
    See also Interstate highway system
Autry, Gene, 77, 86
AWARE, Incorporated, 36–37

Baby boomers
    birth of, 28
    holidays, 71–72
    importance of television, 12, 75, 182
Bad Day in Black Rock, 177
Ball, Lucille, 28, 29(photo), 42
Bambi, 47
Barthes, Roland, 3
Bass, Sandra, 184
Bat Masterson, 87, 147
Battle Report—Washington, 22
Berg, Gertrude, 37
Berle, Milton, 17–18
Bernhard, Nancy, 21
The Big Picture, 31
The Big Valley, 162
Black Codes, 9–10, 187–188n20
Blacklisting, 36–37
Black Panther Party, 181
Blacks
    civil rights, 9–10
    civil rights movement, 37, 117, 181
    colonization movement, 9
    cowboys, 116, 145–147, 148
    freed slaves, 141, 187–188n20
    history in United States, 8–9

legal status, 171
marginalization, 67–73
migration to northern cities, 10
in military, 11–12
neighborhoods destroyed by highway
    construction, 68–69
passing for white, 3
prison inmates, 184
seen as subhuman, 123–124
social invisibility, 10, 69, 180
stereotypes of, 164
white fear of, 8, 9, 121, 123–125
See also Racial discrimination;
    Segregation
Black soldiers
    cavalry, 146, 149, 151(photo), 151–155
    in Civil War, 152
    importance, 149–150
    Indian wars, 149–150
    portrayals in adult Westerns, 150–155
    treatment of, 149
    in West, 146, 148–150, 152
    in World War II, 11–12, 152
Blacks on television
    absence, 70, 115, 116, 130, 137, 144, 146,
        147–148, 182
    Amos 'n' Andy characters, 7, 15, 16(photo),
        37
    controversies, 37, 38–39
    in current programming, 183
    in early years, 7, 37
    musical performers, 7, 37, 38
    news coverage of civil rights movement,
        117
Bogle, Donald, 7
Bolger, Ray, 28
Bomb shelters, 160–161
Bonanza
    absence of blacks and Native Americans,
        168
    absence of females, 171–172
    conflicts between Northern and
        Southern sympathies, 164, 170
    family, 163–164, 173(photo)
    first episode, 163–165, 169
    historical characters and events, 169

"House Divided," 169
"The Mill," 165–167
Ponderosa, 162, 163, 164, 165, 169,
    170–171
popularity, 162, 174
property rights theme, 170–171
significance, 167–168
similarities of Cartwrights and
    Kennedys, 162–163, 165, 173
"Springtime," 167
temporal setting, 168–170
Bonino, 28
Borgnine, Ernest, 101–102
Bowers, Claude, 124
Bowie, Jim, 78, 79
Boyd, William (Hopalong Cassidy), 77, 86
Broadcasters Advisory Council, 22
Broadcasting, 20, 32
Bronco
    location, 147
    "The Shadow of Jesse James," 126–128
    timeframe, 170
Brown v. Board of Education of Topeka, 84,
    113–115, 118, 122, 125, 137, 147
Buffalo soldiers. See Black soldiers
Burns, George, 28
Burns and Allen Show, 28
Byrnes, James F., 124

Cable television, 183
Caddigan, James, 24–25, 26, 30
California
    growth, 64
    multiethnic population, 63, 73, 169
    See also Disneyland; Los Angeles
Camelot, 164
Capitalism, 49, 65, 107, 108
Captain Midnight, 31
Captain Video, 31
Cashman, Sean Dennis, 117
Catholic Church, television programs, 17,
    31
Cattle trails, 107, 145, 146
CBS (Columbia Broadcasting System)
    course on how to use television, 159
    Disney Christmas specials, 72

employment discrimination, 37–38
The Facts We Face, 22
The Goldbergs, 37
radio network, 18–19
Robin Hood, 32
"What to Do during a Nuclear Attack,"
    23
Central Intelligence Agency (CIA), 30
Cheer detergent, 143
Chef Boyardee, 24
Chevrolet, 175
Cheyenne
    "The Blind Spot," 129–131, 132
    timeframe, 170
Chicago
    bombings of black-owned houses, 11
    Hyde Park, 1
Christensen, H. G., 23–24
Christianity. See Religion
Christmas, 44, 71–72
CIA (Central Intelligence Agency, 30
Cinderella, 47–48
Cities
    federal policies promoting expansion,
        66
    neighborhoods destroyed by highway
        construction, 68–69
    property value declines, 69
    race riots, 181
    residential segregation, 10–11, 68–69,
        73
    urban planning, 50, 61–62, 64
Citizenship, 42
Civil rights movement, 37, 117, 181
Civil War
    aftermath depicted in adult Westerns,
        126–128, 129–131, 133–134, 135–136,
        137–143
    black troops, 152
    Confederate surrender, 138
    reflected in Bonanza, 164, 168, 170
    role of race and slavery, 128–129
    significance, 5
    Southern views of, 123, 129
    veterans as characters in adult Westerns,
        102, 126–128, 132–133, 137–144

Cold War
  blacklisting, 36–37
  bomb shelters, 160–161
  containment strategy, 30, 35, 64–65, 66,
    97
  Disneyland as representative of West,
    49–50
  integration and, 112–115
  international criticism of racial
    segregation, 113, 114
  military role, 150–151
  motifs in television shows, 31
  surveillance state, 23, 25, 28–31
  suspicion of nonconformists, 30–31
  warriors, 64, 76
  See also Containment policy
Cold War ideology
  advantages of private ownership, 21
  in Davy Crockett story, 82, 112
  Disneyland as symbol, 65
  emphasis on conformity, 6
  families seen as response to
    communism, 16–17, 32, 72, 99–100
  presented on television, 31, 83, 100, 129,
    153, 167
  superiority of capitalism and democracy,
    65
Cole, Nat King, 38, 183
Collins, Winfield H., 125
Colonialism, 98
Colonization movement, 9
Colt .45, "The Judgment Day," 94–96, 97,
  100
Columbia Broadcasting System. See CBS
Comanche Indians, 152–155
Commercials
  integrated with programming, 24
  whiteness themes, 41, 143–144
  See also Sponsors
Communism
  American Communist Party, 36
  anti-, 16, 23, 31, 97
  Disney on, 60
  See also Cold War; Soviet Union
Confederate Army
  surrender, 138

veterans as characters in adult Westerns,
    126–128, 132–133, 137–144
Conformity
  during Cold War, 6
  at Disneyland, 60, 70–71, 73
  influence of television, 53, 67
  in suburbs, 66
Congress
  House Un-American Activities
    Committee, 37, 60
  Southern Manifesto, 125, 171
Constitution, U.S., 5
  Second Amendment, 122
  Ninth Amendment, 119
  Thirteenth Amendment, 9
  Fourteenth Amendment, 9, 114
  Fifteenth Amendment, 9
Consumers
  Davy Crockett products, 75, 76(illus.), 93
  at Disneyland, 60
  middle class, 55
  production by television, 39, 75
Containment policy, 30, 35, 64–65, 66, 97
Cooks, on cattle drives, 146
Cowboy films, 74, 77
Cowboys, black, 116, 145–147, 148
Crest, 41
Crockett, Davy
  death at Alamo, 76, 91, 92
  Disneyland series on, 47, 74–83, 84–85,
    86, 91, 112
  "journal," 78
  motto, 122
  national craze for, 74–77, 76(illus.), 93
  reasons for going to Texas, 79–80
  symbolism, 76, 77, 84
Cronkite, Walter, 23
Custer, George C., 149

Daily Worker, 36
Davies, Ronald, 119, 131
Davis, Sammy, Jr., 38, 152, 153
Deane, Bill, 179–180
Death Valley Days, 90, 91(photo)
Declaration of Independence, 5, 157
Deer, Mark, 80

Defense, Department of, 22–23
Democracy, 65, 98
Democratic National Convention (1960), 157–158
Denton, Nancy, 10–11
Depression, 11
Derby Foods, 46
De Roos, Robert, 47
Desegregation. *See* Integration
Detroit, neighborhoods destroyed by highway construction, 68
Diedesheimer, Philip, 169
Dillon, Matt. *See* Gunsmoke
Discrimination. *See* Racial discrimination
Disney, Walt
    approach to film as family entertainment, 55–56
    as Cold War warrior, 64
    on communism, 60
    control obsession, 60–61
    on Davy Crockett shows, 112
    on Disneyland, 59–60, 90–91
    on fantasy, 63
    on history, 61, 63, 93
    innovations, 47
    introductions to *Texas John Slaughter* series, 92–94, 99–100, 106–108, 148–149
    on limitations of film, 57
    objectives for Disneyland, 83–84
    relationship with FBI, 192n53
    television appearances, 12, 48
    view of television, 55–56
Disneyland
    ABC financing, 44, 45
    Adventureland, 44, 66
    Autotopia, 54–55
    construction, 45, 182
    design, 56–58, 59–61, 73
    as destination, 53–54, 83
    engineering of visitors' responses, 58–59, 60
    Fantasyland, 44, 66
    FBI access, 192n53
    Frontierland, 44, 66, 74
    highways leading to, 12–13, 53–54, 62–63, 72

idealization of past, 52
integration, 83, 84
jungle cruise, 56–57
Khrushchev's visit prohibited, 49–50
lack of black employees, 70–71, 84, 171
Main Street, 52, 54, 56, 59, 60, 62, 73
narratives, 57–58, 61
as ongoing project, 57
realism, 59–61, 90–91
relationship to television, 58, 59, 61, 62
significance, 12–13, 49–50, 63, 64, 66
site, 53–54, 182
staff, 60, 61, 70–71
success, 62
Tomorrowland, 44, 54–55, 66
    as urban model, 64
    vision of future, 54–55
    Western character, 67
Disneyland (television show)
    The Adventures of Davy Crockett, 47, 74–83, 84–85, 86, 91, 112
    audience, 70
    Emmy awards, 45
    popularity, 75
    promotion of Disneyland, 44–46, 48–50, 56, 66, 90–91
    significance, 12–13, 75
    sponsors, 45, 46
Disney Productions
    absence of minorities, 112–113
    animated features, 46, 47–48
    Christmas specials, 44, 72
    growth, 12
    nature documentaries, 47, 48, 65–66
    shareholders, 108
    technological innovations, 48, 65–66
    television productions, 55
    Texas John Slaughter series, 91–94, 99–100, 106–108, 148–149
Dodge City (Kansas), 89, 144–148, 169–170
Doherty, Thomas, 17, 36
Dortort, David, 164, 171–172
Douglas, William O., 114
Du Bois, W. E. B., 114
Dudziak, Mary, 113–114
Dulles, John Foster, 17

DuMont network, 22, 23, 37, 43, 190n1
Dunlap, Orin E., 34
Dyer, Richard, 2–3

Earp, Wyatt, 94, 147–148, 169. See also *The Life and Legend of Wyatt Earp*
Education. *See* Integration, school; Schools
Educational television, 21
Eisenhower, Dwight
    inauguration (1953), 26, 42
    interstate highway system, 68
    Nixon as running mate, 159
    on religion in government, 17
    troops sent to Little Rock, 132
Ellender, Allen, 123
Ellison, Ralph, 5, 69
Entrepreneurs, 107, 108
European socialism, 32, 33
Exceptionalism, 118–119

Family life
    bomb shelters, 160–161
    Cold War symbolism, 16–17, 32, 72, 99–100
    effects of television, 46
    idealized, 99–100
    togetherness, 16–17
    white nuclear family as norm, 32
Farber, David, 159
Farnsworth, Philo, 15, 39
Father Knows Best, 40, 99, 172
Faubus, Orval, 116, 117, 118, 119–121, 122, 125, 131–132, 144, 171
Faulk, Odie, 145–146
FBI (Federal Bureau of Investigation), 23, 30, 37, 192n53
FCC. *See* Federal Communications Commission
Federal Bureau of Investigation. *See* FBI
Federal Communications Commission (FCC), television license freeze, 7, 26, 32–33, 37, 43
Federal Housing Administration (FHA), 11, 66, 69
Federal Radio Commission, 19
Fehrenbach, T. R., 79

FHA. *See* Federal Housing Administration
Film
    biblical epics, 195n20
    Cinemascope, 43
    comparison to television, 43–44
    stagecraft, 56
    studios, 43, 44, 45, 67
    Westerns, 74, 77, 86, 177
    See also Disney Productions; Telefilm
Findlay, John, 54, 56, 60, 61–62, 64, 65, 67, 83
Fireside Theater, 39
Fitzgerald, Ella, 38
Foner, Eric, 141
Ford, John, 65, 133
Foreign policy
    American influence in other countries, 98
    connections to individual Americans, 31–32
    containment strategy, 30, 35, 64–65, 66, 97
    desegregation and, 113–114
    reflected in television Westerns, 96–99
    See also Cold War
Fort Dodge, 144, 145
Free blacks, fear of, 8, 9
Freedom Riders, 117
Freeways. *See* Interstate highway system
Frontier
    as border between new and old worlds, 111
    future seen as, 159
    heroes of, 77
    manifest destiny, 81, 82, 167
    New Frontier (Kennedy), 157–158, 159–161, 174
    relationship to Disneyland, 52
    television as, 158
    temporal concept, 63–64, 157
    weapons, 108
    See also Western United States
The Fugitive, 177–181, 179(photo)
Fugitive Slave Laws, 9

Gannon, Mary, 39–40

Garroway, Dave, 27
Gates, Henry Louis, 6–7
General Foods, 36
General Motors, "Futurama" exhibit at
    World's Fair, 50–51, 51(photo)
Geronimo, capture of, 148–149, 152
Gipson, Henry Clay, 39
Giroux, Henry, 112
Goddard, Stephen B., 68
Godfrey, Arthur, 27
Goldberger, Paul, 62
The Goldbergs, 37
Goldenfield, David, 120, 137
Gone with the Wind, 120
Gossett, Thomas, 124
Graebner, William, 64
Graham, Billy, 59
Grant, Ulysses S., 133, 138
Greene, Lorne, 172, 173, 173(photo). See also
    Bonanza
Grey, Zane. See The Zane Grey Theater
Gunsmoke, 86, 144, 162
    concept, 88–89
    location, 147
    Matt Dillon character, 99, 178
    popularity, 88, 174
    radio show, 88
    timeframe, 169–170

Hackney, Sheldon, 125–126
Hall v. De Cuir, 121
Harris, Cheryl, 3
Harris, Neil, 53
Hartnett, Vincent, 36–37
Have Gun, Will Travel, 134–135, 178
Hayes, Rutherford B. See Tilden-Hayes
    compromise
Hench, John, 58–59
High Chaparral, 162
Highways. See Interstate highway system
Hispanics
    characters in Westerns, 146, 198n62
    cowboys, 116
HOLC. See Home Owner's Loan
    Corporation
Holidays, 44, 71–72

Home Owner's Loan Corporation (HOLC), 11
Horsman, Reginald, 81
House Beautiful, 35
House Un-American Activities Committee
    (HUAC), 37, 60
Housing
    destroyed by highway construction,
        68–69
    federal policies, 66
    mortgage assistance programs, 11, 66, 69
    segregation, 10–11, 68–69, 73
    single-family, 66
    suburban, 69
Houston, Sam, 78, 79
HUAC. See House Un-American Activities
    Committee

I Love Lucy, 28, 29(photo), 42
Imperialism, 97–98
Indians. See Native Americans
Indian wars, 148, 149–150, 169
Individualism, 109, 110, 115
Integration
    Cold War and, 112–115
    at Disneyland, 83, 84
    in Western communities, 147
Integration, school
    Brown v. Board of Education of Topeka, 84,
        113–115, 118, 122, 125, 137, 147
    implementation of, 116–117
    resistance in Little Rock, 118, 119–121,
        122–123, 125–126, 131–132, 144
    resistance to, 116–117
    in Western states, 147
Interstate highway system
    access to Disneyland, 12–13, 53–54,
        62–63, 72
    cloverleaf intersections, 70(photo)
    driving times reduced by, 62–63
    financing, 68
    growth, 182
    legislation, 68
    neighborhoods destroyed by, 68–69
    social impact, 69–70
    standardization, 53
    unification of country, 53

James, Jesse, 126
Janssen, David, 177, 179(photo)
Johnson, Lyndon B., 82
Jordan, George, 149–150
Jordan, Winthrop, 8
J. Walter Thompson, 40

Kaiser Industries, 110–111
Kansas
    abolitionism, 145
    black population, 146, 147
    Dodge City, 89, 144–148, 169–170
    Fort Dodge, 144, 145
    racial tolerance, 146–147
    segregated schools, 147
    Westerns set in, 147
    See also Brown v. Board of Education of
        Topeka
Kennan, George, 35, 64–65
Kennedy, John F.
    acceptance speech, 157–158, 160–161
    Camelot image, 164
    civil rights issues, 117
    inaugural address, 165
    New Frontier theme, 157–158, 159–161,
        174
    use of television, 158–159, 160(photo)
Kennedy, Joseph, 162, 173
Kennedy administration, civil rights issues,
    117, 171
Kennedy family, similarities to Cartwrights
    of Bonanza, 162–163, 165, 173
Khrushchev, Nikita, 49–50
Kilgore, Dan, 91
King, Martin Luther, Jr., 171, 181
King, Rodney, 13–14
Koon, Stacy, 13
Korean War, 22, 23, 36–37
Kovacs, Ernie, 27
Ku Klux Klan, 141

Lake, Stuart, 87
Lee, Peggy, 38
Lee, Robert E., 138
Leibman, Nina, 16, 40
Levittown, 11

The Life and Legend of Wyatt Earp, 86, 87, 89,
    94, 147–148
Life Is Worth Living, 17
Lincoln, Abraham, 5, 169
Lipsitz, George, 55, 57, 63, 72
Little Rock Central High School
    conflict over desegregation, 116, 119–121,
        122–123, 131–132
    federal troops at, 132, 133(photo), 149
    National Guard at, 119–120, 122, 125
    television news coverage of conflict, 117,
        118, 125–126
Loeb, Philip, 37
Lone Ranger, 134–135, 181
Long, Jeff, 79–80
Look, 57
Los Angeles
    diverse population, 63, 73
    film industry, 44, 45, 67
    freeways, 53–54, 62–63, 72
    residential segregation, 73
    Rodney King incident, 13–14
    suburbs, 73
    See also Disneyland
Lynchings, 1, 2(illus.), 38, 124, 125,
    176–177

MacDonald, J. Fred, 31, 86, 133
Mademoiselle, 39–40
Make Room for Daddy, 28
Manifest destiny, 81, 82, 167
Marable, Manning, 116–117
Marc, David, 32, 63
Marling, Karal Ann, 47, 50, 56–57, 59, 74,
    83
Marx, Groucho, 17
Mary Kay and Johnny, 28
Massey, Douglas, 10–11
Masterson, Bat, 87, 147
Matthews, Christopher, 159
Maverick, "The War of the Silver Kings,"
    108–111
McCall's, 16
McNeil, Alex, 89
Meet the Press, 23
Menken, Adah, 169

Meredith, James, 117
Meston, John, 88–89, 144
Mexican Americans, 73. *See also* Hispanics
Mexico, war with Texas revolutionaries, 78–79. *See also* Alamo
Middle class, 49, 55, 67, 69
Military
    National Guard, 119–120, 122, 125
    occupation of South after Civil War, 135–136, 149
    role in Cold War, 150–151
    segregation, 11–12, 152
    television documentaries, 31
    troops sent to Little Rock, 132, 149
    See also Black soldiers
Military adventure programs, 31
Monaco, James, 39
Monopolies, in television, 18–21, 32–33, 118
Moore, Charles, 62
Morrison, Toni, 2
Movies. *See* Film
Mowbray, A. Q., 53, 68
Muir, Jeanne, 36
My Three Sons, 172, 173–174

NAACP, 114
Nashville, neighborhoods destroyed by highway construction, 68
National Association of Radio and Television Broadcasters, 34–35
National Broadcasting Company. *See* NBC
National Guard, in Little Rock, 119–120, 122, 125
Native Americans
    Apache, 148, 149–150, 153–154
    Comanche, 152–155
    cowboys, 116
    Geronimo, 148–149, 152
    Indian wars, 148, 149–150, 169
    portrayals in adult Westerns, 152–155
    racist attitudes toward, 153, 155
The Nat King Cole Show, 38, 183
Nature documentaries (Disney), 47, 48, 65–66
NBC (National Broadcasting Company)

Amos 'n' Andy, 15, 37
Battle Report—Washington, 22
blacklisting of actors, 37
Disney Christmas specials, 44
The Goldbergs, 37
The Nat King Cole Show, 38, 183
Texaco Star Theater, 18
Nelson, Ozzie and Harriet, 27–28
Nevada
    black population, 168
    Bonanza set in, 162, 169
    settlement, 168, 169
New Frontier, 157–158, 159–161, 174
New Frontier Westerns
    The Fugitive, 177–181
    Route 66, 174–177, 181
News. *See* Television news
New York Times, 113
Ninth Cavalry, 146, 149, 151(photo)
Nixon, Richard M., 158, 159
Normality, role of education, 115
Norms
    at Disneyland, 60, 73
    presented on television, 17, 28–31, 32, 33–36, 42, 161
    religious values, 100
    whiteness as, 3–4, 12, 41
Nuclear weapons
    bomb shelters, 160–161
    documentaries on potential attacks, 23
    intercontinental ballistic missiles, 160–161
    U.S. supremacy, 97–98

O'Brien, Hugh, 87
O'Hara, John, *Appointment in Samarra*, 7
Oklahoma, black population, 147
Oregon constitution, 1
Othello, 24

Pennsylvania supreme court, 121
Peter Pan, 46
Peter Pan peanut butter, 45, 46
Pinza, Ezio, 28
Pledge of Allegiance, 53
Plessy v. Ferguson, 113, 114, 121, 196n3

Popular culture, Davy Crockett craze, 74–77, 76(illus.), 93
Powell, Dick, 89–90, 150
Pregnancy, absence from television, 7, 28
Product placement, 39–41
Property Westerns, 162, 171. *See also Bonanza*
Protestant ethic, 167
Public interests, 21–22
Public service announcements, 21, 100
Purification
   at Disneyland, 59–61, 71, 72–73
   in suburbs, 71
   of television, 71

Quantrill, William, 126, 132
Quantrill's Raiders, 102, 126, 129, 132

Race
   classifications, 3, 4, 8
   relations in South, 10, 121–122, 123–125, 141
   role in Civil War, 128–129
Racial discrimination
   Black Codes, 9–10, 187–188n20
   at Disneyland, 70–71, 84, 171
   effects, 184
   in employment, 37–38, 70–71
   history in United States, 1–2, 9–11
   international criticism of, 114
   by law enforcement, 1, 184
   in real estate, 11, 69, 73
   See also Segregation
Radio
   Amos 'n' Andy, 15
   audiences, 32
   FM, 20
   Gunsmoke, 88
   networks, 18–19
Radio Corporation of America, 18, 19
Ransom, Roger, 129
Rawhide
   characters, 99, 146
   historical realism, 90
   "Incident of the Golden Calf," 103–106
   timeframe, 170
RCA (Radio Corporation of America), 18, 19

The Rebel, 137–144, 140(photo)
Reconstruction
   end of, 10, 137, 141
   land ownership policies, 141
   Southern views of, 120, 124, 129
Red Channels, 36–37
Regulators, 129–131
Religion
   holidays, 71–72
   norms presented on television, 28–31, 100
   secular status, 17, 72
   television programs, 17, 21, 30, 31, 35
   as theme of adult Westerns, 100–106, 167
   as theme of films, 195n20
   in U.S. government, 17
Residential segregation, 10–11, 68–69, 73
Reston, James, 114
The Rifleman, 94, 95(photo), 99
Roach, Hal, Jr., 44
Roberts, Pernell, 168, 173(photo)
Robin Hood, 32
Rod Brown of the Rocket Rangers, 31
Rogers, Roy, 77, 86
Route 66, 174–177, 181
   "Black November," 176–177
Russell, George, 80, 82
Russell, Katheryn, 184

Santa Ana freeway, 53, 63
Schickel, Richard, 60, 71
Schools, segregated, 115, 147. *See also* Integration, school
Scott, Hazel, 37
Scott Paper, 40–41
Scottsboro boys, 1
Screen Gems, 40
Segregation
   absence from television, 38
   effects, 115, 184
   international criticism of, 113, 114
   of military, 11–12, 152
   protests against, 114
   residential, 10–11, 68–69, 73
   schools, 115, 147
   "separate but equal" facilities, 113, 114

Supreme Court cases, 113, 114, 121
    See also Integration
Seldes, Gilbert, 25
Self-censorship, by television, 7, 22, 28, 30,
    33, 118
Serling, Rod, 38
Shackford, James, 78
Sheen, Fulton J., 17, 31
Short, Luke, 145
Situation comedies
    The Adventures of Ozzie and Harriet, 27–28
    celebrity stars, 27–28
    families, 99, 161
    Father Knows Best, 40, 99, 172
    laugh tracks, 27
    live audiences, 27
    My Three Sons, 172, 173–174
Skin color, 3
Slaughter, Texas John, 91–94, 99–100,
    106–108, 148–149
Slavery
    abolitionism, 9, 145
    in colonial period, 8–9
    Fugitive Slave Laws, 9
    role in Civil War, 128–129
    in Texas, 80, 81–82, 112, 145
Slotkin, Richard, 111
Small towns, idealized, 52, 99–100
Smith, Cecil, 137–138
Snow White, 47
Social Darwinism, 49, 88–89
Socialism, 32, 33
Soldiers. *See* Black soldiers; Military
Sorensen, Ted, 159
Southern Manifesto, 125, 171
Southern United States
    Black Codes, 9–10, 187–188n20
    black labor force, 141, 187–188n20
    Confederate Army, 126–128, 132–133,
        137–144
    lynchings, 38
    occupation by Northern troops, 135–136,
        149
    race relations, 10, 121–122, 123–125, 141
    Reconstruction, 10, 120, 124, 129, 137,
        141

representation in adult Westerns, 119,
    144
segregated schools, 116–117
sponsors' fear of alienating audience in,
    7, 37, 118
television stations, 43
values, 144
victimhood, 120, 124–125, 129, 131, 141,
    143, 144
white supremacy, 120, 123, 137, 141
Soviet Union
    criticism of racism in United States,
        114
    Khrushchev's visit to United States,
        49–50
    See also Cold War
Space adventure programs, 31
Spigel, Lynn, 16, 71
Sponsors, 20–21
    of adult Westerns, 110–111
    automobile companies, 175
    desire for large audiences, 33
    of *Disneyland*, 45, 46
    fears of alienating Southern audiences,
        7, 37, 118
    product placement, 39–41
    See also Commercials
Spy series, 31
Standardization, 53
Stanford Research Institute, 53
State Department, U.S., 113–114
State sovereignty, 122
States' rights, 119
Steelman, John, 22
Suburbs
    access to interstate highways, 68
    consumer culture, 55
    development, 66, 69
    extension of settlement of West, 99–100
    lack of diversity, 66, 69
    mortgage assistance programs, 69
    purified communal spaces, 71
    racial discrimination in, 11, 73
Sugrue, Thomas J., 68
Sullivan, Ed, 7
Superman, 31

Supreme Court
  Brown v. Board of Education of Topeka, 84,
    113–115, 118, 122, 125, 137, 147
  Hall v. De Cuir, 121
  Plessy v. Ferguson, 113, 114, 121, 196n3
  ruling on racial discrimination in
    housing covenants, 11
Surveillance state, 23, 25, 28–31
Susskind, David, 37

Taylor, Quintard, 116, 146, 149–150
Telefilm, 44, 45, 48, 49, 55
Television
  conformity promoted by, 53, 67
  cultural influence, 74, 182
  eternal present, 63
  FCC license freeze, 7, 26, 32–33, 37, 43
  federal regulation, 19–20, 21
  first broadcast, 15, 39
  fragmentation of audience, 182–183
  as guest in homes, 34, 46
  immediacy, 24–25, 26, 42, 43–44, 55
  interpretations of history, 155–156
  intimacy, 27
  as medium of truth and reality, 23–28,
    31, 35, 40–41, 46–47, 87
  monopoly structure, 18–21, 32–33, 118
  norms presented by, 17, 28–31, 32,
    33–36, 42, 161
  purification, 71
  reality constructed by, 42
  self-censorship, 7, 22, 28, 30, 33, 118
  spontaneity, 25–26, 27
  technology, 18, 19, 20, 33
  viewer participation, 41–42
  vision of America, 6–8, 12, 17, 33
  waning of authority, 13–14
Television code, 34–35
Television networks
  DuMont, 22, 23, 37, 43, 190n1
  efforts to attract large audiences, 32–33
  monopoly, 18–20, 32
  See also ABC; CBS; NBC
Television news
  in Cold War context, 22, 23
  coverage of racial conflicts, 116–118,
    125–126, 181
  government influence on, 22–23, 35
  intelligence gathering model, 30
  objectivity, 22
  as public service, 21–22
  spontaneity, 25–26
Television programs
  action-adventure series, 31
  anthology shows, 38–39
  military adventure programs, 31
  religious, 17, 21, 30, 31, 35
  space adventure programs, 31
  spy series, 31
  See also Adult Westerns; *Disneyland*;
    Situation comedies; Westerns
Television sets
  manufacturers, 19, 20
  proportion of households owning, 26,
    43, 99
Tenth Cavalry, 146, 149, 151–155
Texaco Star Theater, 17–18
Texas
  adult Westerns set in, 92
  Alamo, 47, 76, 77–82, 91, 92, 142
  annexation by United States, 81–82
  black population, 145, 146, 147
  federal occupation, 149
  Regulators, 129–131
  revolution, 78–79, 81, 122
  settlement by Americans, 79–80
  slavery in, 80, 81–82, 112, 145
  Southern culture, 145
  Western imagery, 92, 145
  Westerns set in, 147
Texas John Slaughter, 91–94, 99–100, 106–108,
    147, 148–149
Texas Rangers, 92–94
Thanksgiving, 71–72
Theme parks. *See* Amusement parks;
    Disneyland
Thomas, Danny, 28
Thompson, William Irwin, 59
Tilden-Hayes compromise, 137, 141
Till, Emmett, 38
Tillman, "Pitchfork Ben," 123
Time, 25

Today, 27
Togetherness, 16–17, 27
Tombstone Territory, 90, 133–134, 147
Torme, Mel, 38
Tracy, Spencer, 177
Transcontinental coaxial cable, 26–27, 43, 61
Travis, William, 79
Trolley companies, 52
Truman administration, 22–23
TV Guide, 44–45, 75, 76, 77, 86, 87, 112
Twain, Mark, 169

UHF frequencies, 19, 20, 21
United Nations, *An Appeal to the World,* 114
U.S. Army Signal Corps, 31
U.S. government
    influence on television news, 22–23, 35
    regulation of airwaves, 19–20, 21
    religion in, 17
    urban development policies, 66
    See also Foreign policy
Upward mobility, 51, 68–69
Urban planning, 50, 61–62, 64. *See also*
    Cities
Utopianism, 42, 49, 50, 53

Vardaman, James Kimble, 123
VHF frequencies, 19–20
Video recordings, authority, 13–14
Vietnam, 82, 97
Virginia City (Nevada), 168, 169
The Virginian (television series), 162
The Virginian (Wister), 116
Visual representation, faith in, 23–24
Voice of America, 113

Wagon Train, 99, 101(photo)
    "The Coulter Craven Story," 133
    "The Orly French Story," 102–103
    timeframe, 170
    "The Willie Moran Story," 101–102,
        132–133, 144
Walker, Sam, 93
Wallace, George, 117
"Walt Disney Presents." *See Texas John*
    Slaughter series

Wanted Dead or Alive, 94, 178
Watts, Steven, 58, 61, 64, 65, 74, 83
Wayne, John, 89
Weapons, 93–94, 108
    See also Nuclear weapons
Weaver, Pat, 41–42, 58, 90
West, Cornel, 1
Western bloc
    American leadership during Cold War, 64
    associated with Western frontier, 64,
        99–100, 111
    capitalism, 49, 65, 107, 108
    Disneyland as representative of, 49–50
    televised images, 83
Westerns
    children's, 77, 86
    Davy Crockett series on *Disneyland,* 47,
        74–83, 84–85, 86, 91, 112
    films, 74, 77, 86, 177
    Hispanic characters, 146, 198n62
    New Frontier, 174–181
    in 1960s, 174
    novels, 116
    property, 162, 171
    See also Adult Westerns
Western United States
    black presence, 145–147
    black soldiers, 146, 148–150, 152
    idealized, 88–89
    integrated communities, 147
    settlement, 64, 84, 87
    spiritual redemption in, 101–103
    Texas as representative of, 92, 145
    urban growth, 61–62
    See also Frontier; *individual states*
Westward expansion, 54, 99–100
"What to Do During a Nuclear Attack," 23
Where's Raymond, 28
Whiteness
    in adult Westerns, 143–144
    of Christmas, 72
    in commercials, 41, 143–144
    of Disneyland, 70–71, 84, 171
    myth of, 2–3
    as norm in television programming, 3–4,
        12, 41

Whiteness (*continued*)
  of public space, 4
  superiority, 8
White supremacy, 81, 120, 123, 137, 141
Wild West shows, 116
William Morris Agency, 20
Williams, Raymond, 75, 99
Wister, Owen, 116
Wizbar, Fred, 39
Women, absence from *Bonanza*, 171–172
World's Fair (1939)
  General Motors' "Futurama" exhibit,
    50–51, 51(photo)
  as precursor to Disneyland, 50, 53
  television broadcast from grounds, 15,
    39
World War II
  air wardens, 34

blacks in armed forces, 11–12, 152
defense plants, 73
German prisoners of war, 176
murders of Japanese Americans, 177
*Wyatt Earp. See The Life and Legend of Wyatt
  Earp*

Yancy Derringer, 126, 134–135
  "State of Crisis," 135–136
Yoggy, Gary, 165, 170, 172
Younger, Cole, 127–128
Yuma, Johnny. *See The Rebel*

The Zane Grey Theater, 89–90
  "The Mission," 150–155